GRAND DELUSIONS

GRAND DELUSIONS

A STORY OF MENTAL ILLNESS, HOPE AND LOVE

DENNIS JOHN MULHEARN

HARD NOCK PRESS

NEW YORK

Grand Delusions: A Story of Mental Illness, Hope and Love

Copyright © 2014 by Dennis John Mulhearn

Published in the United States of America by
Hard Nock Press, LLC

Hard Nock Press, LLC
P.O. Box 665
Orangeburg, NY 10962
www.hardnockpress.com

Printed in the United States of America

10 9 8 7 6 5 4 3 2 1

ISBN: 978-0-692-21284-4

First Edition

DISCLAIMER AND WARNING

This book contains the author's recollections of his journey into mental illness. As Dennis John Mulhearn makes clear, he was not always able—even with the benefit of hindsight—to distinguish reality from fantasy. Any critical references to individuals, and/or their actions towards him and/or others, may thus be the product of Dennis's delusions. For these reasons, no one should rely on the truth and/or accuracy of any facts or opinions contained in this book.

Likewise, if you or anyone you know is suffering from mental illness, or believe that you may be suffering from mental illness, you should seek immediate medical attention from a physician or mental health provider. Similarly, if you or anyone you know experiences, or may be experiencing, delusions of grandeur or messianic delusions, you should seek immediate medical attention from a physician or mental health provider.

Any person diagnosed with mental illness should follow his or her physician's instructions and directions and take all prescribed medications.

Publisher's Note: Dennis depicted certain authority figures during his high school years in a most positive light. He had no knowledge that some of these men engaged in despicable behavior. Had Dennis learned of the darker facts about these individuals' acts and omissions, there is no doubt that some of his characterizations would have been quite different.

CONTENTS

PREFACE

Grand Delusions is a work of non-fiction which chronicles my experiences from October 1990 to October 1991.

All the people depicted in this book are real. I have taken the liberty of changing certain names at my personal discretion. The places I have written about are real. The events described in this book reflect my understanding of what happened to me but—in view of my mental illness—cannot and should not be relied upon for factual accuracy.

To emphasize this point, I'd like to apologize to the members of my family for at times depicting them in a very negative light. It should be apparent that these unfair and untrue characterizations and the subsequent conclusions I drew from them were the direct by-product of my illness and do not in any way reflect my true feelings.

Please bear in mind that *Grand Delusions* was not intended to be an objective account of the tumultuous period of time I have described. It is, instead, my own unapologetically biased perspective of a time when the world as I knew it was fragmented into millions of separate, yet interconnected pieces. Amidst these fragments lies some element of truth. How much truth—even I'm not sure. As you turn these pages, I invite you to take a journey inside my mind, examine the facts I have presented, and then decide for yourself.

Dennis John Mulhearn

1

ESCAPE

I had to do something; they were coming for me. I thought about calling home but couldn't risk the phone being bugged. How could I get out of there? The elevator was the only exit and it passed directly by the security desk. I sat motionless in my bed, too terrified to move a muscle.

I glanced at my alarm clock and saw that it was 3:05 a.m. Suddenly, I heard a noise coming from the hallway. I was out of time; the security guards were on their way. I hastily slipped on a pair of sneakers and a jacket and climbed through a window.

The screen was bent inward, so it was easy to push open. I crawled over to the edge of the roof, making sure no one could see me. Fortunately, I was able to jump down onto a stack of wooden crates that were placed against the building.

I crouched low atop the sturdy boxes and hesitated for a moment, taking a long and careful look in all directions. The broken window screen and conveniently placed crates seemed almost too advantageous. I was fearful that an armed security guard would emerge from the dark shadows the instant my feet touched the ground. When I was finally certain that no one was out there with me, I leapt onto the hard pavement and started frantically running to the nearest hotel room.

"Let me in, please, someone's trying to kill me," I said, pounding on the hotel door. I didn't know which building I was in, but I knew I had to get inside the room.

"Who are you? What do you want?" squeaked a frightened male voice.

"I can't tell you. It's too complicated. I'm not going to hurt you. I just need to use your phone. Here's some money." I shoved fifty dollars underneath the locked door in a gesture of good faith.

"I just called security," the man replied. "They'll be here any minute."

"No!" I yelled. Now they knew precisely where I was. I ran out the doorway and into the woods. If I could just get to a phone in town, I could call my brother Sean and have him come pick me up. The woods were sloped slightly uphill and a recent rainfall made the ground wet and slippery. Nevertheless, I was moving extremely fast. They'll never catch me, I thought, as I continued up the slick terrain.

My right sneaker got caught in the mud and came off, but I continued running. Oversized pine tree branches swooped down and scratched my face and body, yet I ignored the pain and kept moving. I was running for dear life.

After running for about a half hour, I glanced back over my shoulder and was horrified to see the back of The Pines's main building less than fifty yards away. Had I been running in circles? Then I remembered that the resort was surrounded by woods—there was no way out.

I crouched low to the ground and listened for sounds. I heard a noise that sounded like a rock thudding against the trunk of a tree. Someone was in the forest with me. By this time the whole security staff had probably been rounded up and was out there looking for me. I tried to dig a hole and camouflage myself with leaves but my bare hands were unable to uncover more than a few handfuls of dirt form the hard ground. Not knowing what else to do, I ran deeper into the woods at full speed. I tripped and fell a number of times, banging my head against various rocks and tree stumps.

As I raced into the heart of the woods, I suddenly pulled to a screeching stop. Wait a minute. Even if I make it out of these woods they'll have someone waiting for me on the outside. This is a multi-million dollar drug ring. These hick cops from South Fallsburg have to be a part of the operation. I thought back to my meeting with Bruce Smythe. He said that he and Eve Cantor had worked at The Pines for twelve years. They've been doing this for a long time. I have to get out of here to tell people about what's going on and put an end to this madness.

You're a great athlete, Dennis. You can do it. Think like Rambo; what would he do? I asked myself. While I continued to rack my brains as to what survival tactics I could utilize, I detected a large figure lurking ominously in the light of the moon. Despite the darkness, I clearly recognized Charlie, the Chief of Security. He was holding a pointed object that appeared to be a gun with his left hand and throwing stones into the trees with his right.

Charlie was a burly, three-hundred pound Goliath who would not have needed a weapon to overpower me. The sight of his imposing frame almost made me stain the front of my pants. I did not know for certain if there were any other guards with him, but I wasn't going to wait to find out. With a surge of adrenaline, I ran back down the slope toward The Pines again. I emerged from the woods at the far west end of the complex.

ESCAPE

The blackness of this uninhabited section of the resort worked perfectly to my advantage. Half-running, half-crawling on the ground, I made it into the parking lot. To my astonishment, my Chevy was still parked exactly where I had left it. Someone had been inexcusably sloppy to have forgotten to get rid of my only mode of transportation.

The rapidly descending temperature had created a thin layer of frost on my windshield. I didn't have time to allow my defroster to kick in, so I turned the ignition key, stuck my head out the side window, and floored the gas pedal. After a few minutes, I turned onto Route 17 East, the main highway leading to the New York State Thruway. I drove at fifty-five miles per hour in order to avoid any unwanted attention. After continuing on Route 17 for another two or three miles, I saw a caravan of approximately twenty police cars speeding toward The Pines from 17 West.

I didn't hear any sirens, but the flashing red and blue lights on the hoods of the police cars were all activated; the colorful, bright lights almost blinded me. South Fallsburg can't have that many police cruisers. The New York State Troopers must be in on this operation as well. They're all going up to The Pines to try to flush me out of the woods, I reasoned. The realization that I had escaped with only ten or twelve minutes to spare made me shudder.

A thick, dense fog made visibility poor but I didn't mind that one bit. I knew that the fog made it nearly impossible for anyone to notice my Florida license plates, a distinction that—in this part of the country—would have called attention to my car as surely as a neon sign. I drove cautiously and stayed in the right lane in case I had to make a quick maneuver.

I finally reached the Garden State Parkway just as the sun was rising. I felt somewhat safer having made it into New Jersey but still could not relax. They're going to come looking for me. I have to warn my family. I turned off the Parkway at Exit 153, and entered a small town called Clifton. I had previously worked in Clifton and, because of my familiarity with the area, felt it would be a good place from which to call home. I drove through the town's business district for a few minutes but couldn't find a public phone. Damn, I'm wasting valuable time. At most I've got a two or three hour head start on these guys. I've got to move fast.

Fortunately, I saw an elderly woman who was out early walking her dog. I pulled over to the curb, explained as calmly as possible that someone was trying to kill me, and asked to use her phone. My frightful appearance must have convinced her that I was speaking the truth. Without a moment's hesitation, she graciously invited me into her home and led me straight to the kitchen telephone. I took a fifty dollar bill from my wallet and offered it to her as compensation for her help but she politely told me to put my money away. The kind woman was genuinely concerned for my safety.

I called my mother in Manalapan, New Jersey. "Mom, get everyone out of the house. Go to a motel or to Mary's if you want, just get out! You're in danger. The people I was working for are trying to kill me. They're going to come looking for you." My mother wanted to know more but I told her that I didn't have time to explain the details. "Just listen to what I'm saying and get out of the house. Do it!" I yelled.

Next, I called my father in New City, New ork and relayed the same message to him. He wanted me to drive to his house and go with him to the New York State Police but I told him that that was not possible. "Just please get out!" I implored. "Hurry, they'll be coming for you soon."

While I was calling my parents, the elderly lady went next door and called the Clifton Police Department for assistance. Two uniformed policemen arrived at the front doorstep within minutes. When they asked me what the problem was, I tried to summarize what I had been through. Unfortunately, they didn't believe a word I said.

"Okay, buddy. Tell us what really happened. How did you rip your clothes and get those cuts and scratches all over yourself?" asked one of the officers.

"I told you what happened. Some people at The Pines Hotel in The Catskills are involved in a major drug operation. They tried to kill me because I found out too much," I repeated.

The incredulous cops took me into their squad car and, despite my vehement objections, placed a call to the front desk of The Pines. Shit, now they know exactly where I am. The "powers-that-be" at The Pines knew what any cop would do if I told such an outrageous story. I watched one of the officers nod as he spoke into the phone. "We're taking you down to the station to ask you some questions, Dennis. The person I spoke to at the hotel says you were fired because you were volatile and unstable," he said disdainfully.

At this point, I was convinced that this misinformation was proof that my suspicions were correct. The only volatile thing I had done at The Pines was slam my notes onto my desk after I had been fired. I needed to get back to my car and into a motel room. Maybe I could get in touch with Mike McAlary, the investigative reporter for the *New York Post*, and reveal my story to him.

An overweight sergeant led me to a desk and told me to sit down. "So what really happened, Dennis?" he inquired. I reiterated what I told the two patrolmen but, of course, he didn't believe me either. "Let me ask you again, what really happened?" he persisted. I took a quick glance at the round-faced clock on the wall. The goons from The Pines were already on their way; I had to get out of that police station as soon as possible.

Using my imagination, I fabricated a story that I was beaten up at a Parkway rest stop. The sergeant seemed to accept this more plausible explanation of my physical appearance. He called a few of the nearest service areas to find out if anyone had seen the alleged brawl.

After a few minutes another police officer came over and told me that he had called my father who would soon be coming to take me home. I looked at the clock again and observed that it was exactly 8:30 in the morning. The drive from New City to Clifton should have only taken my father twenty minutes; that would give me plenty of time to leave before the thugs coming from South Fallsburg arrived at the station. I breathed a huge sigh of relief.

At 9:15 I started to get worried; by 9:45 I was distraught. Where the hell was my father? Had the New York police intercepted him and killed him? Were my mother, brothers, and sister also dead? Were the forces behind the drug operation waiting to ambush me outside the police station?

Relax, I told myself. I had to think rationally—my life depended on it. I needed to think of a way to stall for time. No one could touch me as long as I was in the police station.

I walked over to where one of the officers was standing and made an intentionally half-assed attempt to pull his gun out of his holster. Had I really wanted to take the gun, I could have easily done so. But that wasn't necessary. The pretense of going for the weapon was enough to achieve my objective.

Within seconds, five cops surrounded me, restrained me roughly and cuffed my hands behind my back. I was thrown into an isolated cell but, nevertheless, I was quite pleased with myself. I figured that if they were still alive, I had just bought enough time to save the lives of my family as well as my own.

While I was sitting alone in my cell, I gave further thought to my situation. It's not over yet. This is a multi-million, maybe even billion-dollar operation. Who else was involved? The F.B.I.? The C.I.A.? Maybe the federal government? I didn't know and there was no way of estimating the magnitude of the operation with any degree of certainty.

What are the extradition laws in this state? Can they take me back to New York on unrelated charges? Of course they can. They're going to take me back to the New York State Police barracks and quietly put a bullet in my head. They'll tell my family that I had become violent again and that they had no choice. I had made it easy for them by going for the Clifton cop's gun. There was nothing else I could do now—I was a dead man. My life was coming to a brutal and sudden conclusion.

Shortly after 10 a.m. my father arrived at the police station with his wife, Willie. They were both dressed as though they were going to a ballroom dance. My dad was wearing a beige suit and a fancy brown tie. Willie wore a low-cut red dress and numerous pieces of gold jewelry. One of the policemen took me to the interview area, where I was able to talk to my father through a plexiglass window. He seemed nervous and shaken.

My father was the first to speak. "What happened, Dennis?"

"All I can tell you is that I'm going to die, Dad. I found out too much, too soon," I said, trying to protect him by not divulging too much information. I was both physically exhausted and mentally drained. My father wiped away a tear from his eye. The only other time I had ever seen him cry was the day his mother died.

"Dennis, I love you. You can talk to me. Please tell me what happened."

I relented and told him the whole sordid story in vivid detail. When I was finished, he smiled brightly and told me not to worry. He was going to take care of everything.

"I'll call Ernie Anastos and all the news people. Nobody's going to lay a finger on you, son," he assured me. "Just leave everything to me. I'm going to take care of a couple of things right now but Willie is going to stay here with you."

Willie sat and talked with me while my father left for a few minutes. She seemed interested in what I had to say yet I sensed a certain amount of fear in her as well. When I told her that we were "going to nail those drug bastards," her steadfast smile disappeared and turned into an ugly frown. Why was she upset about me beating them? Why wasn't she ecstatic? Her reaction to my triumph was unsettling. I was relieved to see my father return.

He came back with a small, bookish woman from the social service office. She wrote feverishly in her black log book as I recounted the details of my adventure from start to finish. From the wondrous expressions on her face, I assumed that she believed me. She was one of the first persons to learn about the biggest drug crackdown in the history of the United States and was privileged to hear my personal account first-hand.

When I had finished speaking to her, she asked me if I would permit the police to take me to Saint Mary's Medical Center for a thorough psychiatric examination. Oblivious to the hidden dangers that awaited me there, I agreed without hesitation. I was confident that the examination would verify my sanity, and thereby confirm my accusations against The Pines.

As I was riding in the police cruiser I speculated on what was in store for me at Saint Mary's. I imagined a horde of photographers and reporters hungrily awaiting the doctors' analysis that I was completely sane and that my story was one-hundred percent true. I prepared answers to some of the questions I might be asked: When did you first realize that you were involved in a drug operation? How did you manage to escape? I planned on being a modest hero, but smiled when I thought about what my friends from Chi-Chi's were going to say when they saw me on television. They would all be so proud to know me.

When I arrived at the hospital I was shocked that I didn't see any media people there. I saw no one but nurses and orderlies carrying out their routine duties. What happened? Didn't the news stations know I was coming? I was ushered into a white room and seated in an uncomfortable chair. A tall, geeky doctor with thick horn-rimmed glasses came in and started the interview.

He began by examining my eyes and asking me one inane question after another: "Do you hear voices? Get headaches? Are you seeing things? Do you get blurred vision? Do you take drugs? Is there any previous history of mental illness in your family? Have you even been mentally ill before?" I scoffed at such ridiculous queries and came to the conclusion that the interview was a joke. I'm as sane as you, you moron, I thought bitterly as I responded "no" to each question.

"Uh-huh, uh-huh … listen, Dennis, why don't you just tell me why you grabbed the officer's gun," he asked coolly. I again explained my discovery of the drug operation and why this knowledge placed me in danger. His response was cold and business-like. "I see. You feared your employers from the resort in The Catskills because you thought that they were conducting something of a drug cartel. Is that correct?"

"Yes, that's right," I responded through gritted teeth.

This guy's patronizing attitude was infuriating. He was talking to me as if I were some idiot who had lost his marbles and I resented the hell out of him for that. I had just survived a night fraught with unspeakable danger and this close-minded jackass was questioning my sanity. In my opinion, regardless of his medical degree, he was unqualified to pass judgment on the facts I had presented to him.

When the impassive physician had finished interviewing me, a short female doctor of Oriental ethnicity entered the room and repeated most of the same questions he had asked. Once again, I answered the questions as truthfully as possible but I detected similar skepticism from her that made it apparent she didn't believe me either.

By the time she had finished her examination, my entire family had arrived at Saint Mary's. I remained in the white room, and they came in to see me one at a time. When each of them had talked with me, I asked to see Kevin again. He was the person I trusted the most.

In addition to being extremely concerned and worried about me, my twin brother was also very confused. After comforting him, I explained the situation. "Turn off the tape, Kevin," I instructed. He had brought a miniature tape machine with him and recorded our previous conversation about the drug operation at The Pines. "Kev, what I'm going to say to you now is going to be very painful, but listen carefully. Daddy is involved in the operation. He and Willie are both afraid of me. They know that I know too much. He's out there right now trying to convince you guys to put me away in a mental hospital, isn't he?"

"Well, y-yeah," Kevin stammered. "He thinks that you're sick and that you need help."

"Do I look sick to you? I haven't slept for two days but I'm as sharp as a razor. Do you really think I could make up a story this bizarre?" I asked my brother. "I'll tell you what really happened. I beat them. I was never supposed to make it out of that place alive. Now too many people have heard my story, so they can't kill me.

"If I die, people will go to The Pines and investigate. Then they'll be screwed. Their only hope is to make it look as if I went crazy. They probably paid off Daddy a million or two to put me in a hospital. I'm not sure, but they may have even paid off these doctors here—we're talking about a lot of money."

Kevin looked at me and contemplated what I had said. "You know, you may be right. Willie keeps talking about her daughter Melissa being in a mental institution in New York. She and Daddy are really pushing hard to put you in a hospital."

I considered the implications. God, I loved my father. How could he sell out his own son? The thought was breaking my heart, yet I was determined not to let him or anyone else beat me. I was tough, though. I would not go down without one hell of a fight. As I watched Kevin exit the room, I thought about the series of events that led me to this point. Had it really only been two weeks since this nightmare had begun?

2

A NEW
BEGINNING

The smell of stale nachos lingered in my car as I sped down Route 18 towards my rented East Brunswick home. I unlocked the front door and walked into the empty house, which had been deserted for the evening by my three roommates. After pouring myself a glass of milk in the kitchen, I noticed the steady blinking of the green numeral one on my answering machine. It's probably for Bob or Chris, I thought, as I reached over and pressed the play button. "Hello, Dennis, this is Steve Richman from The Pines Hotel. I'm calling you in regard to the resume you sent us. Please call me back at (914) 434-6000. Thanks." Excited, I hung up the phone and raced upstairs to search for the classified advertisement to which I had responded. I rummaged through the shoebox in which I kept my important possessions and soon found the square strip of newspaper I was looking for:

HOTEL RECREATION DIRECTOR
Athletically-inclined individual, with public speaking skills,
to work in upstate resort. Send resume to P.O. Box ---

The classified ad had run in the September 23, 1990 edition of the *New York Times*. Maybe this is the break I need. I took off my dirty uniform and changed into a fresh T-shirt and a pair of shorts.

I had been employed as a waiter at Chi-Chi's, a Mexican restaurant, for more than two years. The money was adequate, but each night I worked there, mindlessly and without purpose, more and more of my self-esteem gradually withered away.

Before I returned my makeshift file cabinet, which had once contained a pair of suede Puma sneakers, to its storage space in my closet, I examined one other item of note—the resume I had sent out:

Dennis John Mulhearn
11 Tunison Road
East Brunswick, N.J. 08816
(201) 390-1013

Education:	Albright College, Reading, Pa. B.S.- Business Administration May, 1986
Honors:	Dean's List, 3.8 Grade Point Average
Work Experience:	Financial Analyst for New York Life Insurance, NY, NY; Marketing Specialist for Education Aides Publishing Co., Clifton, NJ; Waiter and bartender for various food establishments
Athletics:	Varsity Baseball, Varsity Football
Leadership:	Resident Adviser and Dormitory President, Coordinator for The Muscular Dystrophy Association

However humbling it was to see my life's summary typed onto a single sheet of paper, reading the resume brought a smile to my face. I momentarily reflected back to my college days, those four short yet wonderful years that seemed to pass by in a blink of a pretty girl's eye.

Then, within the isolated walls of Albright's picturesque campus, I was someone important: jock, scholar, and leader of the community. The world was mine for the taking; all I had to do was decide which path to travel on the proverbial road to success and happiness. I was a can't miss hot-shot. Yet now, those days of promise seemed faint and distant. Where had all my potential disappeared?

When I earned my degree in 1986, I really had no idea of what I wanted to do with my life. Following graduation, I accepted the first job offer I received and became a faceless New York commuter, armed with an exquisite leather briefcase (excellent for carrying sandwiches), and a pair of winged-tip shoes shiny enough to double as a mirror. The title of Financial Analyst for a highly respected insurance firm sounded impressive to my friends and family, but I was ill-suited to sit in front of a computer screen all day.

After a year and a half of unrelenting boredom, I left New York Life and accepted a position as a Marketing Specialist with a New Jersey-based reading company. Although I enjoyed visiting elementary school classrooms and giving reading lessons to the children, I was diametrically opposed to management's "sales at any cost" attitude in which ethics were trampled upon in the name of profit. Unwilling or unable to adopt this mindset, I quit after just eight months there.

Disillusioned with the business world, I took a part-time job at Chi-Chi's while I figured out what to do next. I continued serving burritos, chimichangas, and fried ice-cream until November 1989, when I decided to make a "Ralph Kramdenish" career change. After arranging a transfer with the local Chi-Chi's manager, I moved to Kissimee, Florida in a wildly naïve, yet wholehearted attempt to become a professional golfer.

I sincerely believed that if I devoted my life to the game of golf, it would not be long before I could beat all those skinny guys on T.V. After seven months of slaving away at the driving range for an average of ten hours a day, however, I still had difficulty breaking eighty. At that point I knew it was time to return home. I did so in May of 1990.

Now it was October 6, 1990 and what I had hoped would only be a temporary job at Chi-Chi's was becoming a disappointing, dead-end career. I knew I had the ability to achieve so much more in life, both in terms of social status and personal fulfillment. As I bided my time with customer after customer I never stopped believing that there was something much better awaiting me. Steve Richman's message filled me with hope that maybe my luck was finally changing.

I sat in my chair and thought about this new job prospect: Recreational Director of an upscale resort hotel. Compared to the drudgery of waitering, it was a dream come true. The thought lulled me into a deep sleep.

I woke up at 9:30 the next morning and immediately dialed The Pines's number.

"Hello, my name is Dennis Mulhearn. I'm responding to the message you left last night." Steve Richman answered me in calm, assured tone. He said he was very interested in my resume and wanted me to come to The Pines for an interview.

"How about tomorrow morning, Dennis?" he asked. It's a good thing I was speaking to him on a telephone—an ability to drool was definitely not one of the job requirements.

The roads were delightfully peaceful at 6:30 a.m. on the first Sunday of October. My 1980 Chevy Citation had been running well, and I was confident that my canary yellow car, which I had purchased in Florida, would survive the three-hour drive. When I stopped for gas on the Garden State Parkway, I looked at myself in the rear view mirror. Very sharp, Den. Very sharp.

I was wearing my best suit: light gray pinstripes blended stylishly into the navy blue garment. A neatly pressed white shirt and red power tie completed the ensemble. I was usually my own harshest critic, but even I had to admit that today I looked damned good. I thought nothing was going to stop me now.

I was wrong.

I made an inexcusable blunder and somehow thought I was supposed to get on the Palisades Parkway rather than the New York State Thruway. I drove for an hour before I realized my mistake. Panic-stricken, I pulled over and phoned The Pines to inform them that I would be delayed because of "car trouble."

Discouraged, I began to drive again. Great first impression—show up an hour late, I thought somberly as I picked up speed.

An hour and a half later I arrived in South Fallsburg, New York. Instead of seeing the wealthy, upper-middle class community I had imagined, I discovered that South Fallsburg was, actually, an impoverished ghetto. Most of the residential homes and all of the stores and shops were dilapidated and void of fresh paint, making the town appear as if it had never progressed beyond the year 1965. As I drove through the streets leading to my destination, I observed a dozen or so people shuffling aimlessly along the sidewalks. Not one of them seemed to be in any hurry to go anywhere or do anything.

I was relieved to see that The Pines, on the contrary, looked as classy as I had imagined. When I parked my car and walked through the open front gate, I felt as though I were crossing an invisible line that separated me from the depressing town of South Fallsburg and, indeed, from everywhere else.

The hotel's main structure consisted of one large building with four adjoining wings. A small, circular flowerbed was planted in front of the steps that led to the entrance. I entered an immaculate lobby and observed two young bellhops, both nattily dressed in black vests and matching bowties, joking with each other at the front desk. They stopped abruptly when they saw me approaching.

"Morning, fellas. Can you tell me where I can find Steve Richman's office?"

"Yea, sure. Go through the main office and Mr. Richman's is the first door on the right." I found the door and knocked on it.

"C'mon in."

The office was large yet not fancy. Steve Richman looked up from playing a game with his young daughter and acknowledged my presence with a nod. His youthful face and trim build befit a man of his position but his attire surprised me. Instead of a fancy corporate suit, he was dressed casually in a red polo shirt, khaki slacks, and brown loafers.

"Nice to meet you, Dennis? I'm Steve," he said, extending his right hand. I shook it and replied, "Hi, I'm sorry to keep you waiting."

"Don't worry about it. You won't need a car up here." He swiveled in his chair and directed my attention to a woman seated at a desk adjacent to his. "Bobbi here is our Group Sales Manager. She's going to give you a quick tour of the hotel, Dennis, and then bring you back here in about fifteen minutes."

Bobbi appeared to be in her mid-to-late forties and had short blond hair that was starting to turn gray. She was also casually dressed in a red polo shirt similar to Steve's. Her informal tour was impressive. The facilities at The Pines were an athlete's fantasy come to life. A golf course, indoor and outdoor pools, a skating rink, tennis and basketball courts, baseball diamonds, and numerous ski slopes, were spread throughout the resort.

At the conclusion of the tour, we walked through the nightclub. An older, squat woman was on stage conducting a masquerade contest. "That's Eve Cantor," Bobbi said, pointing toward her. "She's a wonderful lady whom you'll be working with closely." We were almost back to Steve's office and I still had a few questions I wanted to ask.

"Is this a new position or will I be taking someone's place?" Bobbi smiled at me and shook her head slowly.

"Evan Harris is the current Activities Director. He has a problem with cocaine. The poor guy just can't function anymore." That wasn't the answer I was expecting. I didn't say another word during the remaining walk back to the office.

"Well, what did you think?" Steve asked.

"You have a beautiful hotel here. I'm very impressed," I replied.

"C'mon, Dennis. Let's go for a walk outside," Steve said, motioning toward the door.

When we climbed a small hill overlooking the golf course, I noticed a number of people staring at me. It must be the way I'm dressed, I surmised. Nobody else around here wears a business suit on a weekend morning. Steve walked into the Pro Shop and returned with two putters and four golf balls. I took my jacket off and tried out the practice green. The unusually hot October sun beat down on the back of my neck as I crouched over my ball.

"This sure isn't a typical interview," I said as one of my Titleists clicked into the cup. I was enjoying myself immensely.

"No, I guess not," he answered. "We have a great hotel here and, although it takes quite a bit of work to keep things running smoothly, we also have a lot of time to kick back, relax, and enjoy ourselves. Generally, we keep things as informal as possible."

He started asking me question as we continued putting. I was surprised by his line of questioning. He didn't ask me anything about my background or my previous work experience. Instead, he asked me questions such as: "How do you feel about moving into a room here in the hotel? Can you speak in front of a large crowd? Would you be able to teach an aerobics class to

Senior Citizens?" I, of course, responded affirmatively to all of these questions. I had been on many interviews in my life but never before had I wanted a job this badly.

"I really like your resume. It's very diversified," Steve said, as we began walking back to the main lobby. I was heartened by his tone of voice as well as by his attitude towards me. It almost seemed as if the job were mine if I wanted it.

"My mother and father started this place up years ago. Back then, there were so many hotels up here in the Catskills, you could hardly keep track of them. Now The Pines is one of the few that are still open. My brother Cliff and I try to make sure all our guests are happy, so they'll continue to come back," he said. "I became involved in the business end of the hotel right after I graduated from The University of Colorado, but I've lived here since I was a kid." We were back inside the lobby when he spotted his brother and introduced me to him.

Cliff Richman was a few years younger than Steve—perhaps in his late twenties. His thinning brown hair and small pot belly, however, made him noticeably less attractive than his older sibling. He and I talked privately for a few minutes, while Steve left to take care of some business. Cliff told me basically the same things I had already heard from Bobbi and Steve. The only difference was that he spoke to me with far less enthusiasm than they had. After we had talked for a while, he looked down at his watch. With an apathetic sigh, he said, "It's 12:30, Steve wants me to take you into the dining room for lunch."

I dutifully walked behind him through the upper lobby into the dining room. The room was majestic. It reminded me of The Ferncliffe Manor, an elegant catering hall in which I had worked hundreds of weddings as a banquet waiter during my teenage years in Brooklyn. From the multitude of chandeliers, light jumped at me from every angle. The tables were covered with snow white linen and fine china, and the lights were dimmed to improve the ambiance.

Cliff directed me to a round table just to the right of a large dais. Seated at the table were Steve Richman and his wife and kids, Cliff's wife and kids, and a man named Bruce Smythe who was introduced as the General Manager of the hotel.

At this point, my primary concern was to get through lunch without spilling anything or doing something brilliant like dipping my tie in sauce. Fortunately, I encountered none of these problems. While engaging in a genial conversation, I learned that Bruce Smythe had a wife who was expecting a child within days. I also found out that he and I shared the same birthday: on October 20, I would be turning twenty-six and Bruce would be thirty. He seemed like an agreeable person. I envisioned no difficulty in working with him as my immediate boss.

The only thing that bothered me at lunch was the condescending manner in which Cliff treated the waiters: "Get me this," "Get me that," he demanded, without even bothering to say please or thank you. As a waiter myself, I cringed every time he called one of them over and barked out orders like a bad-tempered drill sergeant. At the conclusion of our lunch, I was told by Steve that they would be making a decision about the vacant position soon. He said he'd call me with an answer by early next week.

I drove home with the radio off. I wanted to absorb my unusual interview and think about the job for a while. The salary was acceptable, although far from spectacular. They were paying four hundred dollars per week in addition to providing free room and board. Money, however, was not the most compelling consideration. I was excited by the perks of the job. I imagined getting up and playing nine holes of golf every day before work. At night, I envisioned getting a good workout at the gym, eating dinner, and then going over to the nightclub to watch a show. Yes, I could easily get accustomed to this kind of lifestyle.

My only fear was that I wouldn't get the job because of religious discrimination. The Catskills was a predominantly Jewish area and I was worried that Cliff might take one look at my Irish-Catholic name and say: "Forget this guy." Nevertheless, I wasn't too concerned. From what I had observed, Steve was the person with the final decision and I could tell that he liked me quite a bit.

I pulled into my driveway and walked into my house. One of my roommates, Bob, was home watching a Giants game on television. "Did you get the job?" he asked.

"I don't know, it was just an interview." I took off my tie, sat down on the sofa, and told Bob everything I could remember. In the background, we watched Phil Simms methodically march his team down the field for a score.

"You're gonna get it. This job sounds made for you," he said, munching on a Doritos chip. I said nothing but could not have agreed more.

When my phone rang on Tuesday morning, I pounced on it on the first ring. To my disappointment, the caller was my younger brother Sean. I hadn't told him about The Pines interview, so he was simply calling to say hello. Even over the telephone, it didn't take long for him to sense my anxiety.

"Are you all right, Den? You sound as if you're on pins and needles."

"Yeah, I'm fine. I'm just waiting to hear about a job prospect. I'll let you know more about it if I get hired. Thanks for calling."

Although eighteen months my junior, Sean was often mistaken for my older brother. I still called him "little" brother, but at 6'2" and two hundred pounds he was far from little. In addition to his physical size, his sharp features and blue eyes made him extremely desirable to the opposite sex. My sister's friends referred to him as a "hunk" so frequently, one might have thought it was his middle name.

I suppose I felt some envy toward Sean sometimes, but this envy was tempered with respect. I admired his affable, easy-going personality and enjoyed hanging around with him. After living on the west coast of Florida for a year and a half, he had recently moved back to New Jersey. I was glad to have him home.

I received the call I had been waiting for later that afternoon. My palms turned as sweaty as a teenager on his first date when I heard Steve Richman's voice on the other end of the line.

"Hi, Dennis, this is Steve Richman from The Pines. We've narrowed our candidates down to two people. I want to just ask you one question: how soon can you start if we give you the job?" I told him I would have to give Chi-Chi's a week's notice but I could start on Monday. "All right then, c'mon up on Monday morning at nine o'clock. I'll get rid of this other guy. Bye."

I could hardly believe my good fortune. I was the new Activities Director of The Pines Hotel!

I spent the rest of the week preparing for the transition. Besides finally starting a career position, I was also moving to the Catskills. After being born and raised in Brooklyn, New York, New Jersey had seemed like "the country" to me, so I could only imagine the culture shock I would soon experience.

The only negative aspect of being hired by The Pines was the distance I would be separated from my family, with whom I was very close. When I told them about the new job and my impending move, however, my brothers Kevin, Sean, and Thomas, and my sister Deirdre (aged twenty-five, twenty-four, sixteen and twenty-one) were supportive, enthusiastic, and excited for me.

My mother was concerned that I would never be able to find the time to come see her but I tried to dispel her fears by promising to visit as often as possible. I planned on keeping my word.

My mother, Mary Ann Montello Mulhearn, was rapidly approaching fifty years of age, yet her energy and enthusiasm for life never failed to amaze me. After an excruciatingly painful divorce from my father, she had decided to boldly move forward and make some drastic changes in her life. Replacing self-pity with action, she was now doing all the things she had never had time to do while she was married. Participating in a theater group, socializing with friends, traveling, etc.

It took a while to get accustomed to the "new Mary Ann," but the bottom line was that she seemed truly happy. That was good enough for me. Thomas resented that his mother wasn't home every night to cook him dinner, but I tried to explain to him that she needed to do things for herself now. She had always made countless sacrifices for us, now it was our turn to be understanding. No matter how much she was enjoying her newfound independence, I knew that her five children would always remain her first priority.

On Saturday morning, I woke up early and went shopping with my sister. Deirdre was flattered that I had asked her to help me choose a new wardrobe. She conscientiously selected slacks, dress shirts, shoes, and sweaters that she thought would be appropriate for my new executive position. As always, her fashion taste was impeccable. I thanked her by treating her to lunch.

"Don't be a stranger. Make sure you call us every week and drop by for a visit every once in a while," she said while we waited for our meals to arrive.

"Don't worry, Deirdre. Once I learn the ropes at the hotel, I'll come by to annoy you and Mommy. The two of you won't be able to get rid of me that easily." She laughed blithely and tossed her red hair back from her face. Her hard-earned summer tan was gone now, leaving her Irish complexion as white as freshly fallen snow. Fortunately, she bore no resemblance to any of her brothers. She was a beautiful girl.

One of the few rays of light that came out of my parents' divorce was Deirdre's improved relationship with our mother. Growing up as the only girl among four brothers, she had always felt as if she were on the periphery of our male-dominated family. Because her three older brothers were star athletes, attention was shifted even further away from her. In her estimation, since she could not put a ball through a hoop or hit a curved pitch, anything else she did was insignificant and second-rate.

When she reached her teenage years, her self-esteem was extremely poor. She became increasingly distant from her family and especially from our mother, whom she viewed as her chief adversary. My mother tried to reach out and get Deirdre to talk about what was bothering her, but no amount of coaxing could get her to open up.

During holidays, Deirdre would disappear at the first opportunity to escape with her friends. She felt closer to them than to anyone in her own family. After many years of struggling to come to terms with her true feelings, she was finally able to develop a positive self-image, but the impenetrable wall that she had carefully built, brick by brick, grew higher and thicker with each passing day.

It took the trauma of the divorce to bring that wall crumbling down. Deirdre was deeply hurt when our father left home but she provided our mother with great strength and compassion during her time of need. For the first time, they talked to each other and shared their innermost feelings not just as mother and daughter, but as friends. Their friendship has continued to solidify with the passage of time.

I drove to New City, New York that Sunday evening. New City was halfway between East Brunswick and The Pines. Since my father and his wife rented a house there, I figured I could stay at their place on Sunday night, and then only have to drive another hour and a half on Monday morning. My father greeted me at the door.

"Glad to see you finally made it. We couldn't wait any longer, we already ate." Seated on the couch were my twin brother Kevin and my father's second wife, whose real name was Awilda, but whom everyone called "Willie." They were watching the last quarter of a tight Giants–Redskins game.

I stepped inside and made myself comfortable. I was no stranger to the house. Nearly every Monday morning, I'd drive up and play golf with my father. When we returned from the links, Willie always had a hot lunch ready for us.

"Sit down and relax. I'll go get your dinner, hon," Willie said. She stood up and walked into the kitchen.

"Thanks, Willie," I replied. I treated her courteously, if not outright cordially.

My father, Thomas Lee Mulhearn, met Willie in New York, in the fall of 1987. She, too, was married and had four children of her own. At that time, he was going through a major transition. Within the span of a few months, he had retired from the New York ity Police Department and then suffered a mild heart attack. I noticed a change in him immediately after his release from the hospital. Medically, he was fine, but the frightening brush with his mortality left him questioning the direction of his life. I wasn't that surprised when I found out he was involved with another woman.

Although I felt that my parents still had some love for each other, I had known for quite some time there were serious problems with their relationship. My mother and father were both terrific persons and very devoted parents, but as the years progressed it became obvious to me that, aside from their five children, they had virtually nothing else in common.

In fact, in many ways they were exact opposites. My mom loved the Arts and was extremely sociable, while my dad was a sports junkie who liked nothing better than to sit home and watch a ballgame on television. It is not fair of me to speak for either of my parents, so I won't try. I can say, however, that ever since my high school graduation, I feared the possibility of them splitting up. From my vantage point, a key undefined ingredient in their marriage seemed to be missing. The unexpected pecks on the cheek and hugs of affection I had frequently witnessed in my idyllic childhood had become relics of the past.

Willie was a radically different person than my down-to-earth mother. She was a flashy and cosmopolitan woman. Her sense of style and sophistication were qualities my father found highly attractive. After knowing each other for a brief period of time, they began to have an affair.

Soon thereafter, my father left home to live with Willie. A year and much turmoil later, divorce papers were finally processed by my parents' respective attorneys. When Willie's divorce was also made final, she and my father were married by a New City justice of the peace.

While the emotional upheaval of the ugly divorce was devastating to all the children in our family, my youngest brother, Thomas, suffered the most. He was only thirteen when everything started. As the only minor, his custody was fiercely contested, and was the cause of many venomous arguments between our parents.

The daunting specter of choosing sides between the two people in the world whom he loved the most was an impossible task. But Thomas courageously refused to allow himself to be used as a pawn in his mother and father's war. He maintained a rigidly neutral position, never budging one way or another. Through the worst of times, Tom displayed a gentle toughness that I found remarkable in such a young boy. Although often thrust into the unenviable role of peacemaker, he always conducted himself admirably.

Nevertheless, his underdeveloped psyche was greatly damaged by our parents' breakup. When the divorce mercifully became final, it was decided that he was going to continue to live with my mother. Within two months, he became acutely depressed and gained thirty pounds. My mother had quite a bit of difficulty just getting him out of bed in the morning for school.

Gradually, Thomas was able to snap out of his depression and return to a more normal routine. Although he was still very immature in certain ways, he had come a long way in the past few months. I noticed him laughing and smiling with much greater frequency. His weight gain effectively ended what had been a promising baseball career, but he showed an artistic talent that none of his siblings possessed. He planned on using that talent to become an architect. I wouldn't bet against him.

There's a saying that goes: "Time heals all wounds." What the saying fails to mention is that sometimes deep wounds leave jagged scars. These scars can be covered up but they are always there, penetrating beneath the surface of the skin as an unpleasant reminder of one's pain.

Despite the lasting scars, in time I was able to forgive my father for his infidelity. Although his armor coat had been unceremoniously stripped away before my eyes, I still loved him very much. His relationship with Willie did not alter the fact that he had always been a terrific father. I continued to attach disproportional importance to his approval of me.

My attitude toward Willie was also markedly improving. The unabashed hostility that I had initially felt toward her was slowly changing into a reluctant understanding of what had actually taken place between her and my father. I still didn't like the situation, but I was going to have to learn how to accept it.

"Here you go sweetheart, I hope it's hot enough for you," Willie said as she returned to the living room with a bowl of beef stew. My father, Kevin, and I talked football as I ate my dinner and watched the end of the game. The Giants secured the win with about a minute left on the clock, when they picked off a hurried Redskins pass.

"Well, that's it. I'd better get going. I've got some work to do tonight," Kevin said, standing up and stretching. "Would you mind giving me a ride to the bus stop, Dad? I can catch the 8 o'clock into the city if we leave now."

"Sure, Kev. Get your coat and let's get going."

Kevin pulled on his overcoat, congratulated me once again, and wished me luck.

"Once you get settled, give me a call and I'll come and visit you on a weekend," he said.

"Sounds good. I'll talk to you next week."

We have often been asked the standard question, "What's it like to be a twin?" We always respond by asking, "What's it like to not be a twin?" Kevin and I have always been very close. We are one another's best friend, yet have distinct differences in personality. He is much more outgoing and emotional than I am. With the facility to talk one's ear off, he aptly earned the nickname "KOB" (King of Bull). In contrast, I have always been much more quiet and introspective than my older (by seven minutes) brother.

Ironically, our decision to attend different colleges probably brought us closer than any other single event in our young lives. Throughout our elementary and secondary school days in Brooklyn, we were known as a pair—a dual entity known as "The Mulhearn Twins." By separating, we were finally able to establish our own individual identities; as a result, we both enjoyed a great deal of success and popularity at our respective institutions of higher learning.

After graduating from Mulhenberg College, Kevin enrolled at Villanova Law School, where he continued to excel. He thrilled our family by delivering a rousing speech at the school's Spring 1990 Commencement. He then began working at a prestigious New York City law firm in September of that year.

Although my achievements in life paled in comparison to his, I felt no jealousy towards him. My entire family and I were extremely proud of everything he had accomplished. We knew how hard he had worked.

I chuckled as I thought back to Villanova's graduation ceremony. "Great speech, Kev," I heard about a hundred times. After a while, I played along. "Thank you," I responded with a straight face. "Thank you very much." I had to laugh. Except for a slightly different hairstyle and the ten extra pounds he carried on his five foot eleven inch frame, my brother and I were virtually identical. We even had the same beauty mark on our left cheek.

"So tell me about the position," Willie said, sitting down next to me on the sofa. I did not like to be alone with her—it made me uncomfortable—but, nevertheless, I was anxious to talk about my job.

"Its sounds like its right up my alley. The Pines is said to be the second best resort in the Catskills, right behind The Concord." I paused for a moment, and tried to remember what Bobbi and the Richman brothers had told me.

"The place is huge. There are more than eight hundred rooms in nine different buildings that are all connected by tunnels. Best of all, it's an athlete's paradise. All the sports facilities are right on the premises." After I described the golf course, tennis and basketball courts, and the baseball field, I told her about the six ski slopes. "I'm gonna finally get a chance to learn how to ski this winter," I gushed. "I've always wanted to do that."

Willie stopped me there. She asked to see the resume I had sent. I went down to my car and retrieved it along with the ad I had answered, and proudly handed both pieces of paper to her.

"This is very impressive," she said as she examined my resume, her tone indicating sincerity.

In truth, it was nothing special. Although I had quite a few academic and athletic accomplishments while at Albright College, I could not hide that I had never stayed with one job for much more than a year. Thus, my diverse work experience was a liability as well. Despite this flaw, I felt that Steve Richman had chosen me because of my enthusiasm and intensity. During my interview, I made it easy for him to see how much I wanted the job.

My father returned in a few minutes and questioned me some more about The Pines. I enjoyed repeating all the details to him. I would have probably continued to talk all night long if he and Willie had not had to get up early. When they retired to their bedroom, I flopped onto the living room sofa and fell right to sleep.

3

SEVEN DAYS
AT THE PINES

I awoke at 6:30 sharp and was on the road by 7 o'clock. The time passed quickly and I was at the entrance to The Pines before I knew it. While I parked the car in the main parking lot, I noticed for the first time that the resort was encircled by a wooded area that stretched for miles. An abundance of tall pine trees provided a beautiful and natural setting for the hotel's facilities, but also isolated the complex from the rest of the community. I walked briskly through the front gate and into the main lobby.

"Good morning," I said to an elderly woman working behind the front desk, "my name is Dennis Mulhearn. I'm the new Director of Activities."

"It's a pleasure to meet you. Come around back here," she said, pointing to an adjacent door. Behind the door was the office for the hotel's activities and administrative departments. A small, round woman who bore a striking resemblance to Dr. Ruth Westheimer was seated at one of the desks. She looked vaguely familiar but I could not immediately place her face. When she was introduced to me as Eve Cantor, however, I remembered that she was the woman I had seen on the stage the day of my interview.

"Finally, my new assistant. Excuse me   co-director," she said happily. Steve had told me that Eve would teach me the administrative aspects of the job. He had said that her expertise was as an entertainer, and that she was excellent at overseeing the various social events that took place at the hotel.   Eve brought me behind her desk and showed me what she was working on. "Do you type" she asked as she sat down in front of her electric typewriter and punched in some corrections with her index fingers. I shook my head. "Well these papers are called Activities Sheets. All daily activities are listed according to a very tight schedule. Every day, we have to make sure there are enough copies of these sheets. If the guests can't find them, they throw a fit."

That was the extent of the information I received from Eve. Later that morning, tour buses arrived from the Pennsylvania towns of Reading, Bethlehem and Perkiomen. All three of the buses were filled with groups of senior citizens that were going to be staying at the hotel until the weekend. It was the job of the ctivities staff to see to it that they were entertained with card games, Bingo, and other various types of leisure activities.

As Activities Director I was responsible for greeting the newly arrived guests, informing them of the day's schedule, and showing them to their rooms. Most of the people were quite pleasant considering that they had endured an uncomfortable bus ride of six or more hours. One gentleman complained about the flight of stairs he and his wife had to climb to get to their room. I quickly called the front desk and had the couple's accommodations relocated to the main floor.

Most of the staff I met on my first day seemed indifferent to my arrival. I met people from all the departments: housekeeping, food and beverage, front desk, sales, and payroll, to name just a few. My head spun amidst handshakes and introductions.

"So, you're taking Evan's place," a mousy girl in her late twenties said to me as I was being introduced to the payroll department employees.

"That's right, my name's Dennis."

"Joyce," she responded. "Good luck. Your department is the only one in the hotel with a high turnover rate. People from Activities come and go every couple of months." I nodded and moved on.

By lunchtime I had met my three activity assistants: Ciji, Lawrence, and Joe. The first two were sloppily dressed and unshaven young black men in their early twenties. I was surprised and disappointed by their appearance. Their jobs required close interaction with the guests, and neatness and good grooming should have been a priority. When introduced to Joe, I was further shocked by what I saw.

Joe was a forty-three-year-old man of Italian descent with salt and pepper hair, glasses, and a big gap where a front tooth was strikingly absent. His baggy jeans and old gray sweatshirt hung from his body like a potato sack.

"So, you're the new boss, huh," he said, smiling. I recoiled from the offensive amount of alcohol on his breath.

"That's right," I said, unsure of what to make of his comment. He smiled again and resumed working. I watched as he posted the sign for Tuesday morning's speaker. In spite of his appearance, I would soon learn that Joe was the one indispensable member of the Activities Department. He had been at The Pines for a year and a half, the other two guys had been there less than a month. Joe knew precisely what, where, and how to set up for each event. After he did what needed to be done, he would go back to his room and grab a beer. He would then reappear just in time to break down or set up for the next activity.

Joe's last name was Martello but, because of his supposed penchant to consume large amounts of cocaine, he was known by everyone at The Pines as "Joe Crack." I sincerely hoped that the nickname was either a false rumor or a gross exaggeration. Drinking a couple of beers was one thing, but smoking crack was an entirely different matter.

In the afternoon, I accompanied Ciji and watched him give a tour of the hotel. I was going to be doing that job myself in a couple of days. To the left of the tennis courts, I noticed a run-down brick building that looked as though it should have been condemned.

"What's that? I asked Ciji.

"That place is called the Annex. I'd stay away from there if I was you."

Later, I approached a security guard and asked him what he knew about the Annex.

"You want to forget you ever heard of that dump," he said. "Ya see, they got a scam goin' here. They hire illegal aliens from South America to work in the kitchen. Even the waiters are spics. You won't find more than a handful who can speak decent English. They pay 'em only two bucks a day, but they got 'em all living over there in the Annex. It's rat-infested and there's more drugs in there than in a fuckin' pharmacy."

Despite the appearance of my assistants and the distressing information about the Annex, I was still enthusiastic about the job and the potential I saw for myself at The Pines. That night, before I went to bed, I jogged around the outer circumference of the hotel. I felt free and alive, ready to take on whatever challenges might come my way. I was assigned room number 261 in the main building. The 8' x 12' room was cramped, yet sufficient to meet my basic needs. It was going to be my home until I was able to save enough money to move into an apartment.

The next couple of days were extremely busy but enjoyable. I taught an aerobics class in the morning, made announcements in the dining hall at lunch and dinner, and entertained guests with Trivia and Bingo in the afternoons. Although the work was hectic, I found it satisfying. It was fun to help people have a good time on their vacations. The energetic senior citizens reminded me of my own grandparents.

The resort was buzzing with activity. There was always something going on in one area of the hotel or another. In the main lobby, Eve held a variety of talks on topics ranging from "Superstitions" to "Helpful Vinegar Tips." The South lobby was prearranged with an assortment of exhibits such as cartoonists, needlepoint, and tarot card readings. For those of a competitive nature, ping-pong, shuffleboard, and bocci ball tournaments were held daily.

I enjoyed being in the middle of the action but was upset by my lack of training. Eve hadn't spent any time whatsoever teaching me my job duties and responsibilities. She was such a nervous wreck, I was amazed she could function at all.

The Activities desk was unorganized and chaotic. Important papers and supplies were strewn all over the place. Whenever Eve needed something, she'd yell at one of the assistants, and he would scurry behind the desk looking for what she wanted. During the staffer's frantic search, Eve's heavy, impatient breathing was a not-so-subtle reminder of her annoyance with his incompetence.

On Wednesday, Evan Harris left The Pines along with his pregnant girlfriend, Anita. I found out that Anita was a former Activities staffer who had been fired on Monday morning. They were both removed by security at the urging of Eve Cantor. She wanted them off the grounds immediately.

Although I had never met Evan, I felt sorry for him. From various sources, I had heard many wild stories about his ability to party, and wondered how much truth was in those stories. Also, I regretted that I didn't have the opportunity to meet with him and ask him some questions concerning the job. His perspective would have been illuminating.

Joe was very close to Evan and was extremely upset by his friend's termination. Despite his alleged addictions, I was starting to like Joe quite a bit. He was honest, funny, and forthright. More importantly, he not only knew his own job, but also how the entire Activities Department should be run.

To his credit, he was eager to share his knowledge with me. He would pull me aside and tell me how certain aspects of my job should be handled. He taught me how to run the Bingo games, how to prepare for different guest speakers, and how to set up for Lou Goldstein, the Simon-Sez guru who worked at the hotel.

In addition to familiarizing me with my job duties, he also helped me understand how The Pines's corporate politics worked. Joe pointed out all the influential people to me, and related some of the unspoken rules he thought I should know. None of this information was earth-shattering, but it certainly didn't hurt to be well informed.

That afternoon, I was looking forward to attending my first Department Head meeting in the dining room. Ciji failed to show up for work, however, so I was forced to watch the front desk in his absence. Eve finally relieved me with ten minutes left in the meeting. When I walked into the dining room, all eyes became fixed on me.

Steve Richman personally introduced me to everyone present: Claudia (dining room), Lois (front desk), Frank (registration), Charlie (security), Kevin (night club), and Roberta (bar). Bruce Smythe served as moderator. He had passed around next week's memo and was discussing the upcoming week and what was expected from each department. Since I had missed most of the meeting, I didn't understand much of what was being said. I bit my lip and cursed Ciji under my breath. His irresponsibility had created needless extra work for me.

After the late afternoon Bingo game, Joe informed me that we had to get the lobby ready for Lou Goldstein's show. Lou was quite an interesting person. Upon being introduced to him, I immediately perceived him as a man worthy of my respect. His sixty odd years appeared to be an optical illusion. Indeed, his muscular and well-proportioned physique and his apparently bottomless reservoir of energy were the envy of many men half his age. I could readily see that this man's personality was the root of his success as an entertainer.

Although Lou was friendly and polite, he was also inordinately fastidious about the way he wanted the lobby prepared for his show. He demanded that the chairs be precisely eighteen inches apart in rows facing the stage. The microphone wire had to be taped to the floor in just the exact location. Joe was familiar with the routine. Working efficiently, we quickly arranged the room to Lou's specifications.

I stopped into the dining hall, hurriedly ate my dinner, and then returned to the lobby to watch Lou perform. His act was hilarious. The audience howled with delight. Following the show, I had planned on going back to my room to watch the second game of the World Series between the Oakland A's and the Cincinatti Reds, but Joe persuaded me to change my mind.

"Hey, Dennis, why don't you go with me to the night club. I'll show you a few things you might find interesting," he said. I really wanted to see the game, but I didn't want to miss an opportunity to learn more about The Pines.

"All right, Joe, lead the way." He took me out the back door of the lobby, and we proceeded toward the night club entrance. The cool night air was delightful. It was the kind of perfect evening in which one felt fortunate to be alive.

When we reached the night club, I was escorted into a soundproof control booth to the left of the stage. Through a glass window, I observed a colorfully attired musical group singing and dancing their way across the platform. Joe again introduced me to the manager, Kevin Stack. Kevin was in his mid-thirties. He had black hair that was just beginning to gray on the sides and a thick mustache. In addition to being the night club manager, he also served as the Master of Ceremonies, and thus was dressed in a black tuxedo.

"How are you, Dennis?" he said, shaking my hand. A small black and white televison in the corner of the room was tuned to the baseball game, but Kevin focused his sight squarely on the control panel in front of him. Despite his attention to his job, he made a generous effort to befriend me. We talked about the World Series, the hotel, and other various topics as he manipulated the buttons and levers of the panel. He didn't seem to mind my presence in the middle of a performance.

When the production ended, I thanked Kevin and said goodnight to him, and then turned to Joe.

"Thanks for everything, Joe. I'll see you tomor ..."

"Not so fast, boss. You gotta see my place before you go back tonight. It's not far from here at all," he said animatedly.

Not wanting to offend him after everything he had done for me, I followed him into a building called the Ritz, in which he and some of the other employees were housed. I was curious why he was so anxious to have me go with him, but decided that there couldn't be any harm in seeing where he lived.

The Ritz was only about seventy yards to the right of the night club but the difference in atmosphere was indescribable. As I entered the building I was unprepared for the dank, musty odor. The building didn't look any better than it smelled. The dilapidated walls appeared poised to crumble at any moment, and I had all I could do to keep from tripping over the debris on the floor. Among this debris were numerous compact vials that had been emptied and haphazardly discarded.

"Welcome to the Ritz," Joe said proudly as we entered his room. "It doesn't look like much, but it's a helluva place to party. Ciji and Lawrence live upstairs, and Evan used to live right up the hall. You'll be moving in as soon as you get settled."

"I don't think so, Joe. I'm as straight as an arrow. I don't even drink."

Joe just smiled and said, "Yeah, right ... we'll see about that. This is where you can make your money. You can make more money here than you ever imagined." I didn't like where the conversation was headed, so I nervously excused myself and rushed back to my room.

When I laid down on my bed, countless thoughts ran through my head at a substantially accelerated pace. I was disturbed by what I had seen at the Ritz. In the middle of all the natural beauty of The Pines and its facilities was what appeared to be a powerful drug culture. I hadn't even seen the Annex yet, but after getting a brief glimpse of the Ritz, I didn't want to go anywhere near it.

Having grown up in Brooklyn, I had a particularly strong aversion to drugs and what they did to people. I had witnessed so many classmates and friends with unlimited potential throw away their lives, desperately attempting to escape from reality through the bottom of a bottle or the other end of a spoon.

I was also becoming increasingly perturbed by my lack of training. Eve hadn't made the slightest attempt to help me get acclimated to my new position. When she left at four o'clock every day, I was on my own. I was responsible for the entire Activities Department, but I didn't have any knowledge of the proper procedures. Without Joe's help I would have been lost. With him, I managed to barely muddle through. Nevertheless, I was determined to excel at this job despite the drugs and despite Eve's ambivalence towards me. I was going to show everyone exactly what Dennis Mulhearn was made of.

I woke up early on Thursday, got dressed in a new sweat suit, and jogged around the hotel. I had heard that Thursday was an unusually busy day, since it was the last full day for most of the seniors. Despite the previous night, I was still full of zest for my job. Joe's impromptu tour of the Ritz was relegated to the back of my mind.

The day started on a bright note, as the people in my morning aerobics class showed an unusual amount of verve. The spry senior citizens responded enthusiastically to the *Rocky* soundtrack I blasted from my portable cassette player. The inspirational music allowed me to push them a littler harder than I had in any of my previous classes.

While I walked back through the lobby on the way to my room, scores of guests stopped me to say a few words. Some expressed their appreciation for helping to make their hiatus an enjoyable one, others simply wanted to extend a heartfelt goodbye in case they didn't see me again before they checked out. Their sincerity and kindness made me feel as if I had finally found a home at The Pines. I hadn't felt this good since my senior year in college.

I took a five minute shower and returned to the main lobby in time to see Eve frenetically looking for a roll of masking tape. As the grand finale to their vacations, some of the guests were entered in a costume-contest show, in which various categories included "Zaniest Pajamas," "Funniest Hat," and "Best Costume Overall." While a packed audience waited in the lobby, Eve was trying to line up the contestants and place numbers on their backs. When she finally found the tape, she proceeded to roughly slap a number on the backs of each of the participants.

When she stepped out onto the stage, Eve threw her slight shoulders back and flashed a big smile. She joked with the guests and seemed quite comfortable with a microphone in hand. Judging by their collective response, the audience found her very entertaining.

The show concluded with the presentation of "Best Costume Overall." A woman, who I later learned was eighty-four years old, captured the prize by wearing her original wedding gown.

The wrinkles and lines on her well-worn face didn't matter, not even the tenacious sands of time could detract from this woman's beauty. As she stood on the stage in her white remembrance of a time long ago, large teardrops cascaded from her venerable eyes. Trying to decide if she was happy or sad, I realized that she was a little of both. It was not possible for me to comprehend the labyrinth of emotions she must have felt at that moment.

Right after the show, I went downstairs to the support staff office. One of my responsibilities was to calculate each employee's payroll every other week, and I wanted to make sure I learned how to do it correctly. I was fully cognizant that nothing could aggravate an employee more than a deficient paycheck.

Joyce kept the book I needed locked in a safe. When I asked her about it, she graciously retrieved it for me. I immediately noticed some inconsistencies. Aside from the Activities Department, all the other employees were paid a decent salary. Joe, Ciji, and Lawrence, however, were paid a flat rate of just twenty dollars per day. Since they worked between eight and ten hours daily, this was far below the legal minimum wage.

In addition, Lou and Jackie Goldstein (who taught an advanced aerobics class), and Terry Suratt (The Pines's organist) were listed under the Activities Department. Each of them had little red checks next to their names in lieu of a numerical rate of pay. No other employees in any department had such a vague record of his or her earnings. I was curious as to the reason for this discrepancy.

"Cliff Richman's the person you need to see if you have any questions. He's in Manhattan this week, but he'll be back on Monday," Joyce said, taking the book from me. I nodded, assured her that I had quite a few questions for Cliff, and then went back to work.

Later that afternoon, Eve returned to the Activities desk with a stack of Friday's Activities sheets. To my dismay, she had changed the heading of the sheets. All week I had been listed as "Co-Director of Activities," but on Friday's sheets I was listed as "Assistant Director." Angered by this paper demotion, I immediately confronted her about it. She looked at the sheet and said, "Assistant Director, Co-Director, what's the difference?"

"There's a big difference, Eve. I would appreciate it if you'd change it back tomorrow." She walked away without saying another word.

Although it was only my first week of work, it appeared that Eve was going out of her way to make my transition difficult. I kept asking her to show me how to do the Activities sheets, which was one of the primary functions of my job, but she kept telling me she didn't have any time. I even offered to come to the office early in the morning, but Eve rejected this idea as well, saying she had a hard enough time getting to work by eight o'clock.

Thus, I had to learn by continually asking questions, talking to numerous people, and relying heavily on Joe. Ciji and Lawrence were both consistently lazy. They tried to get away with doing as little work as possible. I did not foresee long futures at The Pines for either of them.

At 7 p.m. I attended the weekly cocktail party in the private board room. Eve didn't even have the courtesy to inform me about this important event. Not surprisingly, I learned about it from Joe an hour before it was scheduled to begin.

The elegant party was intended to leave one final lasting impression on the departing guests. Only the leaders of the respective tour groups and the heads of the departments were invited. At the beginning of the hour, each staff member was briefly introduced to the honored guests.

Normally, Bruce Smythe handled the Mc-ing, but his wife had just delivered their first child, so Bobbi was filling in for him. When it was my turn to be acknowledged, she introduced me as "Danny, Eve Cantor's new assistant." Embarrassed, my face turned beet red.

I wanted to correct her and set the record straight, but I could not speak above the volume of her microphone. I wasn't positive, but I guessed that Eve had something to do with what I thought was clearly an intentional slight. I saw her whispering in Bobbi's ear right before Bobbi began the introductions.

Although I was furious by these women's thinly veiled attempt to subjugate me, the formal cocktail party was not the proper venue to do anything about it. Still seething, I collected myself enough to chat amiably with some of the guests for a few minutes. When the first opportunity presented itself, however, I unobtrusively slipped away from the festivities, rolled up the sleeves of my white shirt, and walked down to my office.

I turned my anger into something productive by staying up late and working. I stayed up until two o'clock that morning, teaching myself how to type so I could do the Activities sheets myself. If Eve wasn't going to help me, I would have to learn how to do everything on my own.

The only people down in the office with me were Bill, the nighttime operator, Leroy, the head janitor, and Terry Suratt. Terry did not look like a typical entertainer. He was at least fifty pounds overweight and had a severe case of adult acne. When I asked him what he was doing down in the office so late, he told me he was working on a few songs for some friends. I didn't say anything to him but I found that rather odd. I hadn't pegged him to be the ambitious type.

The sporadic clicking of typewriter keys gradually increased in tempo. I went to bed only when I thought I could do a passable job of typing, even if I just used my two index fingers.

I didn't sleep well that night. Too many thoughts were haphazardly floating through my brain. I started planning every single thing I was going to do the next day. Get up early, jog, eat breakfast, clean office, etc. Everything had to be done perfectly.

I found out at the breakfast table that Eve had stayed overnight at the hotel. She fell asleep in her bathtub and had let the water continue running. It took a maintenance crew nearly all morning to clean up the flood that spread throughout the entire floor.

After breakfast I went down to my office and tried to rearrange the disorderly desk my predecessor had left me. I was going through some papers when Steve Richman walked in.

"Hi, Dennis. How's everything going?"

"Fine, thanks, Steve. I'm just trying to get organized here."

"Good, you're doing a great job. The department's all yours. I want you to run with the ball." He smiled and walked into his office. His compliment emboldened my already strong resolve to establish a standard of excellence in my work. It was gratifying to know that the boss was firmly in my corner.

Friday was even more hectic than Thursday had been. The senior citizens were all leaving, and a number of different singles groups were checking in for the weekend. I was running around with unbridled nervous energy, trying to figure out what to do, when I learned that Eve had left the hotel at twelve noon. Without so much as a word of advice, she left all the responsibilities squarely in my lap.

In stark contrast to the mellow seniors, the young men and women from the various singles groups bombarded me with an endless array of demands and questions. My insufficient (almost nonexistent) training left me ill-prepared to say anything to them other than, "hold on a minute," or "I'll see what I can do." I tried valiantly to maintain my composure and professionalism, but my blatant ignorance of the check-in procedures made this extremely difficult.

Once again, Joe came to the rescue. He had been through similar situations many times before and knew all the intricacies associated with checking in the various groups, contacts, special instructions, and which facilities needed to be adjusted for the weekend. With him as my guide, I was able to respond to all of the questions to everyone's satisfaction and project a rather convincing illusion of competence.

As grateful as I was to Joe for his invaluable assistance, I was even more furious at Eve for leaving me in such a quandary. I had been at The Pines for five days now and she hadn't given me one morsel of useful information. Had she shared some of her vast experience with me, my productivity would have increased substantially and, also, her own workload would have been significantly reduced. I couldn't fathom why she was unwilling to provide even a modicum of help.

Later that evening I called my dad in New City and told him what was happening. "Don't let some pushy broad give you the run around. Stand up to her and tell her how you feel," he advised. He was absolutely right. The next morning, I was going to speak with her and set things straight. First, there was a large quantity of work to be done. I went back down to the office and immersed myself in a stack of papers.

I stayed up all night doing various work. At 1 a.m., Anita, an attractive girl who worked at the front desk, came down and started talking to me. Since she was easily the prettiest girl at The Pines, I didn't mind the diversion.

"Why don't you come to the nightclub with me and have a drink or two? I'd really like to get to know you better," she said coquettishly. The offer was very tempting but I had too much work to complete.

"I'm sorry, Anita. I can't tonight. Maybe tomorrow night." She looked at me with a startled expression on her face. This was a girl who was not used to being turned down.

"Have you ever tried cocaine?" she asked me from out of nowhere.

"No, I stay away from that garbage. It's poison," I replied.

"Yeah, you're right. I used to be really into coke, but I haven't done it for two years. I was just curious, that's all." After she said goodnight and left, I pondered why she would blurt out a question like that. Was she trying to turn me on to the white powder? "If you are, you picked the wrong guy, baby," I muttered under my breath as I returned to the papers on my desk.

I looked through a month's worth of old Activities sheets and finally figured out how to prepare them correctly. I then wrote down approximately ten pages of notes that outlined some of my ideas for The Pines. In addition to a few general organizational changes that I felt would increase efficiency, my notes included a detailed marketing strategy.

Finally, I finished off the Activity sheets for the upcoming Sunday and Monday, and posted a half-dozen new signs all through the hotel. In short, I was a working juggernaut. I had just completed three or four days worth of work in one sleepless night. Unlike the dreaded all-night sessions I had reluctantly pulled in college with the aid of a two-liter bottle of Mountain Dew soda, I wasn't even that tired. I didn't know where I was getting my energy from and, frankly, I didn't care.

Saturday, October 20, 1990 was a gorgeous day. The sun was shining brightly, the birds were singing, and—as far as I was concerned—all was right with the world. It was my twenty-sixth birthday and I felt terrific about myself and the job I was doing at The Pines.

As I jogged around the hotel that morning, my thoughts turned to my family. I was going to make them all so proud of me when they saw how well I was doing. I was not a high-powered attorney like my brother Kevin, but The Pines was a place where I could make my own distinctive mark.

I confronted Eve Cantor at 9 a.m. I plainly told her I didn't think I was being treated fairly and that I shouldn't have to learn the job by myself. I was decidedly calm and cool. Eve was not. She exploded in a fit of rage.

"If you don't like the way I do my job, let's take it up with the Richmans, you little snot-nosed bastard," she hissed in a shrill voice.

"That's fine with me," I retorted angrily. I didn't know why this woman wanted to fight me, but I didn't intend to back down from her. In the brief week I had been there, the quality of my work spoke for itself. I strode confidently through the lobby and made my way toward the main office. Eve lagged right behind me, her short legs struggling to keep up with my pace.

"They come and they go," Eve repeated again and again as we approached the Richmans' office. "They come and they go," she said once more, loud enough for all the other employees in the room to hear, before we entered the office.

Steve was seated at his desk and his father, Jerry Richman, was standing in the far corner of the room. They were both caught off guard by our unannounced appearance, but it did not take them long to see that a serious problem was brewing. Eve immediately began screaming about my insubordination and I yelled right back, questioning her honesty and her motives for failing to train me properly.

"You're trying to make yourself look better by making me look bad. You're threatened by me, aren't you?" I shouted above her shrieks of protest. When some semblance of civility was temporarily restored, Eve and I sat down and presented separate versions of our dispute.

Armed with nothing except lies and rhetoric, she mumbled something incoherent about how difficult I was to work with. I laughed in her face and then apprised the Richmans of a number of specific instances in which she had lied to me, and in which she had purposely withheld important information.

I reached into my pocket, showed them one of Friday's Activities sheets, and asked if they had been aware of my sudden demotion. The two men looked at each other and shook their heads forlornly. If the debate had been scored, I would have won in a landslide. While Eve spoke in vague generalities, I had overwhelming evidence to support my assertions.

Since she couldn't dispute the facts with me, she shifted gears and went on the attack. "I can't work with him. I want him out of here," she whined.

"Relax, Eve, we'll work it out," Jerry Richman said with a carefree smile. Those were the first and only words he spoke, but they were of great comfort to Eve. She sat back in her chair and gave me a self-satisfied smirk. I found out later that she and Jerry's wife had been close friends for many years.

Steve, on the other hand, was taking my side in the argument. He chided Eve for giving me what he termed "misinformation." Although he was trying to be a fair intermediary, he definitely agreed that I wasn't treated the way I should have been. After another few minutes of hostile dialogue between Eve and me, Steve told me to go back to my room and calm down.

An hour later, Bruce Smythe called me into his office. When I arrived, Eve was already sitting down. I could tell that she was still fuming. "Okay, Dennis, we're going to try to iron out this little difference and get back to work," Bruce said sternly. "You're the head of the Activities Department. All the responsibilities will be yours. You'll split the commissions from exhibits 50/50 with Eve. How does that sound?"

"That's fine, Bruce, but I need to work with Eve, not against her. I need to know that she'll try to help me out, and that she won't sabotage my work."

Bruce turned to Eve, looked her straight in the eyes and said, "All right, Eve, will you be able to work with Dennis and get the job done?"

Eve stared at me with her dark eyes. I could almost see right through her pupils. Never before had I seen such a look of pure hatred. "Yesssss," she answered with a low guttural tone that seemed to emanate from the very bowels of her soul.

"That's exactly what I'm talking about," I said, my voice quivering with anger. "She says, 'yes, I'll work with him' but her tone of voice and the expression on her face says, 'I'm going to make your life miserable, you rotten son-of-a-bitch!'"

Bruce had no response. He saw that we were not making any progress but, to my surprise, he sided with Eve. "Look, Dennis. Eve Cantor has been here for twelve years, the same amount of time as me. If she says she'll work with you, then dammit, she'll work with you. If you can't work with her, then we've got problems. I want to talk to each of you individually. Come back in fifteen minutes."

As I walked back to my room through the main lobby I was thoroughly disgusted. Why was Bruce turning everything around and making me look like the bad guy? Didn't he see the way she was looking at me? I made a detour at the Activities desk and grabbed the notes I had written the night before. If Bruce wouldn't listen to reason, then I would have to win him over with my ideas for The Pines.

When I knocked on his door and walked back into his office, Bruce was seated at his desk with his head bowed. "Sit down, Dennis," he instructed. I was about to show him my notes, when he interrupted me. "I'm sorry to have to do this but we're going to have to let you go. Here's a four hundred dollar cashier's check. I hope there are no hard feelings."

My hand went numb as he handed me my check. My lack of sleep had finally caught up with me. I instantaneously became dizzy and a terrible migraine headache pounded inside my skull.

"So that's it," I said bitterly, "you don't even want to hear my side of the story, do you?" I didn't wait for an answer. I stormed out of the office and angrily threw my notes onto my desk. My big chance for success had blown up in my face. I couldn't believe it. I had worked like a maniac, done a fantastic job, and still hadn't make it through my first week. What the hell was going on here?

Badly in need of some air, I walked out the back door and started heading toward the tennis courts. Behind the courts, two singles groups were playing a game of volleyball. Everyone was laughing and having fun. I did not want to make a spectacle of myself in public, so I fought hard to retain control over my emotions. However, my frazzled nerves were overpowered by a feeling that can best be described as "utter grief." As I mourned "what might have been," I broke down and started sobbing loudly.

While I stood there crying like a baby, Joe came over and put his arm around my shoulder. "What's the matter, Dennis? What's wrong?" he asked. I explained what had just happened. He looked at me thoughtfully and grinned. "Don't worry, Dennis. You'll be able to get your job back. All you got to do is kiss Eve's ass. There's a ton of money to be made here. This can be a good deal for you."

I thanked Joe for his support and began the long walk back to my room. How could I explain to him that I could never kiss anybody's ass, especially not Eve's. I had too much pride to debase myself that way. I returned to my room and slept until dinner time.

When I awoke, my pillow was soaking wet from my free-flowing tears. Although I was embarrassed by my temporary loss of emotional control (it had been many years since I had last allowed myself to shed even one tear), the crying provided a release that actually made me feel much better. It helped alleviate the enormous despondency I was experiencing. I gathered myself, brushed my teeth and washed my face, and changed into a fresh shirt.

My brown eyes were still bleary and red when I entered the employee dining room, but I walked with my head held high. I knew I had done absolutely nothing wrong. Eve was seated at one of the front tables with Lou Goldstein and his wife Jackie. The two women quickly looked away, but Lou looked me in the eyes like a man.

"Hey, Lou," I greeted him. "Hi, Dennis," he said softly, in a sad, unfamiliar voice. He suddenly looked very old. I spared the man further awkwardness by hurriedly moving away from his table, without acknowledging Eve or his wife.

I sat down at a table with Anita and Roberta. "I'd better enjoy my food. This could be my last meal," I joked. Neither of the women cracked a smile. Instead, they gloomily stared down at their plates.

When dinner was served, I politely asked Roberta to pass the pepper. She did so, but made a concerted effort to avoid looking at my face. I took a closer look at her and noticed that there were tears welling up in her eyes. Why was she so upset about my dismissal? She had only been at The Pines a week longer than I had been and hardly even knew me.

Throughout the meal, I felt many pairs of eyes staring at me coldly, as if I were an exhibit in an art museum. This made me uncomfortable, but I defiantly ate my food at my usual, unhurried pace. Before I excused myself from the table, I made plans to meet Anita and her friend, Ann, at a nightclub in nearby Monticello. "Happy Birthday" I said to myself as I stepped into the elevator that transported me back to my room.

I had been in my room for no longer than ten minutes, when Steve Richman phoned me. He asked me to meet him in his office in a half hour. The phone call lifted my spirits. Maybe it wasn't too late to save my job! I hoped to impress Steve enough to make him overrule Bruce's senseless decision to fire me. I excitedly gathered my notes and prepared to make the most of my opportunity to speak directly with the boss.

The meeting was a major disappointment. I talked about my ideas for over an hour, while Steve took notes. I spoke with a rapid fire delivery, anxious to share my entire vision of what I thought The Pines could become. He seemed interested in what I had to say, at times expressing unabashed esteem for some of the changes I proposed. When push came to shove, however, it became apparent that Eve was staying and I was going. He told me he was sorry to have to lose me.

"I really think you're getting a bum rap here, Dennis," he said. "You've shown me that Eve Cantor is a real shrew, but there's nothing I can do. The hotel is booked solid for the next couple of months and we need Eve's experience."

I argued that I'd work hard enough to learn the job in a very short time, but Steve was unmoved by my desperate pleas. His decision was final. Before I left his office, I asked him if I could stay at the hotel for a while, since I had no place to go. He said, "Sure, stay for as long as you'd like. We don't want to kick you out on the street." I thanked him for his time and went back to my room.

As I got dressed to go out I thought about my immediate future. My friends had already rented out my room in East Brunswick, so I really didn't have any place to live. I could never move back with my mother or father. Moving home with my tail tucked between my legs was simply not an acceptable alternative. I'd rather live out of the back seat of my Chevrolet than have to endure the humiliation of being dependent on my parents again.

I thought of taking the four hundred bucks and driving back down to Florida, but I hated being so far away from my family. Once again, I considered myself an absolute failure. Twenty-six years old with no job, no home, and no woman. What had I done to become such a loser?

I drove around Monticello for an hour and a half but couldn't find the damn nightclub. All I found was one dark road after another. Finally, at 11 p.m. I headed back to The Pines. I returned to my room just in time to click on the T.V. set and watch the Reds complete their four game sweep of the Oakland A's. Normally, I was a baseball fanatic, but I had worked so hard this week I had missed the whole series.

I turned off the television and the lights and tried in vain to get some sleep. I kept replaying the events of the past week over and over again in my mind. What had I done wrong? My thoughts were interrupted by the ringing of my telephone.

"Yo, Dennis, it's Joe. Sorry to call you so late, but this is really important. Did you quit or did you get fired?" he asked hesitantly.

"I got fired, Joe. I told you what happened. Why do you ask?" There was a pause at the other end of the line.

"Well, Eve says you quit, and that you'll be off the grounds by tomorrow mornin'. She ain't comin' in tomorrow, so she called to tell me what needed to be set up. I don't understand why she would lie about you." His unexpected call took me by surprise. I told Joe I didn't know what was going on, but assured him that I would check things out and get back to him promptly.

As I hung up the phone I thought about why Eve would lie about me getting fired. What did she have to gain by distorting the truth? Than it hit me—there was a lot more to the job than I had been told. Eve had kept me in the dark for a reason. I wasn't supposed to learn too much too fast. I had ruined her plans by being too ambitious and too smart.

I thought about the previous Activities Director, Evan Harris. The last time anyone had seen him, he was being forcibly removed from the premises by three armed security guards. Where did they take him, and what did they do with him? Oh my God … EVAN HARRIS IS DEAD!

It was all becoming crystal clear. The Pines Hotel was a clever front for management's real business: drugs. Drugs, of course. Huge shipments of cocaine were probably smuggled in from the not too distant Canadian border. They hired young drifter types like me for the Activities positions, got them hooked on crack, and then let them act as the middlemen in the drug transactions. When they knew too much or outlived their usefulness, they quietly disposed of them.

Steve Richman had not hired me because of my credentials to work at a hotel but rather because my resume indicated a lack of direction and high degree of instability. I fit the exact profile he had undoubtedly been looking for to replace Evan Harris.

I reflected back on my initial visit to The Pines, remembered Steve's positively ebullient attitude towards me. Despite keeping him waiting for over an hour, he spoke with me as if my getting the job were a foregone conclusion. At the time, I was too enthralled to notice a setup. But now I could plainly see that my interview had been nothing more than a formality. I wondered if anyone else had even been brought in to apply for the position. Furthermore, I had not been asked to fill out a standard application form, which would have disclosed my social security number, so there was no official record of my employment.

I did not have any tangible evidence but in my one week at The Pines I had seen and heard enough to know that 2 + 2 = 4. Evan's and Joe's addictions, the ridiculously high turnover rate of the Activities staff, the appalling condition of the Ritz building, the suspicious payroll book, Anita's unusual come-on, Roberta's inability to make eye contact with me, and Eve's final lie to Joe, all pointed to one thing: a nefarious drug operation, where human life was a necessary expenditure.

In my zealousness to make a name for myself, I had accidentally stumbled across something bigger than anything I could have ever imagined. How many other ctivities workers had allegedly "quit," never to be seen by anyone again?

4

WELCOME TO THE JUNGLE

I sat alone in my white room and anxiously waited for the doctors to make a determination. The walls were thin enough to allow me to hear muffled voices, but nothing intelligible. Blood from my various cuts and scratches had dried and hardened, and dirt from the woods was caked onto my body. As good as a hot shower would have felt, I was in no hurry to wash or bathe. Indeed, my physical appearance was the only evidence of my struggle. The layer of filth that covered me was my uniform, the cuts and bruises my medals of honor.

Finally, my mother came into the room and gently told me the bad news. I was going to be taken to the Centra-State Medical Center Psychiatric Unit in Freehold. Because I had attempted to take a police officer's gun, I was to be admitted there on an involuntary basis. I didn't have any say in the matter.

"Where's Daddy?" I asked. I was told that he was driving to The Pines to find out exactly what had happened. Yeah, right. He's probably meeting with the Richmans and Eve Cantor to discuss what to do about me. I'll play the game, Dad. I'll outsmart all of you.

I was strapped into a stretcher and placed in an ambulance. I had never been more humiliated, but realized that I was going to have to sacrifice some of my pride to attain ultimate justice. Kevin rode with me in the front seat. I didn't think my father had the time to bug the ambulance, but I couldn't take any chances. I decided to speak to Kevin in code and hoped he understood what I was saying. "Give Daddy the Judas Priest tape, Kevin," I said in a voice barely above a whisper. Translation: I wanted Kevin to give our father the tape he had made about the drug operation. I wanted my dad to think that I trusted him completely. The tape was unimportant. I had all the names and facts memorized.

The ride from Clifton to Freehold took slightly more than an hour. During that time, I devised my plan. If I told the doctors at Centra-State the truth, I'd probably spend the rest of my life in a mental ward. I was going to have to make them think I had really had a minor "breakdown." The sooner I was able to convince them that I recognized I had been "ill," the sooner they would let me out of the hospital.

I was wheeled into a private room in the involuntary wing of the psychiatric ward. With the addition of a few items such as a St. Pauli girl poster or a Playboy calendar, the room could have passed for a college dorm. The walls were painted a soothing peach color and the brand new furnishings included two wooden chairs, a bed, a night stand, and a large dresser. I noticed, however, that every piece of furniture was rounded on the edges to prevent any accidents.

A pretty brunette nurse walked over to my bed and introduced herself. "Hi, I'm Jeannine. I'm the charge nurse tonight."

"Hello. My name's Dennis. This is a lot nicer room than I expected," I said quietly.

"Thanks. It's not the Ritz-Carlton, but we're kind of proud of it." My whole body tensed when I heard the word "Ritz." Why would she say the "Ritz" instead of The Waldorf-Astoria or some other hotel? Did she know about the Ritz at The Pines?

While Jeannine and Kevin chatted, I took a closer look at my room. On the ceiling there appeared to be a smoke alarm. The alarm's red light continually blinked on and off. Nice try guys. I knew that the mechanism was really a sophisticated bugging device. There was probably a tiny camera hidden inside of it as well. I had to be very careful of everything I said and did. My enemies were monitoring my every move.

My mother, Sean, Thomas, and Deirdre arrived at the hospital a few minutes behind us. Thomas worriedly asked me how I was feeling, and I answered him in a soft voice, speaking slowly in between words. I was giving an acting performance worthy of Sir Lawrence Olivier.

"My, this is a lovely room," my mother remarked to Jeannine.

"Thank you. We try to make it comfortable even if it's not too Ritzy," she said, flashing a smile that revealed her dimples.

When I heard the word "Ritzy," I forgot all about the hidden camera and completely lost my cool. "She's in on it! She's involved with the people at The Pines," I yelled as I jumped out of my bed. "Daddy talked to her, didn't he? Didn't he?" I demanded a reply.

"Yes," Sean answered. "He called the hospital while you were on your way in the ambulance."

I looked at my family pleadingly. "Don't you see what's happening? I'm being set up and people are being paid off. I'm not sick. I don't belong here. Could a sick person do this?" I dropped to the floor and started doing one-arm pushups. Normally I could do about twenty of them, but at the moment I felt gifted with Herculean strength. I didn't stop until I had done at least fifty one-arm pushups with each arm. "What do I have to do to convince you I'm sane?" I asked, getting up from the cold floor.

"Look, Dennis. Daddy's not involved in this. He loves you and would never do anything to hurt you," Kevin said grimly. "You've had a mental breakdown and you need to get some rest and some medical help."

"FUCK YOU, KEVIN!" I yelled in his face. My frustration was now turning into resentment and anger. "Did you run through a forest all night, being chased by people who were out to kill you? Did you see twenty cop cars driving up to look for you? You weren't at The Pines all week. You don't have even the slightest clue about what the hell's going on!"

I was disgusted with my whole family. It was easier for them to believe that I had gone nuts than it was to accept the truth about the drug operation. "Get the hell out of here. EVERYBODY OUT!" I commanded. "Dennis the Nut is going to get some sleep."

When everyone had left, an old white-haired doctor came into my room and handed me a paper cup filled with a foul-smelling medicine.

"What's this?" I asked.

"It's called Haldol. It'll help you sleep. Drink it." As first I resisted him with all the strength I had left, but the doctor made it clear that he was going to get the medicine in me one way or another. Two large orderlies were standing outside my door in the event I continued to be uncooperative. The Haldol tasted awful, but I was sound asleep in a few minutes.

When I awoke in the morning, I was given more medication, had my vital signs taken, and was then asked to provide a urine sample in a small plastic container—to determine whether there were any drugs in my system. I grudgingly went into the washroom and complied with this demeaning request. A few hours later, the drug test came back negative.

During my first day of confinement, I was most uncomfortable in the hospital. I could not be sure of who else was directly involved with The Pines's underhanded business, or who had been paid off. I looked at everyone with suspicion and caution and flinched every time one of the nurses came close to me.

Later that morning I spoke with the resident shrink, Dr. Allan Miller. Dr. Miller was a small man with dark, serious eyes, kinky gray hair, and a thick beard. He invited me into his office, which was surprisingly modest, equipped only with an oak desk and two uncomfortable chairs. Where's the couch? I felt like asking. If not for the three framed diplomas proudly displayed on one of the walls, I never would have believed I was in the office of a psychiatrist.

I sat down in one of the chairs, and he immediately started firing questions at me. "Why do you think people are trying to kill you? Did you actually see the drugs? Are you still in danger now?" I felt comfortable with Dr. Miller, who seemed like a man I could trust, and answered all his questions as truthfully as possible. Everything was out in the open now. My acting career was over.

I told him exactly what I had told my family and anyone else who cared to listen. I had stumbled across a drug operation that put my life in danger. Through a miracle of God, I had managed to escape, but I couldn't convince anyone that I was telling the truth. Thus, I was now speaking to a psychiatrist instead of a law enforcement agent. When I had finished talking, Dr. Miller sat back in his chair and gave me his analysis.

"Dennis, I believe you've suffered from a psychotic episode. You're experiencing paranoid delusions brought on by a combination of sleep deprivation and the trauma of losing your job."

"That's a crock of shit!" I said. "I've lost jobs before." It was depressingly clear that this doctor was the same as the rest of them. He had probably seen so many nuts come and go that he didn't know the difference between them and me. Couldn't he see that I was the Real McCoy?

I spend the rest of the day lying in bed, thinking: What the hell can I do about my situation? Nobody believes me. I am going to go crazy if someone doesn't believe me soon. As least I was safe. After careful analysis of my circumstances, I didn't think anyone could touch me while I was in the hospital.

At 8 p.m. a nurse gave me a 10 milligram tablet of Haldol, as well as a medicine called Cogentin to counteract its side effects. I didn't know that Haldol (generic name: haloperidol) was the most potent anti-psychotic prescription drug available. It was commonly administered to the most profoundly disturbed mental patients. Had I known this at the time, I would have never allowed it to enter my body.

The effects of the potent tranquilizer were extremely unpleasant. The Haldol made me feel as if I were trapped in a dense fog. It acutely dulled all five of my senses. Moreover, the drug also made me tremendously fatigued, regardless of how much I slept. As I drifted off into a dreamless sleep I vowed to put an end to this so-called remedy that was, in actuality, invading my mind and body like a synthetic disease.

The clamor of the nurses' pushcart entering my room woke me up on Tuesday morning at 7 a.m. sharp. One nurse read my vital signs while another dispensed my medication. "Sorry to have to get you up so early, Dennis, but you'd better get used to it. This is the daily hospital procedure," said one of the nurses.

Since I was already awake, I decided to stay up and watch the sunrise. The window in my room afforded me a spectacular unobstructed view of the landscape. I felt uplifted as I saw the bright orange glow of the sun glistening above the untouched farmland behind the hospital. Yes, it was good to be alive. I would do anything to stay that way.

After breakfast was brought in to me on a tray, a heavyset nurse named Joyce took the other mental patients and me out for a walk around the hospital. The fresh air was invigorating but I felt vulnerable away from the protective cloak of the mental ward. I stayed close to Joyce and continually darted my eyes back and forth, checking for any danger signs. Fortunately, I found none, or, rather, none found me.

At one o'clock my family arrived en masse to visit me. Everyone was tense and nervous, unsure of how they should act. I loosened them up by telling jokes and making light of my situation. I was happy to see my mother and siblings but was afraid of my father. He wore a blue pinstriped suit and a red tie. It disturbed me that he was still dressed so formally. Who was he trying to impress?

It's good to see you, Den," he said, placing one of his large hands on my shoulder. "I went to The Pines and checked your story out yesterday. What a depressing place. I don't know why you took that job to begin with. Well, anyway, I talked to Steve Richman, nice guy, he said you were an unbelievable worker and he hated to see you go. That other guy, Joe, is a complete moron. He could barely talk."

"Maybe so, but he did one helluva job by my standards," I interrupted.

"Yeah, well, I investigated thoroughly and there's nothing going on up there. They may be involved in a few dirty scams but believe me I would know if they were running a drug operation. I even talked to the security guy, Charlie. There's no way he could have been in the woods with you, he was working at the South Fallsburg police station all night."

I nodded my head but said nothing. Pretty good, Dad, pretty good. If I wasn't so damn smart, you would actually be able to pull it off. But I can see right through your game, and I will beat you. Just wait until I get out of here. Before my family left, my father borrowed one hundred dollars from Kevin. He said he needed it to take Willie to lunch. I found that exceedingly strange. First of all, he usually carried quite a bit of cash with him, and, secondly, since when did lunch cost a hundred dollars?

My mom mentioned that she had called Vicki and told her I was in the hospital. "She wants to know if it's all right for her to come and visit you."

"No, it's not all right. I'll see her when I get out of here," I snapped.

Vicki was my college sweetheart and ex-fiancee. She was a tiny, beautiful girl with pretty auburn hair and piercing brown eyes. We had started dating during my Senior and her Junior year of college. Our storybook romance survived my graduation that Fall, which led to a trying long distance relationship. Nevertheless, through numerous weekend excursions and endless phone calls late into the night, we were able to continue to foster our love for one another.

It was a joyous occasion for both of us when we finally became engaged on a cool September evening in 1988.

My memories of that unforgettable night remain remarkably vivid. We were staying at Kevin's apartment in Devon, Pennsylvania. After I popped the question, we went into the living room, sat down on the sofa, and snuggled like a couple of starry-eyed teenagers. We stayed wrapped in each other's arms for hours and talked about our future life together until the sun of a new day blinded our moist eyes. I was intoxicated with love and felt as though I were living a dream.

Sadly, this "dream" ended all too quickly. Vicki and I decided that since her parents lived in Pennsylvania, it was sensible to break the news to them first. Since I had always gotten along well with her family, I was anticipating a positive reaction from them. Certainly at least something like, "Congratulations" or "Welcome to the family."

Instead, Vicki's announcement of our engagement was greeted first with awkward silence, and then by derisive laughter from her mother. "You have got to be kidding. The two of you won't last six months. What a joke," she said with a vicious tone that left me shocked.

Vicki ran out of the room crying hysterically, while I stood there agape, trying to recover from the violent verbal blow that hit way below the belt. Eventually, I recovered my senses enough to retrieve my fiancée and exit the home in which I had previously spent many pleasant days and nights. While I drove her back to her apartment, Vicki broke the heavy silence.

"Don't worry about my mother, she'll come around. I'm the baby of the family and she just doesn't want to lose me, that's all," she said, placing her feminine hand on my knee.

I brusquely flicked her hand off me. "Screw that! I want an apology, Vicki," I said, as the brunt of my anger began to surface. "She had no right to say that even if she was thinking it. You didn't deserve it and I sure as hell didn't deserve it!"

Vicki quickly replied, "Well, don't expect an apology. You won't get one. That's just the way my mother is. You have to learn to accept it, Dennis."

With those words, I pulled back and retreated into my own private shell. From then on, when I saw Vicki I would have sex with her, but that was all I would give of myself. I no longer shared my thoughts or dreams with her, and all talk or plans for a wedding were indefinitely put on hold. It was not what her mother had said, but rather Vicki's inability to stand up for me and confront her that rankled me most. Just a week after the engagement announcement, Vicki acted as if nothing had happed and went shopping at the mall with her two sisters and her mother.

My bitter resentment was turned inward, and I became a moody, sullen lover. I didn't discuss the dramatic change in my behavior and she didn't press me to explain why I was suddenly withholding tenderness and affection from her. Perhaps if either of us had tried to communicate our feelings, the end result might have turned out differently.

This, however, was not to be. We drifted farther and farther apart, until there was nothing left of our bond to hold onto. Still, I was willing to grasp thin air in a feeble attempt to recapture the love we once shared. Vicki put me out of my misery by unceremoniously dumping me in August of 1989. Although the rejection was quite painful, in my heart I knew she was right.

We had stayed in contact up until a month before I left for The Pines. Inexplicably, she stopped calling me and failed to return my calls. At the time I assumed that her career as a psychologist had kept her too busy to bother with me. But now, I wasn't so sure.

Christ! She's in on it too! She had been paid off by Eve Cantor and the others at The Pines, and was going to try to convince me that I was nuts. I didn't have any proof, but I was certain that Vicki had betrayed me once again. I would have to be careful. I still loved her very much. Those feelings might get in the way of my better judgment.

As my clan was walking down the corridor toward the exit, Willie turned her head around and smiled at me. The woman couldn't help it, could she? She was very happy to see me locked away in a mental hospital. Her plan was working to perfection.

I thought about Willie's family. Her 17 year-old daughter, Melissa, was in a mental hospital in New York. Another daughter, Tara, was finishing up her last year of college as a psychology major. She also had a twenty-two year-old son, David, whom she hadn't seen in three years. Willie had mentioned to me once that he was heavily involved with drugs. Drugs. He was into drugs, of course. It all fits perfectly. Willie must have set up her own son three years ago. David Lawson had been Activities Director at The Pines, but he wasn't as lucky as I. He didn't make it out alive.

My dad and Willie have been in on this from the beginning. They had known I was looking in the *New York Times* and had placed that classified ad specifically for me.

Although this belief was pure speculation, and as much as it saddened me, there was no doubt in my mind that my theory was correct. Unfortunately, this tunnel-vision train of thought led to more unfounded conclusions. Being unjustly locked up in a mental hospital also gave further credence to my conviction that there was a conspiracy against me. Like a snowball rolling down a steep mountaintop, this notion was gaining momentum and growing in stature at a rapid rate.

This has been going on for twelve years. Countless parents had set up their sons with the activities job in exchange for huge payoffs from the Richmans. When their kids mysteriously disappeared, they didn't do any investigating or go to the local newspapers. This brilliant strategy was what had enabled The Pines's brain trust to get away with their diabolical operation for so long.

The postulation that I was probably the first "pigeon" to ever escape from The Pines made me resolve to do something that would break the sickening chain of murder and drugs. In the name of all the previous ctivities directors and staffers, as well as for all the unsuspecting young men who would follow, I needed to expose the leaders of The Pines's drug ring for whom and what they truly were. But what could I do? The fact that two certified doctors had misdiagnosed me as "mentally ill" made my word meaningless. Dismayed, but far from defeated, I devoted much of my mental energy in search of a solution to this perplexing problem.

About an hour after my family had left, Dr. Miller came into my room to talk to me. I reiterated exactly what I had said to him the previous day. He notified me that he was transferring me from the involuntary unit to the voluntary ward down the hall.

"Thanks, Doc, I appreciate that," I said gratefully. My initial negative impression of Dr. Miller was premature. He was the first doctor that had shown me some compassion.

"Since I'm a voluntary patient now, I won't be taking any more Haldol," I said. I knew my rights. Voluntary patients had the legal right to refuse medication. It was time to regain control over my own body.

"I strongly advise against doing that, but I can't force you to take medication against your will," Dr. Miller responded. "I'll inform the nurses of the change."

Although I had been upgraded to so-called "voluntary patient" status, I was still not permitted to leave the hospital until I received a written discharge from Dr. Miller. In addition to being taken off the medication, however, I was given other privileges as well. I was now able to wear my regular clothes instead of the ridiculous hospital gown the nursing staff had given me. I was also allowed to eat my meals and participate in group therapy in the day room with the other voluntary patients. It was a great relief to be removed from the isolation of the involuntary ward.

Despite these improvements and despite Centra-State's well-earned reputation for having one of the cleanest and most modern mental health facilities in New Jersey, I could not escape the haunting atmosphere of gloom that festered within my new surroundings. The fresh paint on the walls and the shiny floors didn't make the environment any less depressing.

Furthermore, the nurses treated me no differently than they did any of the other patients. Their inability to recognize the absurdity of my hospitalization was reflected in their behavior towards me. I was spoken to like a child, not permitted to wear my shoes, and observed closely every morning when I shaved my face. I understood the reasoning behind the strict hospital rules but that didn't make them any less degrading.

Also, after group therapy in the morning there was absolutely nothing to do the rest of the day. I spent hour after hour staring at the walls and lamenting my unfortunate fate.

I was moved into a room down the hall, next to the nurses' station. My roommate was a twenty-eight year-old man named Karl. He was tall, broad-shouldered, and handsome. But, tragically, he was destined to spend the rest of his life confined to a wheelchair. A few years before, he had attempted to commit suicide by swallowing a bottle of pills. The subsequent neurological damage to his brain was severe and irreversible. He was left with hardly any use of his legs and limited functioning of his hands and arms. His speech was also slightly impaired.

Karl was surprisingly friendly and seemed enthusiastic about sharing a room with me. When I was settled in, we engaged in a pleasant conversation about our backgrounds and families. Despite his handicap, he was an extremely intelligent person. I considered what it must be like trapped in a body that didn't work properly and thanked God for giving me one that was strong and healthy.

Later that evening I received phone calls from Vicki and my father. They both sounded quite concerned about my well-being, but I knew better. Vicki advised me to trust my doctor and listen to what he said. "Sure, kid, I'll listen to this quack try to convince me that I went bananas."

My father tried to keep the conversation light. We talked sports for a while until he had to go. When he hung up, the operator came back on the line and spoke two words very softly into the phone, "The Ritz." Son of a bitch, he's trying to drive me crazy! Damn him! How could he do this to his own son?

It wasn't hard to figure out. My father had given the operator the hundred dollars he had received from Kevin and told her what to say. Okay, I'll play the game. I know I'm not crazy. I'm just going to have to be on guard for any other tricks they might pull. I'll let them think they are beating me.

I staggered into the ward's lounge, referred to by the staff as the "day room." This area was intended to provide social interaction between patients. Group therapy was held there each morning, with the patients pulling the sofas and chairs into a makeshift circle. At mealtimes, two large arts and crafts tables were cleaned up, covered with paper table cloths, and used for dining.

In the back of the room, a shelf was stacked with dusty board games, unopened boxes of playing cards, and novels in pristine condition. Not too many patients had either the energy or the attention span to engage in these activities. It was so much easier to passively sit in front of the big screen television set and kill time by watching game shows and reruns of old sitcoms.

I sat down on one of the sofas and tried to watch some T.V., but it was impossible to concentrate on the program. I kept thinking about my father and the people at The Pines. What would they try next?

My thoughts were interrupted by the sight of a nurse's aide walking towards me. He was a stocky, fiftyish black man, with a stylish mustache. Dressed completely in white, he looked like the Good Humor man. "Hi, Dennis, how are you feeling," he said with a smile as he sat down next to me on the sofa.

"Fine thanks. How do you know my name?"

"Oh, I know everything about you, Dennis. My name is Joe. I was with you when you came in on Sunday night." As Joe and I continued talking, I noticed an unusual sparkle in his eyes. There was something intriguing about this man. He spoke to me as if he had known me all of my life.

He related that the hospital had been built in the summer of 1971. "You remember that summer, don't you Dennis?" He asked, playfully winking at me. Of course I remembered. How could I forget?

I recalled being a seven year-old boy on vacation with my family at a resort called Police Camp, in upstate New York. I had ventured off by myself and gone fishing for tadpoles in the local pond. The next thing I knew, my foot slipped on a rock and I was immersed in six feet of water. I struggled for three or four minutes until an heroic off-duty policeman dove into the pond and pulled me out. The doctors said that if I had stayed underwater another minute, I would have died.

While I was underwater, images from my entire short life passed before my eyes, just the way it happens in the movies. I prayed to God for help and promised to make something of myself if only he would give me another chance. How in the Lord's name did Joe know about this?

He didn't stop to explain. He simply continued his conversation. "I understand you're from Manalapan, Dennis. That's beautiful country."

"Well, I'm not actually from Manalapan. I grew up in Brooklyn. My family moved there in 1985. Just my mom and youngest brother live there now," I corrected.

"Right. Well anyway, Manalapan used to be all farmland. Fifteen years ago all you could see were rows and rows of crops and hundreds of sheep grazing by the countryside. It was really beautiful," he said wistfully. I wasn't sure, but it seemed as if Joe knew something that he wasn't telling me. When he finally left to make his appointed rounds, I mused about the secrets to which he was privy.

On Wednesday morning after breakfast, I was invited to participate in a group therapy session with the other patients. Most of the patients seemed harmless enough. They certainly didn't conform to my ignorant stereotype of mental patients. Instead of finding a bunch of violent, dangerous "psychos," all I encountered were troubled, frightened people who had lost their ability to cope with life.

Some of the patients were young, some old. Some were hospitalized because of drugs and alcoholism. Others had simply been beaten up by the realities of life and were suffering from acute depression. In any event, all these people were screwed up in one way or another. None of them was normal like me, or so I thought.

The session itself was incredibly boring. We were each asked to have a goal for the day and were also requested to rate ourselves on a scale from 1 to 10, depending upon how we felt. I rated myself a "10" of course. I had no intention of letting my poor circumstances reflect negatively on my self-image.

At one o'clock Sean and his girlfriend, Starlight, came to visit me. Starlight was a tall, exotic, head-turner with long flowing chestnut hair. A full-blooded American Indian, Star was trying to embark on a career as a professional singer. She and Sean had met while they were both living in Fort Myers, Florida. Currently, they were staying at my Mom's house in Manalapan, until Sean found a job in the New York metropolitan area.

My brother greeted me warmly and seemed happy to see me. "You look pretty good for a nut," he joked, as he and Star sat down next to me.

"Thanks a lot, pal," I returned, smiling. As we talked, it became more and more evident that Sean was on my side. He didn't believe that our father was involved, but he wholeheartedly endorsed my theory that there was a drug operation at The Pines. Finally, I had an ally worthy of trust.

Sean asked me what I had said to the doctor, and I explained that I had told him the truth. He looked at me thoughtfully, shook his head, and offered his advice. "Look, Den, you know you were set up and I know that you were set up, but the shrinks here are never going to believe your story. They want you to tell them that everything was in your mind. Tell them what they want to hear and they'll let you out of this place. You don't belong here."

He was absolutely right. My brother's advice was exactly the same as my original strategy. I had foolishly decided to tell Dr. Miller the true facts. I told Sean that I would rectify this mistake the next time I spoke with the good doctor.

We talked a little while longer until the visiting hour was over. Before he and Star left, Sean gave me a copy of the *New York Post* to help keep me occupied. I returned to my bed and began flipping through the sports pages. I turned to the section on boxing, hoping to read something interesting about the upcoming Buster Douglas-Evander Holyfield bout. I found two boxing articles written by Michael Marley and one by Jerry Izenberg. Their content raised the hair on the back of my neck.

Sean had doodled a blue beard and mustache on Marley's photograph. He also colored in Douglas's mouth, eyes, and ear in a picture of the champ pounding a heavy bag. There was something strange going on here. I did not want to miss anything, so I read each of the articles very slowly. In his article, Izenberg called Las Vegas "Gomorrah West." He talked about The Mirage owner, Steve Wynn, rooting for Douglas. One sentence in particular caught my attention. "If we're the other guy, then after the other guy wins, we'll fight our first title defense at the other hotel." I immediately recognized the double meaning of this sentence. The "other hotel" Wynn was referring to was The Pines and I was the "other guy" who would be fighting the fight.

Marley's lead article listed five reasons why neither contender would win the fight. He finished the article with this sentence, "So you tell me who's got God on his side. Perhaps the Supreme Being likes a draw, which you can get down at 17-1."

As I looked down at the paper I tried to decipher what my eyes were seeing. This was not your typical championship boxing match. The stakes were much higher. It was Good versus Evil, God against the Devil. The battle would help determine the fate of the world!

I took another closer look at the pictures of Marley and Douglas. From their photographs it was clear that they were both unmistakably sinister. The expression in Douglas's eyes uncannily resembled the evil look Eve Cantor had given me.

When Douglas had defeated Mike Tyson, I had asked myself how was it possible for an ordinary, journeyman fighter to beat the invincible Iron Mike. Now I thought I knew the answer to that question. In a contemporary version of *Damn Yankees*, Douglas had sold his soul to the devil in exchange for fame, fortune, and adulation. Conversely, Holyfield was a man of God, a pious, born-again Christian. I prayed that God would give him the courage and the strength to defeat this insidious agent of Satan.

Steve Wynn was another person whom I thought would burn in Hell. I remembered the old saying "the love of money is the root of all evil." Wynn exemplified the accuracy of that quote. He wanted Douglas to win so he could make more money with a Tyson rematch. What the general public didn't realize was that the revenue from the fight barely scratched the surface of his total take. The real money was going to be made by an enormous drug transaction that would take place during the fight. It was a flawless plan.

I looked again at Jerry Izenberg's picture. He was smiling and I could tell from his eyes that he was a kind man, a man who wrote from the heart. I could learn much from his work.

A nurse knocked on my door and said, "Dennis, you have a phone call. It's your brother, Kevin. He's calling from his office." I spoke with Kevin for a few minutes. He was needlessly concerned and felt terrible about me being in a mental hospital. I assured him that I was fine and there was nothing to worry about. "Don't worry, I'll be out of here soon," I said confidently as we said our goodbyes.

I turned the corner just in time to see Joe hurriedly ducking through my doorway. "Good afternoon, Joe," I called out.

"Hi, Dennis," he replied.

When I sat back down on my bed I notice a blue book on top of my dresser. I picked it up and saw that the book was a Gideon Bible. "That's funny, this wasn't here a minute ago." Karl couldn't have put it there, either. He had been in the day room watching T.V. I rushed out into the hallway in search of Joe.

I found him in the nurses' station. "Joe, did you just put a Bible on my dresser?" I asked.

"No, I just went in there to pick up a few things." He smiled brightly and his brown eyes danced around his face as he shuffled down the hallway whistling a soft melody. I was confused as I returned to my room and picked up the Bible again.

It had been quite a white since I had read from the Holy Book. As a kid, I was brought up as a strict Roman Catholic, but I had fallen away from the church during my freshman year of college. My spiritual relationship with God was replaced by an intellectual curiosity about him. At Albright, I took five religion courses as electives and received "A's" in all of them. I was fascinated by all the different religions and the different beliefs of people around the world.

Now I was at a spiritual crossroad. God had obviously saved me from certain death at The Pines, so I decided that it was time to put myself back into his hands. I closed my eyes, randomly opened the Bible and put my right index finger at the top of the page. I opened my eyes and read these words: "If God is for you, who can be against you?" I swallowed hard as the profundity of the words sunk in.

God is with me! I am a powerful and indestructible force. Nothing can stop me. At that moment, all of my paranoia and fear left me. I wasn't afraid of my father, Eve Cantor, or anyone else for that matter. I waited in gleeful anticipation for the victory and glory that would soon be mine.

I was starting to understand my purpose in life. God had given me the brains, strength, and guts necessary to thwart the evil drug ring at The Pines. After that was accomplished, I could concentrate on exposing the drug operation in Las Vegas and other operations all over the country. As a famous American hero, I would have tremendous power to put an end to the horrors of drugs. Whose side is God on, Mike Marley? He's on mine, so you'd better stay out of my way.

I put down the Bible and picked up the *Post* again. I turned the page and noticed that Sean had done some additional drawing. He had drawn a triangular clump of concentric circles over a picture of the basketball player, Derrick Coleman, and had circled the name of the sportswriter, Fred Kerber. The drawing's shape looked exactly like a pine tree, and the circle around Kerber's name must have signified that he, too, was a writer from whom I could learn.

It was remarkable to think of all the information Sean had given me from his innocuous doodling. I was sure that he was unaware of what he was doing and what the doodling meant. His mind was working on a subconscious level. God had made him a human conduit. Through Sean, God was helping me understand bits and pieces about the spiritual battle that was taking place. I still had so much more to learn.

Later than night, after the visiting hour was over and my family had left, I met another nurse's aide named Mary. She was a slim, middle-aged black woman with short, kinky hair. I saw her in the day room talking quietly with Joe. There was an undefined force that drew my attention to her. Noticing my stare, she walked over and introduced herself.

"Hi, Dennis. My name is Mary. Joe's told me a lot about you," she said. She smiled at me and I noticed something peculiar. There was a gap between her two front teeth of at least a half an inch. Her I.D. photo underneath her nametag, however, displayed a set of perfect teeth. How could there be such a discrepancy?

Joe and Mary were still chatting and laughing easily when I turned in to bed. I had much to think about as I adjusted my pillow. Who were Mary and Joe? Were they angels sent by God to help insure the success of my mission? Then a different thought occurred to me. Maybe God had sent the spirits of the Blessed Virgin and her husband, Joseph, themselves. Had he cleverly disguised them in the bodies of two African-Americans?

As bizarre as this premise was, it made some sense to me. Mary definitely had a motherly, spiritual presence. I was almost certain that Joe had left the Bible on my nightstand, and he seemed to have unaccountable in-depth knowledge about me. He had talked of all the sheep in Manalapan. Wasn't Jesus the shepherd who had led the lost flock out of the wilderness? What was Joe trying to tell me? Was I Simon Peter? John the Baptist? I was going to have to be patient and wait for more information to find out for sure, but the possibilities intrigued me. Perhaps I was even Jesus Christ Himself!

Sean visited me by himself on Thursday and again brought a copy of the *New York Post* with him. As soon as he left, I immediately turned to the sports section of the paper. Not surprisingly, the boxing pages were flooded with an abundance of Biblical references. I read all these stories with great interest, hoping to find some clues. But, unfortunately, I wasn't able to elicit any concrete answers from any of the articles.

Later in the day I met with Dr. Miller. This time I was prepared for him. His steely blue eyes were no match for my intellect. I answered each of his questions with clarity and conviction. "The episode at The Pines was all in my mind. There was no drug operation there. All my thoughts and fears were caused by excessive stress."

Dr. Miller was pleased both with my answers and with my appearance. He said that he was going to be able to release me soon. I was ecstatic. There was quite a bit of work to be done and I couldn't accomplish anything lying in a hospital bed.

While I was eating my dinner about 6 p.m., I overheard one of the other patients talking to her friend about Mary. "She's been all over the world, you know. At least fifty or sixty different countries and ...”

“Excuse me, I’m sorry to interrupt you, but are you talking about the slim black nurse with the big gap in her teeth?” I asked.

“Yup, that’s the one. She’s a beautiful woman, ain’t she?” I nodded my agreement and returned to my meal. Was this woman really the Virgin Mary? If she wasn’t, how could somebody on her modest salary afford to be a world traveler?

As late afternoon turned to night, many of the patients were getting excited and had generously doled out the cash to show the bout on Pay-Per-View T.V. When two nurses walked into the day room with three huge bags of popcorn and a package of paper plates, some of my troubled peers smiled for the first time since they had been admitted into the unit. After filling their paper plates with popcorn, everyone sat back in their seats and got ready to watch the action.

Just minutes before the main event was scheduled to start, I stood up from my chair and headed toward the exit. Joe turned away from his conversation with one of the other male nurses and called out to me. “Hey, Dennis! Aren’t you going to stay up and watch the fight?”

“No, Joe. Why should I? I already know that Holyfield is going to win,” I said, grinning broadly. He smiled back at me with the look of a proud father, as if to say, “Very good, Dennis. You are learning, you are beginning to understand.”

I woke up early the next morning and rushed over to the coffee shop to buy a newspaper. “Holyfield Wins!” screamed the headlines. Yes! Glory to God in Heaven! We had won the battle. Evil had been defeated once again. I looked at a picture of the new champ. He was wearing a T-shirt that said, “Don’t Be Afraid of The Gospel.” That’s right, Evander, the Gospel is Truth.

I noticed one other point of significance from the paper. The date was October 26, 1990. Tomorrow was going to be the 27th, a day that would burn forever in my mind. It was the anniversary of my grandfather’s death.

Thomas Joseph Mulhearn was neither rich nor famous. Nonetheless, “Poppy,” as we affectionately called him, was a truly great man. He was incredibly kind, generous, and wise. Although he lived a very simple, relatively obscure life, the man had as much integrity and class as any person I have ever known.

After his wife died of a stroke, my grandfather moved into our finished basement in Brooklyn in the Fall of 1972. My siblings and I spent many days and nights talking, laughing, and learning with him. He seemed to enjoy our company as much as we did his. Whenever something was bothering me, I could always rely on Poppy to provide intelligent and compassionate advice.

October 27, 1978 was the saddest day of my life. Kevin and I had just excelled in a freshman football game at Poly Prep. When our father came to pick us up, we were excited about going home because Poppy was supposed to have been released from the hospital that day.

After experiencing painful chest spasms, he had been in Kings County Hospital for the past eight days. An extensive battery of tests revealed that he had a bleeding ulcer. His doctor put him on medication and told him that his prognosis was excellent.

When Kevin and I shut the doors of my dad's sky blue Oldsmobile, our father spoke slowly and quietly. "Boys, I have some terrible news to tell you. There's been a tragedy in the family. Your Grandfather is dead."

The ride home was painfully silent. Kevin and I both stared straight ahead, our mouths wide open. The jolting shock of what had happened left us unable to utter a single word of comfort to our grieving father.

When we finally arrived home, I heard the ugly details. Apparently, while Poppy was being wheeled out of the hospital by my father and my Aunt Frances, he suffered a major heart attack and collapsed onto the ground, dying instantly.

The wake was agonizing. Kevin was the first grandchild to view the body. He began sobbing and was quickly whisked back to his seat by a compassionate relative. I was next. Through a mighty effort, I managed to fight back the floodgate of tears that were threatening to erupt at any moment. Poppy looked peaceful and serene. I hoped with all my heart that he was somewhere with his beloved wife. If there really was a heaven, he should have been first on line.

I left the funeral parlor early and walked the three blocks to my house. Why, God? Why? Why did you take him so soon? He was such a good man. "I need him," I screamed into the black night. A hollow echo was the only reply. My biggest regret was that I never told him I loved him. There were so many times that I had wanted to, but, because of the macho code I held as truth, I never actually voiced the words.

A few days after the funeral, Kevin found something interesting while he was rummaging through our grandfather's belongings. At the bottom of one of his old shoe boxes was an ancient baptismal certificate that was tattered and yellowed. The writing, however, was completely legible. The certificate read, "Thomas Joseph Mulhearn, Baptized October 27, 1909." Everyone in my family thought that was an amazing coincidence, but I did not agree. To me, it was living proof that my grandfather was a truly special man. He was "born" into God's kingdom way back in 1909. His death, exactly sixty-nine years to the day, was not an ending, it was a new beginning, a fresh start. Although I still missed him terribly, I felt better knowing that his soul was still very much alive.

I folded the *Post* under my arm and hurriedly walked back into my room. Computing the dates in my head, I realized that tomorrow was going to be exactly twelve years since Poppy's death. I remembered what Bruce Smythe had told me; he and Eve Cantor had been at The Pines for twelve years. Twelve years! Something was going down tomorrow. I wasn't exactly sure of what was going to happen, but I knew for certain that there was a connection between The Pines and my grandfather. The drug lords at The Pines didn't dare start their vile operation while he was still alive. I have to get out of this damn hospital now!

As if she had read my mind, a nurse came by and informed me that Dr. Miller had approved my discharge. I would be leaving tomorrow afternoon. All right! I can hold on for one more day. I'm getting out just in time. However bewildered I was about exactly what it was that I had to do, I knew without question that my role was of crucial importance.

Near the end of the evening visiting hour, my former roommate, Bob, and Farruk, another good friend from Chi-Chi's, stopped by the hospital to give me their support. I was pleased to see my two friends, but their discomfort at seeing me in such an unfamiliar environment was quite evident. Although they attempted to conceal it, the tension in their voices was unmistakable. As we talked, I detected other tell-tale signs of their nervousness. Bob had difficulty looking directly into my eyes, and Farruk wore a painted, forced smile on his face.

In an effort to change the somber mood, I took my friends to the coffee shop and ordered three large soft drinks. While we sipped our sodas in a booth, I told them my story in precise detail. There was a sound reason behind my decision to share this information with them. The rumor mill at Chi-Chi's worked like a finely-tuned machine. By Sunday night all my friends would know exactly what had happened to me. The more people who knew the truth about The Pines, the safer I would be. At the conclusion of the visiting hour, I profusely thanked Bob and Farruk for their courage in visiting me in a psych ward and said goodbye.

5

DESTINY

I was released from the hospital at 2 p.m. on Saturday. When Kevin arrived to pick me up, I was packed and ready to go. Tucked away among my clothes was the Gideon Bible I had found. I believed that the Good Book was not only my source of truth, but also that it would help protect me if I should happen to run into any trouble.

The short drive home from Freehold was most enjoyable. I absorbed all the familiar sights and sounds of the outside world with renewed pleasure. After being held against my will for a week, it felt good to be free again.

When I got home, everyone made a big fuss over me. Although I didn't mind the attention, I thought it was unwarranted. Regardless of what anyone else believed, I considered my hospitalization to have been a grave injustice and felt that I was completely normal. Why wasn't this fact easily discernible to my family? I guessed that they were just happy to have me home again. It had been a while since I had lived in Manalapan.

Our house, awarded to my mother in the divorce settlement with my father, was a bi-level ranch design with five bedrooms and two full bathrooms. The exterior had recently been painted an off-white color with royal blue trim, and my mom was currently remodeling the downstairs living room. Other than the kitchen being a tad too small, the ultra-suburban dwelling was a paragon of comfort.

My mother cooked a mouth-watering lasagna dinner that we quickly devoured. Following the meal, my family dispersed in different directions. Deirdre, Sean, and Starlight went out to a club in New York City. My mom decided to catch a movie at a local theater, and Thomas took a walk to a friend's house. I was left alone with Kevin.

We sat down at the kitchen table and had an in-depth discussion on such varied topics as baseball, women, religion, and God. Eventually, after a few hours had passed, the conversation shifted to our family. I told Kevin that I was worried about our father. His betrayal of me had endangered his soul.

"Is it too late for him? Can you save him, Den?" Kevin asked. I smiled warmly. My learned brother looking to me for answers was a welcome change, a change that indicated he was at least subconsciously aware of my new spiritual insight.

"No, Kev, I can't save him, but he can save himself. His fate is not sealed. He just has to turn around and do the right thing." When I spoke those words, Kevin's eyes lit up like a pinball machine.

"Hold on a second, I've got something to show you," he said. He went into one of the bedrooms and returned with a thin notebook. "This is something I wrote for the Freemans. I wanted to give it to them as a wedding present, but I haven't gotten around to typing it yet. Here, read it," he urged, handing it to me.

The short story was entitled *The Slap*. It was about an old man who, seconds before he died, slapped his grandson in the face. The innocent young boy was troubled about why his beloved grandfather would strike him and leave such a bitter final memory. After many years pass and the boy has become a man, he finally comes to understand that the slap was intended to be one final lesson, given out of love. His grandfather wanted to prepare him for some of the harsh realities of an unjust world, and to help him endure despite the inevitable pain and disappointments he would experience.

Kevin's story went on to examine the mysteries of life and death. The ending of his last paragraph, which referred back to the dying grandfather, was particularly poignant. "Having lived life to the fullest and having stared death in the face, he was not afraid of dying. There was nothing to be afraid of."

I felt as if my brother's story had been written specifically for me. He was telling me not to be afraid, to be courageous. Suddenly I knew exactly what I had to do. I told Kevin that I had to go to Bob's house to pick up some money. He was reluctant to let me go out by myself, but I convinced him that I would be all right. I hated lying to him but I had no other choice. I had to confront my enemies tonight and time was running short. It would be midnight in just a few hours.

I put on Sean's black leather jacket and started my car. When I entered the Garden State Parkway a half hour later, I turned on my A.M. radio and tuned into the WFAN sports station. The D.J. was calling it a day of tragedy because of two very sad occurrences. A horse had been killed in the Breeder's Cup Race and, in an unrelated accident, another horse had died at the Freehold Raceway. God was clearly showing his wrath. By destroying those animals, he was giving us a preview of things to come.

I continued listening to the radio and discovered that the Columbia Lions had finally won a football game. There was something significant about this achievement as well. I remembered reading a Biblical passage referring to a pack of lions rising up and claiming a great victory.

While I was making this connection, Kevin's graduation speech also popped into my mind. In the speech, he drew an analogy between law students and *The Wizard of Oz*, noting that the students needed brains, heart, and courage in order to survive the rigors of law school. He concluded his brilliant oration by imploring his classmates to be "lions of the world." Yes, now was definitely the time to be a lion.

As I approached New City, the D.J. reminded his audience that tonight was Daylight Savings Time, so we should remember to turn our clocks back an hour. It seemed poetically appropriate, as if God were giving me an extra hour to take care of business.

I pulled into my father's driveway at precisely 11:57 p.m., just three minutes ahead of my imaginary deadline. October 27 was all but gone; had I made it in time? Without knocking, I pulled open the door and entered the living room. Willie and my father were both in their pajamas, sitting on the sofa. They were startled to see me there so late.

"Wh… What are you doing here, Den?" my father managed to blurt out. It was easy to see that he was afraid of me. His blue eyes revealed his stark fear.

"Oh, I just stopped in to take care of a few things, Dad," I answered coyly. I looked over at Willie, but her eyes remained riveted to the wooden floor. I observed that she was reading a book called *Women of Darkness* and was playing with a white, powdery substance. My instincts were right on target. She was up to something twisted, evil, and sinister. I had stopped her just in time. In another three minutes, at the stroke of midnight, she would have completed her Satanic ritual and my mission would have been a failure.

On the television set, Howard Stern was prancing around in a bra and spitting out crude jokes. Willie remarked how much she hated the show.

"If you find it offensive, why do you watch it?" I asked. She did not reply. I went down into the basement and began loading my possessions, which my father had retrieved from The Pines, into my car. I wondered if he was going to go for his gun. I didn't think so. He still wasn't sure of how much I knew.

When I had finished packing the car, I returned to the living room. My father tried to convince me to stay the night. I responded with a hearty laugh. "Now you know I can't do that, Dad. You see, I know everything. Everything. I know that you and Willie set me up. But that's okay, it's not too late. You just have to listen to me and do exactly what I say."

My father clutched his heart. He was feeling weak and faint. "Jesus, Den, I don't want to die." I moved towards him and put my right hand on his shoulder.

"That's just it, Dad. You're not going to die. Put your faith in God's hands and you will live forever and ever."

Willie looked at me coldly and said, "Can't you see you're upsetting your father? He's got a bad heart."

I laughed again. "It's not his heart I'm worried about, Willie, it's his soul." I looked closely at my father. His ruddy Irish complexion had turned very pale. He looked at me with pleading eyes, begging me to say something. I obliged him.

"Dad, in spite of everything, I love you. You were a great father to me. I know you really didn't want to hurt me." He reached out and hugged me with his once powerful arms.

"Dennis, I love you. I've always loved you so much," he said, choking back tears. "Tell me what you want to do. I'll do anything I can to help you."

I smiled broadly. Deep down in my heart, I always knew that my father would come back to me. After all his pretensions were removed, he was essentially a good man, a man who loved his kids as much as any father I knew.

Gently pulling myself away from his firm hold, I looked him in the eyes and gave him my instructions. "It's very simple, Dad. You're just going to have to turn around and do the right thing. I'll tell you exactly what to do when I know more myself. Listen to me and do exactly as I say. I'm calling the shots now."

I turned to my father's wife and spoke to her. "It's not too late for you either, Willie. Jesus forgives all our sins, no matter how grave they are. Trust my Dad and do as he does." She continued to stare impassively at the floor, not daring to look me in the eyes. I could tell that she was unmoved by what I had said.

I looked over at the clock and saw that it was getting late. "I've got to go now, Dad. I've got a few more things to do tonight. I'll be in touch with you soon," I said, turning towards the door.

"Be careful, son," my father whispered in a hoarse voice.

"Don't worry, Dad. God is with me. Nothing can touch me. Do you know what day it is today?" He shook his head. "It's the day your father died twelve years ago. He's still with us, you know. I can feel his spirit."

Willie looked away. She knew that I had touched her husband. He was not going to betray me again.

As I backed out of the driveway I saw my father's face pressed up against the screen door. I couldn't tell for sure, but it looked as though he was crying. Do what you have to do, Dad. Fight for me. Fight the way you taught me to fight.

When I was a couple of miles away from my father's house, I pulled into a dark Getty station that had been closed for the evening. Moving quickly, I opened the trunk of my car and pulled out two old New Jersey license plates and a Phillips screw driver. I was leaving nothing to chance. Willie knew exactly where I was going. She had undoubtedly called the police or other key people at

The Pines and told them to watch for a car with Florida plates.

I struggled in the dark for nearly twenty minutes before I finally secured the Jersey plates. For all of my athletic talents, God had given me a mechanical aptitude that was only slightly higher than the average chimpanzee's. While I again began the long drive back to The Pines, my thoughts turned to my grandfather.

Aside from obtaining enough evidence to shut down the drug operation at The Pines, was there another purpose for my "homecoming?" Was I going to do something that would release Poppy from some sort of Purgatory he was trapped in? No. That couldn't be true. If God was just as I knew he was, he would have never put my grandfather on any kind of waiting list. The man was a Christian, in the truest meaning of the word.

What then? My mind searched in vain for a definitive answer, but I knew nonetheless that Poppy was somehow involved in all of this. I felt certain that the hows and whys of the equation would be revealed to me later. For now, I was just going to have to concentrate on the work at hand.

I was jolted out of my thoughts by the sickening sight of flashing blue and red lights up ahead. When I slowed down and moved closer, I saw that three police cars had set up a roadblock just two miles from my exit on the New York State Thruway. Once again my hunches had proved correct. Just as I feared, Willie had evidently informed the corrupt cops that I'd be coming this way. Thank God I had thought to change the plates.

The patrolmen were letting cars pass by one at a time. I tried my best to act casual when I came to the barrier, but my heart was pounding fiercely. A burly state trooper with a thick brown mustache stuck a flashlight in my face and waved me through.

Before I resumed normal speed, I noticed a Honda Civic with Florida license plates pulled over to the side of the road. An irate driver seemed to be questioning why he was being detained. Those bozos with badges were either looking for me, or trying to get tickets to Disney World. In her understandably frazzled condition, Willie must have been uncertain as to the make and model of my automobile.

I didn't relax until the police cars became smaller and smaller in my rearview mirror and finally turned into distant dots. Now I was more determined than ever to get to my destination and stop those immoral cowards. I turned off at my exit and headed down the dirt road that led to the den of iniquity, better known as The Pines Hotel.

When I arrived in South Fallsburg it was almost 3 a.m., or 2 a.m., if I took Daylight Savings Time into account. Not surprisingly, the town was desolate and eerily quiet. Gentle rustling of newly fallen leaves provided the only movement in an otherwise still night.

As I drove closer to The Pines I felt a noticeable change in the air. I did not see or hear anything out of the ordinary, but nevertheless I felt the presence of a force that was dirty, evil, and unholy. A gnawing fear gripped my body. I was dancing on the devil's turf. I knew that if I were discovered, I would not live to see the next sunrise.

"Please, God, give me the courage to do what needs to be done," I prayed silently as I pulled into the parking lot. The lot was only half full, not nearly as crowded as it had been a week ago. When I stepped out of my car I realized that the temperature had dropped at least ten degrees since I left my father's house. I put my cold hands inside Sean's jacket pockets and discovered a pair of my brother's reading glasses. "These couldn't hurt," I thought, as I slipped the glasses onto my face. The element of disguise they gave me more than made up for the slight impairment of my vision.

With my hands still in my pockets, I quickly walked through the front gate. The lone guard in the security office was glued to a black and white T.V. and didn't seem to notice me. I opened the back service door and entered the main building of The Pines. Will they be waiting for me? I wondered. No. There's no way they expected me to get past those cops. I continued walking.

As I moved through the main lobby I almost expected to see Eve Cantor jump out from the shadows pointing a 357 magnum at my skull. Her mouth would turn into an evil and crooked grin, her dead eyes mocking my ineptitude. Fortunately, this waking nightmare did not materialize. The hotel was as deserted and quiet as the town itself. Finally, I came to the business office. I took a deep breath and opened the door.

Bill, the night shift operator, was all that stood between me and an empty office. I didn't think that he posed too much of a problem.

"Hi, Bill, how are you doing?" I asked him, trying my best to sound unconcerned.

"Fine, thanks. What are you doing here?"

"Oh, I just came by to pick up a few things I forgot last week." He didn't say anything, so I began searching through my old desk for some incriminating evidence.

I wasn't certain of exactly what I was looking for. But I hoped to find something with names and information that linked individuals to the drug operation. My search netted me an old Activities sheet with a guy named Craig Lawrence listed as the Assistant Director, a handful of department memos, and a batch of sundry papers that I thought I might be of use. I stuffed everything into a large manila folder. After saying goodbye to Bill, I left the office and excitedly walked back to my car.

"I did it. I'm gonna nail these bastards," I triumphantly said to myself as I turned back into the southbound New York State Thruway. Thank you, God. Thanks for letting me get through there without any harm coming my way.

I reviewed the night's events. I had stopped Willie from participating in a Satanic ceremony. My father had been very moved by my words and actions, but had been unable to prevent his wife from contacting her associates. Changing my license plates had probably saved my life. I had been successful in obtaining evidence to prove my allegations against The Pines. Now all I needed was some time to sort through the papers and interpret them. Somewhere, my grandfather was smiling proudly.

I breathed a little easier when I turned off the Thruway and entered the Garden State Parkway. Passing through the state line was a cathartic experience for me. By my way of thinking, all of New York was evil, corrupt, and dirty. New Jersey, on the other hand, was an oasis in the desert. Despite its negative image, the state boasted a plethora of fresh air, tall trees, golf courses, and bountiful land, as well as a never-ending supply of beautiful suburban homes. I hoped to someday own one of these homes.

My condemnation and deification of two entire states accurately reflected how rigidly fixed my thinking had become. Everyone and everything was either good or bad. There was no middle ground. In my simplistic black and white world, not only could I not see all the different shades of gray, I could not even acknowledge their existence.

I exited the Parkway at exit 130 and checked into a cheap motel on Route 1 in East Brunswick. When I was settled into a room, I decided to call home and let my family know that I was unharmed. I was sorry to have to put them through so much worry, but it just wasn't safe to let anyone know what I was doing. It was dangerous enough for me by myself. My mother picked up the phone on the first ring.

"Dennis, is that you? Are you all right? We've been worried sick about you!" she said in a clearly shaken voice.

"I'm fine, Mom. I just had to take care of a few loose ends at The Pines. You didn't really think that I'd just be able to let it go, did you?"

"No, I guess not. Buy why? What did you accomplish by going back there?"

"I have papers with me which will prove that the drug operation exists and that my allegations were not just the product of my imagination, as everybody seems to think."

I asked my mother where Sean and Kevin were and she told me that they had driven up to The Pines to try to look for me. True Warriors, I thought. Those guys would lay down their lives for me.

"Come home, Dennis, or tell me where you are so your brothers can follow you." She was near tears now.

"No, I can't do that. I'm exhausted. I need to get a few hours of sleep. I'll be home by early afternoon. Tell Kevin and Sean to make sure they bring Daddy with them to Manalapan. I don't care if they have to drag him into the car, it's imperative that he comes. He'll be able to corroborate everything I have to say. I love you Mom. I'll be home real soon." I hung up the phone and fell into a deep satisfying sleep.

True to my word, I walked in my front door at one o'clock Sunday afternoon. My family converged on me in an instant.

"It's about goddamn time!" Sean yelled. "We were worried that we'd never see you again." The rest of my family echoed his sentiment. Amidst their relief of seeing me home safe and sound, they were angry at me for pulling what they perceived to be an irresponsible and stupid stunt.

"Oh, what the hell. Thank God you're home," my mother said, hugging me tightly.

Thomas and Deirdre joined in. They were both happy to have their big brother back with them. Kevin was the last to make eye contact with me. One look at him told me what kind of night it had been for my twin. His face looked tired and worn, his hazel eyes struggling to remain open. A two day-old beard further contributed to his shoddy appearance.

"We just missed you, pal," he said quietly, clearly glad to be speaking with me again. "The operator at The Pines said you left fifteen or twenty minutes before we got there." I nodded my head and smiled. It pained me to realize what an ordeal I had put him through. I knew Kevin well enough to surmise that he had blamed himself for letting me go out of the house.

"Where's Daddy, Kev? Why didn't you guys bring him here like I told you?" I asked calmly. He looked at me with an expression that combined annoyance with disbelief.

"Man, you've got some pair of balls! Who the hell are you to go around giving orders?"

"I'm just a regular guy who's going to single-handedly bring down one of the biggest drug operations in the country," I responded evenly. "Now, where is he?" Kevin looked at me and laughed. It was impossible for him to stay mad at me, no matter how hard he tried.

"Look, Den, Sean and I were with him this morning. He's a wreck. You scared the living shit out of him last night. His teeth are falling out. He had to hold his hand to his mouth to keep them in. Willie drove him into Brooklyn to see Dr. Grayson. He won't be coming here today."

My initial reaction was one of sympathy for my father. God had punished him for his sins. Losing his teeth was one of the penances he was going to have to endure.

After thinking it over for a moment, however, I realized that this theory was incorrect. My father's teeth were fine last night. They don't just fall out overnight. He was afraid all right, but it wasn't me he was afraid of. He knew that what he and Willie had done, and were about to do, was wrong. Understandably, he was terrified of God's retribution.

When I left him last night, it was obvious that he had wanted to come clean. I could see the look of desperation in his eyes. Although he wanted to help me, he was powerless to do anything. With one call from Willie, he could be erased as easily as chalk on a blackboard. To her credit, contriving a dental emergency was quite clever. It was the perfect excuse to avoid coming to Manalapan. She knew that if he ever stepped inside our house, he would blow their cover by telling everyone the sordid truth.

I was disappointed that my father hadn't come, but it really didn't matter. I still had all the evidence I needed to end the drug operation at The Pines.

"Here, look at this," I said, handing the thick folder to Kevin. He sat down on the couch and started to read, poring over each piece of paper carefully and analytically, as if he were studying an important legal brief. After a few minutes, he returned with a verdict.

"This is a bunch of crap, Dennis. There's nothing here about any drug operation. All these papers just deal with the daily operations of the hotel."

I tried in vain to argue with him, but inwardly I knew that he was right. Damn, how could I have been so stupid, I thought dejectedly. They're not going to keep any incriminating written records just lying around waiting for someone to discover. I was further depressed when I realized that I had forgotten to take the payroll book. I was certain that the book contained copious tangible evidence.

Unwilling to admit defeat, I quickly shifted gears again. "Okay, that just means I'm going to have to bring Daddy here and let him tell what's going on. He knows the scope of this whole thing," I said to no one in particular. At this point, my family was steadily losing patience with me.

"Look, hon, you don't know for sure that there was a drug operation going on up there. You never actually saw any drugs. Don't you think this could all be a delusion like Dr. Miller says?" my mother asked gently.

"Dr. Miller doesn't know his ass from his elbow," I yelled back angrily. "I tricked that quack into letting me out in a week. I know that there's a drug operation at The Pines. Don't ask me to explain how I know. I just know. God has a plan for me to stop those people. I didn't ask for the job, but it's my destiny to fulfill. Someone's going to have to kill me before I quit trying to expose the truth."

Thomas stared at me intensely and tried hard to assess what I had just said.

"And what makes you so damn special? Do you think you've been touched by God?" he asked sarcastically.

"Yes, Tom. I have been." I could clearly see that my answer had shocked everyone, but I continued, undaunted. "God is working through me. He has already interceded on my behalf more than once. I am just trying to carry out his will." I thought about telling them about Joe and Mary, but they were having a hard enough time understanding what I was saying. I would tell them more when they were ready.

My family sat in disbelief for a minute, until Kevin broke the silence.

"Look, Den, we all love you very much. You're a great person, but you're not dealing in reality here. God had nothing to do with anything that happened last week. If you've been touched like you say you've been, then give us a sign. Show us some proof that what you say is true."

"Now who's got brass balls. You're talking like a lawyer already," I said, chuckling. "God is all powerful and almighty. He doesn't have to prove anything to you or to anyone else. Every breath that you or I draw is proof enough of his existence."

"You're right. I'm not debating that. I'm talking about you in particular. What kind of special knowledge has he given you?" Kevin challenged me to answer.

I pondered his question for a moment, and then told him that the Washington Redskins were going to beat the Giants in today's game.

"There's a 50/50 chance of that happening," Thomas said disgustedly.

"No, Tom. There's a 100% chance of that happening. I know the outcome of the game. God has given me a sign." I was as sure of this prediction as I was of Holyfield winning the fight the other night.

At the hospital, on both Thursday and Friday, a slightly retarded young woman named Jane had dressed in full Redskins regalia. Her burgundy and gold ensemble consisted of a wool hat, sweatshirt and sweatpants, and even a pair of socks. When I complimented her on her outfit, she kept telling me, "The Redskins are gonna win. The Redskins are gonna win." Surely this was a sign from heaven.

"Yeah, right, Den. We'll see about that," said Sean.

Normally, Kevin and I were the only Giants fans in the house. Sean and Tom had always been die-hard Jets fans. On this particular Sunday, however, I was the only Mulhearn not pulling for the Big Blue of New York.

I went into my bedroom and took a brief nap before the game started. When I came back downstairs to the living room, my three brothers and even my sister were huddled in front of the RCA television set. Only our mother remained upstairs, preparing dinner in the kitchen. She had always been amazed that a silly football game could have such a big impact on so many people's lives.

Before the opening kickoff, the announcer spoke of how important the game was to both teams. The stakes were much higher in my household. Unbeknown to them, the Redskins and the Giants were playing to determine whether or not dear old Dennis had gone crazy.

I sat down at the end of the couch and put my feet up on the coffee table. While I was certain that Washington was going to win, I had no idea what the final score would be. I expected a close, hard-hitting contest.

At halftime, my family clung to their unrealistic hopes. The Giants were ahead and theoretically they could easily hold on for the win. Kevin excused himself and went upstairs to make a phone call. When he returned to his position in front of the television, he asked me if I would mind if Jim and Sandi came over later.

"No, not at all. Maybe I can convince some impartial observers that my story is true."

Jim Freeman was Kevin's former roommate from Muhlenberg. Although tall and thin, his fine features, bright smile, and rosy cheeks make him appear much younger than he actually was. Even now, he looked closer to eighteen than to his twenty-six years of age. Jim's personality matched his apple pie looks. He was always extremely friendly and polite. In short, he was the prototypical type of young man whom every father would like to see his daughter marry someday.

Unfortunately for all of those would be fathers-in-law out there, he had already taken a wife. He met Sandi at a party in the basement of the Jefferson Medical Center in Philadelphia. She was a registered nurse there and he was completing the first year of a medical internship. It must have been love at first sight, because they were married less than a year later.

Sandi was a cute, petite redhead with alluring freckles and a bubbly personality. She complimented Jim perfectly. Traveling all the way from Philadelphia just to see me was a selfless gesture above and beyond the call of friendship, but the Freemans thought nothing of it. They left their apartment a few minutes after they received Kevin's urgent phone call.

The football game was living up to its hype. It was a classic battle between two powerful teams. Late in the fourth quarter, the Giants scored a touchdown to reclaim the lead. Pandemonium broke loose in my living room. I hadn't seen my brothers this excited about a football game since the 1987 Super Bowl. Nevertheless, I was not the least bit worried. There was still plenty of time left on the clock, and I was sure that Washington was going to win the game with a dramatic comeback.

True to form, the Redskins mounted an impressive drive and moved the ball all the way down the field against the stingy Giants defense. "Here we go, boys. This is it," I said with gleeful anticipation as the Redskins broke their huddle. I could hardly wait for the winning play to unfold in front of my eyes. Instead of seeing that happen, I watched a Giants cornerback intercept the ball in the endzone. The game was over and the Giants had won a thriller.

"You see, Dennis? You don't have an inside track to God, nobody does," Deirdre said, without a trace of gloating in her voice.

"Got any more hot picks for us, Den?" Thomas piped in. Sean and Kevin joined him in relieved laughter. They all felt that now I would finally see the futility of my warped sense of reality.

My head was spinning. How could I be wrong about this? It never occurred to me that there might actually be something wrong with my brain. My mind was as sharp as it had even been. Sharper actually. I seemed to have achieved a higher state of awareness. All five of my senses were operating at their maximum levels. So what went wrong?

My confusion abated after a minute or two, when I finally recognized where I had made my mistake.

"Well, you were wrong about the game. How do you explain that?" Sean asked.

"It's very simple. I was tricked by the devil. The girl who gave me the sign was an apostate of God, who now works for Satan. She was sent by him to fool me. She obviously succeeded, but next time I'll know better."

"That's the most ridiculous logic I've ever heard," Kevin bellowed. "If I wasn't so pissed off at you, I'd be rolling on the floor laughing."

The expressions on my family's faces left no doubt that they were all extremely concerned about me. I tried to enlighten them further.

"Let me give you an analogy. What's going on here is like a cosmic chess game between God and the devil. I'm just a pawn on God's side. The problem is that they are not playing by the same rules. When God takes his hand off a piece, his move is final.

"The devil, on the other hand, cheats any way he can. He'll change his move at the last minute, and he'll even move pieces around on the board when he thinks God isn't looking. He still can't win, however, so when God invariably gets ready to put him in checkmate, he'll knock the pieces off the board and they'll start all over again."

"When does it end?" Deirdre asked.

"It ends when God wants it to end. He'll force the devil to play to completion, defeat the beast, and rid the world of evil and sin. The devil can't keep stalling forever." My unfounded theology lesson was interrupted by the arrival of Jim and Sandi. We greeted them warmly, and then moved upstairs to enjoy an eggplant parmesan dinner.

After a quiet dinner in which most of the conversation centered on the Freemans, everyone retreated into the family room to discuss my situation. I recounted for Jim and Sandi my week at The Pines, my father's and Willie's involvement, and my special relationship with God. They listened patiently and sympathetically for over an hour. When I had finished, Jim put his hand on his chin and spoke to me, carefully choosing each of his words.

"I understand what you're saying, Dennis, and there's a possibility that everything you say about the drug ring is true. But there is also the chance that you may be having a delusion, as your psychiatrist thinks." I started to protest, but Jim interrupted me. "Hear me out. I'm not judging you. I'm sure that a lot of bad things happened up there in the Catskills, but I also know your father. I don't think he would ever try to hurt you."

I felt a dull headache coming on as Jim continued. "I've talked to Kevin about this and he and everyone else thinks that you should go back to the hospital for a while. If what you say is true, then it won't hurt you at all. If it's not true, you will get the help you need by trained professionals who know what they're doing." My family nodded their approval in unison. I was hurt deeply.

"The hospital is for sick people, nut cases, wackos. I am none of the above, so there is no way I'm ever going back to that prison," I said defiantly. My mother started crying.

"Please, Dennis, please. Go to the hospital. You need help," she said in between sobs. I looked at my brothers and sister. Tom and Deirdre were near tears themselves. Kevin was sweating profusely. He had aged five years in the last two days. I hated seeing my family in such a sorry state. I never doubted their love for me, it was their judgment that I questioned. At that moment, I realized just how much I loved my family. It was killing me to see them suffer like this.

I pondered my predicament for a moment. God only knew how much I hated being cooped up in that hospital, but, was it my destiny to go back there? Maybe it was part of God's plan for me to obtain more knowledge from Joe and Mary. Yes, that must be it. There was no other reasonable explanation.

"All right, all right. I'll go back to the damn hospital," I finally relented. My family breathed a collective sigh of relief.

Sean left to go pick up Starlight at work. The rest of us went downstairs into the living room and continued talking. I agreed to cooperate fully with Dr. Miller. Unfortunately, this included taking the medication that he had prescribed for me. I disdainfully remembered how terrible the "medicine" had made me feel. "What exactly is this Haldol they gave me? What does it do?" I asked Jim.

He explained that Haldol was an anti-psychotic drug used to treat delusions and hallucinations. Its primary function was to block the Dopamine receptors to the brain. In layman's terms, it was supposed to slow down the brain and reconnect any loose wiring. The possible side effects included severe fatigue, blurred vision, dry mouth, and extreme restlessness. Jeez, why wasn't I told about this when I went to Centra-State? Didn't a mental patient have any rights? It was rather ironic that I didn't like to take aspirin, but now I was being forced to consume a drug that was messing with my brain. I wondered grimly if I could wind up like a lobotomized Jack Nicholson in *One Flew Over the Cuckoo's Nest*.

It was nearly ten o'clock when I was escorted into the Centra-State emergency room by my mother, Kevin, Jim, and Sandi. While my mom took care of the appropriate paperwork at the reception area, I turned to my brother and said, "I want to tell you something, Kev. Remember this, I'm the toughest sonofabitch who ever walked down the pike. They won't beat me." He smiled and assured me that he didn't think anyone could beat me.

After a half hour, Kevin left with the Freemans. My mother and I talked while we continued to wait in the lobby of the emergency room. A nurse came over and informed us that there was a problem. They didn't have any beds available on the psych unit and it was going to be a while before I could be admitted there. She told us we could wait in an empty room down the corridor until a bed was ready. We found the room and, after a brief argument, I convinced my exhausted mother to go home. Shortly thereafter, I fell asleep on a green examination table.

I dreamed of being on a cobblestone street happily tossing a pink rubber ball, known as a "spaldeen," back and forth to my paternal grandfather. Both of us were bright-eyed thirteen-year-old boys, brimming with hopes and dreams. Neither of us spoke a word. We just threw the ball over and over again against the backdrop of a setting sun.

My dream was no doubt inspired by the short story I had written a few months before. In the fictional piece, I was married and had a three-year-old daughter. I somehow became a boy again and was magically transported back into Brooklyn, in the year 1922. There, I met three other boys, who just happened to be my grandfather and his younger brothers, Harry and Jimmy. I greeted the boys, careful not to divulge my true identity, and then joined them as they challenged their neighborhood rivals to a friendly game of stickball.

It was a joy to see Tommy (my grandfather) running freely in his youth. At age twenty-one, while working on a construction site, he fell off the roof of a three-story building. His doctors said he was lucky to have lived, but the fall damaged his spine and left one of his legs six inches shorter than the other. The resulting limp severely limited his physical activity.

While not quite as athletic as their older brother, my great-uncles, Harry and Jimmy, played the game with remarkable enthusiasm and intensity. Their spirit was infectious. I was having a great deal of fun being a part of the Mulhearn team.

In the final inning, I ended the game and preserved our team's victory by making a spectacular over-the-shoulder catch on a ball hit three sewers. While the ball was still hanging in the air, Tommy had yelled, "Check the standings. Make sure you check the standings, Dennis." An instant after I caught the ball, my head slammed into a lamppost, and I was returned to my bedroom in 1990. I sat up with my wife Susan and tried to figure out what Tommy had tried to tell me.

Finally, in desperation, I found a recent issue of the *Sporting News* and turned to the baseball standings. My beloved team, the New York Yankees, were solidly entrenched in last place, or what's known in baseball vernacular as "the basement." I jumped out of bed and ran down the steps to my basement. A stack of old newspapers left by the previous owners had been ignited by a carelessly discarded cigarette butt, and the fire was starting to spread. I extinguished it just before the flames reached the boiler. In another few minutes, the authorities would have had to identify my family and me by our dental records.

Greatly relieved, I tiptoed into my daughter's room to check on her. She was wide awake. When I reached down to pull her covers over her shoulders, I saw that she was clutching a pink rubber ball in her delicate fingers.

"Where did you get the ball, sweetheart?" I asked.

"A nice old man with white hair and funny walk gave it to me, Daddy," she answered innocently. I smiled, kissed her on top of her forehead, and went back to my bedroom. Susan soon fell back asleep, but I stayed up for a while and thought about my grandfather.

"I'll see you again soon, Pop. Next time we'll play a little baseball," I vowed. "Just wait until you try hitting with an aluminum bat." And that was the end of my story.

I don't think Poe or Hemingway had anything to worry about, but I was quite proud of my work anyway. It was my tribute to Poppy. Mysteriously, the notebook in which I had written the story had disappeared when my father took my belongings from The Pines. It was my most cherished possession and the lone item that was missing. I was furious when I realized that my untitled work was either lost or stolen. Why would anybody want that notebook? Did my story have any spiritual significance?

6

THE SIGN OF THE CROSS

I was awakened at 4 a.m. by a female hand tugging gently at my shoulder. When my eyes had opened, I saw that the hand belonged to a thirty-something nurse name Toni. Immediately, I knew that this nurse was a good person, a woman of God. I made this assessment based on the way her face glowed and the caring way she looked at me with her hazel eyes.

She propped me into a wheelchair and began pushing me down the hall. "You're a Christian, aren't you, Toni?" I said, turning my head back toward her.

"Why, yes. I'm a born-again Christian. How did you know that?" she asked, smiling shyly.

"You have a certain aura about you. It's really rather obvious." Her smile grew wider. She was extremely pleased.

I had always been intrigued by born-again Christians.

Theirs is a religion of passion and zeal. Indeed, it is more a philosophy of life rather than a religion. I admire the born-again for their devout faith and strict adherence to Christian principles, yet am turned off by their "holier than thou" attitude towards outsiders. They believe that in order to be "saved," a person has to accept Jesus Christ into his life as his personal savior. Of course, the converse of this means that all Jews, Buddhists, Muslims, and others with conflicting beliefs, are damned to hell for all eternity. I could never accept this doctrine as fact. Still, Toni had an inner peacefulness that I envied. Maybe she was onto something.

Finally, we arrived at the psychiatric unit. I chuckled when I saw the sign that read, "Retreat and Recovery." I guess it was better than calling it "El

Nuthouse," but no sugar-coated name could change the irrefutable fact that I was reentering an institution reserved for the mentally unbalanced. I didn't care if it was part of God's plan, it was depressing as hell to be back again. I was moved back into my old room with Karl. The fear and uncertainty I had felt the previous week was replaced by anger and frustration. I vowed to avenge this injustice as I fell back to sleep.

My first day back at the hospital was spent in a mindless void. The dosage of Haldol I was given made me so groggy, it was difficult to think at all. I wandered around the unit looking for Joe or Mary, hoping one of them could enlighten me as to my next course of action. But they were nowhere to be found. I never saw either of them again.

Dr. Miller stopped by my room to pay me a visit. His manner was deliberate and cautious. I had already burned him once. He wasn't going to let that happen again.

"Hello, Dennis. I've scheduled a Catscan and an EEG exam for you tomorrow morning," he said stiffly. I was amused by his new strategy to try to figure me out.

"So, now I'm a laboratory rat. Why don't you just dissect me while you're at it, Doc?" Either my delivery was off, or Dr. Miller did not have much of a sense of humor. He gave me a puzzled look and left the room.

My mood turned dark when I found out one of the details of EEG test. Apparently, the EEG was most effective when the patient was sleep deprived. Since I was being heavily sedated, I didn't see how I could stay up much past eight o'clock, never mind all night. Somehow, however, three nurses managed to keep me awake by taking turns walking me around the hospital. By the time morning arrived I felt as if I had been hit by a truck.

I was wheeled down to the radiology department, which was located in the basement of the hospital, in a wheelchair. There, I was greeted by a medical technician, a pleasant blond-haired woman who did not give me her name. She informed me that the Catscan simply involved taking an X-ray of my brain, while the electro-encephalogram waves (EEG) monitored my brain activity. The Catscan was no problem. All I had to do was stick my head inside a round machine for ten or fifteen seconds, while the technician took the picture.

The EEG was a bit more unpleasant, but not unbearable. The technician attached thin wires to my head and then flicked on another machine that measured my brain's activity. It was all over in a few minutes. I was told that it would take two or three days to get the test results back.

While I awaited those results, I settled into a predictable routine. I ate my meals, participated unenthusiastically in group therapy, worked out in my room, and visited with my family after dinner. The Haldol was working very effectively. I felt as if my brain was working in slow motion. I had no desire to do anything, or even to think about anything. All I wanted to do was sleep. Sleep was replacing food, sex, and love as my primary need. My fear of returning to the hospital had been justified. I was becoming a pathetic shell of the energetic person I had once been.

My spirits were lifted slightly by the nursing staff. Although Joe and Mary had gone back to wherever they had come from, the rest of the nurses, male and female alike, were extraordinarily kind, warm, and understanding. They expressed empathy for what I was going through and did everything they could to make me as comfortable as possible. At times they were still a bit condescending, but I accepted this without bitterness. After all, to them I was now a two-time mental patient.

Much to my surprise, I even developed a friendship with Jeannine, the young woman whom I initially thought was involved with The Pines. I had misjudged her badly. She went out of her way to talk to me and to put my troubled mind at ease.

On Friday, Dr. Miller came in with the results of my tests. One glance at his facial expression indicated that the news was not going to be good. He'd be a lousy poker player, I thought as he gingerly sat down in the chair next to my bed.

"I received the results of your tests this morning. I'll be frank with you, Dennis. Nothing showed up on the Catscan, but I'm concerned with EEG results. You have brainwave activity that is extremely abnormal."

"Just what the hell is 'normal,' Doc?" I said angrily. "How valid could that stupid test be?" He pulled at his beard and looked at me pensively.

"I'm not sure at this point. I've ordered another test for you this afternoon. It's called a Catscan with contrast. That should give us a better idea of what's going on," he said, still pulling at his beard.

The Catscan with contrast was almost identical to the first Catscan I had taken. The only difference was that I was injected with dye prior to the test being administered. Supposedly, the dye provided a more detailed picture of my brain. I wondered why they hadn't just injected me with the dye the first time.

My weekend was spent in quiet reflection and solitude. I spent many hours reading my Bible, hoping to find some verses that could explain my predicament. Although I did not come across any truisms pertinent to me, the words of the Bible comforted me anyway. While many of the parables were confusing, the most basic, repeating theme was that love was the most important thing in life. Over and over again, Jesus preached the importance of loving your fellow man. I agreed with him wholeheartedly. The love I felt for my family and friends was what kept me going.

I had a couple of daily routines that I'm sure a few of the nurses found amusing. In the morning and evenings, I spent a half hour fastidiously washing my face and brushing and flossing my teeth. In the afternoons, I devoted an hour to doing push-ups and sit-ups on the floor on my room. I didn't care if anyone thought my behavior was unusual or eccentric. I had always had very bad skin and teeth, so I had to take extra time to improve my appearance. Likewise, I was proud of the physique I had built up over the years and was determined to not let myself go soft.

Dr. Miller labeled this behavior of mine as "obsessive-compulsive" and, therefore, dangerous. He felt that it was the reason I was compelled to return to The Pines. While I'm sure he had my best interests at heart, he was missing the whole point.

I have always had an obsessive-compulsive personality, but I viewed it as a strength rather than a weakness. As a boy, I spend thousands of hours swinging my baseball bat in my backyard and shooting countless baskets at the local playground. It was this obsessive drive to excel that enabled me to become a fine athlete. I didn't want to change this facet of my personality. It was an important part of my identity.

On Monday, November 5, Dr. Miller flagged me down in the day room while I was eating lunch. He said he wanted to discuss my test results with my mother when she came in to visit me tonight. He left quickly before I had a chance to ask him any questions.

My mother arrived at seven o'clock, looking tense and nervous. She drove into Brooklyn every day to teach a kindergarten class composed of five year-olds. Now, she was further burdened by my unnecessary hospitalization. Despite her long days of teaching and commuting, she had faithfully visited me every night since I had been admitted. Regardless of how tired I was feeling, I always looked forward to seeing her. She was my link to the outside world.

We talked quietly for a few minutes until Dr. Miller entered the room. He exchanged perfunctory pleasantries with us and then sat down next to my mother.

"I am extremely concerned by what we found on the last Catscan, Mrs. Mulhearn. There seems to be some foreign matter lodged in the middle of Dennis's brain. For lack of a better term, we'll call it a cyst. Here, look at this," he said, lowering his clipboard and revealing a black X-ray of my head. On the X-ray there was a white spot in the center of my brain about the size of a dime.

"What does this mean?" my mother asked. I stole a glance at her. She looked tired and frightened.

"Well, in my experience, the cyst is in the area of the brain that is often responsible for psychosis," Dr. Miller explained. I stared blankly into his eyes. That was the first time I had heard anyone described me as "psychotic." If I hadn't understood the gravity of my situation before, I certainly did now.

"What are Dennis's options, Doctor? Can the cyst be removed?"

"No, I don't think so. The cyst is in an area that makes it all but inoperable. Before we explore other options, I think Dennis should have an M.R.I. done."

"What the hell is an 'M.R.I.'?" I shot back. I was getting sick and tired of having to take all these damn tests. The doctor explained that the M.R.I. (Magnetic Resonance Imaging) was a new procedure which was far more advanced than a simple Catscan. It provided many different pictures of the brain, all at various angles. The only catch was that the test cost over a thousand dollars, payable in advance.

"I don't care about the money. I'll chip in with Kevin and Sean," my mother said, with determination in her voice. "When can he get it done?" I smiled broadly at her. She would have robbed a bank for me if she had to. Friday was the earliest day Dr. Miller could schedule the M.R.I. That meant another week of sitting around and waiting.

A few minutes after my mother and Dr. Miller left, I received a phone call from my father. I was surprised to hear from him. I hadn't spoken with him since my impromptu visit last week. His mood was cheerful and upbeat. It was as if he had gotten selective amnesia about what had happened the last time I saw him. I was confused. Why wasn't he discussing The Pines or God's plan for me?

"Willie and I are coming to see you tomorrow morning, son. If you can get a pass from your doctor, we'll go out to the Freehold Raceway and have a nice lunch."

I'm gonna have to be real careful tomorrow, I thought, as I walked back to my room.

I was uncertain as to how much control Willie now exerted over my father. Was he still working against me, or was he just looking for a window of opportunity to help me defeat Willie and the evil people involved with the drug operation? I would find out soon enough.

The next morning, I approached Dr. Miller in his office and asked him for a day pass. Since I had told him about their role in the drug operation, he was pleased that I wanted to spend time with my father and his wife.

"Sure. Go out and have an enjoyable day. Stay out for as long as you want. Just make sure you're back by eight o'clock tonight." I called Sean and told him and Tom to meet us at the track. I'd feel much safer having my two brothers there along with me.

My father and Willie arrived at Centra-State at eleven o'clock sharp. As usual, they were both dressed to kill. My father was wearing a charcoal gray suit, and Willie wore a stylish blue dress and a fancy hat.

"Hello, son, it's good to see you," my father said, clapping me on the back.

"Hi, sweetheart, how are you feeling?" asked Willie.

"Fine, thanks.

I was befuddled. Why were they being so nice to me? They both acted as if nothing had happened last week. Were they hoping that the drugs I was taking had made me forget as well?

Thankfully, the drive to the track only took ten minutes. During that time I was asked how Haldol was making me feel and how the hospital staff was treating me. I was taken aback by Willie's attitude toward me. She seemed genuinely concerned about the care I was receiving. Could this be the same woman who had gotten her own son killed at The Pines? I was still fairly certain that she was but now some doubts, which had not been there before, crept into my mind.

"Melissa's on that Haldol, isn't she, Hon?" my father asked his wife.

"Yes, she is. She hates it. But it stops the voices," Willie answered. My heart went out to Willie's youngest daughter. Melissa was a sweet and innocent young girl who had been besieged by hallucinatory voices. The voices began bothering her a year ago, right after her seventeenth birthday, and she had already been in a psychiatric hospital in New York for more than six months now. I thought of her whenever I started feeling overwhelmed by self-pity.

"The track looks great," my father remarked as we pulled into the parking lot of Freehold Raceway. He was right. A brand new grandstand had recently been completed, leaving no evidence of the fire that had burned the old one to the ground.

We met Sean and Thomas at the front gate. They were anxious to go inside and place a couple of bets. My two younger brothers both shared my father's passion for the ponies, but I didn't enjoy the track scene nearly as much as they did. I just didn't find the action that riveting.

I expected to go down to field level, but my father had different plans. He directed me and my brothers up the escalator to the upper mezzanine. We bought five racing programs, made a quick right, and entered an elegant restaurant called The Jockey Club. The maitre'd came over to us immediately.

"Good morning, Mr. Mulhearn. Please come right this way sir," he said. He seated us at a large round table in the center of the room.

"Whenever we go, they always remember your father," Willie said, smiling proudly. I nodded my agreement. He was an outstanding tipper. People in the food service business usually remembered and appreciated generous customers and made an extra effort to accommodate them.

The expensive yet tasteful décor of the restaurant reminded me of some of the lavish New York establishments in which I had occasionally dined. The only difference was that there were approximately twenty television sets scattered throughout the room and three betting windows strategically located near the front entrance.

We made it to one of these windows just in time to place our bets on the fourth race. I didn't have any money with me, so I had to settle for watching everyone else pick the horse of their choice. A few minutes later, I stared up at the closest monitor and cheered my father's selection to a wire to wire victory. He handed me the winning ticket and instructed me to collect for him. I came back to the table with four crisp one-hundred dollar bills.

In between races, a pretty waitress took our orders. Although I was famished, I ordered a tossed salad. Another of the revolting side effects of the Haldol was that it caused excessive weight gain. Despite my exercise, I noticed the beginnings of a spare tire forming around my mid-section. This development made me feel increasingly self-conscious and unattractive. However many Dopamine receptors the Haldol may or may not have been blocking, it caused me to swallow a bitter pill: the drug was making me fat.

Nobody at our table picked the winner of the fifth race, but it didn't really matter we were all having fun. The conversation shifted from how Thomas was doing in school to how Sean's job search was going. He had received offers from two different companies and was trying to decide which one he should accept.

"Whatever company you choose will be lucky to have you, Sean," said my father. "That goes for you, too, Dennis, when you're ready to go back to work." I smiled thinly. Getting another job was the last thing on my mind at that point. There were still so many things I had to figure out first.

My father hit the daily double in the sixth race, winning over eight hundred dollars. He said he hadn't won that much money at the track in quite some time. I must have been his good luck charm.

"Treat yourself to something nice," he said, handing me a fifty-dollar bill. I thanked him, turned to Sean and said, "would you mind taking me home? I'm feeling really tired. I need to go to sleep." My brother was disappointed to have to leave before the last races, but unselfishly agreed to drive me back to Manalapan.

"That was fun wasn't it?" Sean said as we stopped at a red light on Route 9.

"Yeah, it was," I replied. It really was. I wasn't sure of exactly what I anticipated, but I certainly hadn't expected to enjoy myself so much. I didn't know what to make of my father and Willie. They had both been so warm and friendly. Were they finally getting ready to come forward and expose the truth about The Pines? Or were they merely setting me up for another fall?

When we walked into my house, I bounded up the stairs and collapsed onto my bed. I slept soundly until 7:30 p.m. Sean woke me up and hustled me into his car. He dropped me off in front of the hospital at five minutes before eight. I signed in at the front desk and trudged back to my room. The gloomy atmosphere of the ward made me feel as though I were returning to a jail cell, rather than to a hospital. Being out for just a few hours reminded me how much I missed my freedom.

I was surprised to see Karl lying down in his bed. He usually watched T.V. in the day room until at least eleven o'clock. "Hi. How ya doin', Karl?" I said. He looked at me with sad, red eyes.

"Not so good. I just want to be normal like everybody else. I want to be able to walk again." I wanted desperately to say something that would comfort him, but what could I say? If he was lucky, with a prodigious effort he might some day be able to walk with a walker. That was the most he could realistically hope for.

"Don't give up, Karl. Pray to God and ask for his help. You've got to keep fighting," I said, without much enthusiasm. It was easy for me to give this poor guy advice. I had two healthy legs that could take me anywhere I wanted to go. As I rolled over and closed my eyes I wondered exactly what God had planned for Karl. Why was he burdened with so much pain and mental anguish? Once again, there were no answers to my questions.

The next couple of days moved by slowly. I impatiently waited for Friday to come so I could take my M.R.I. exam and be discharged. On Tuesday night I was sitting on my bed, reading a book, when I heard a knock on my door. "C'mon in," I said loudly. I smiled when I saw a dark-haired woman named Mary enter my room. Mary was a stout, middle-aged Italian-American who was one of my favorite nurses. She always seemed to have a big smile planted on her face and a kind word for every person to whom she spoke. "Hi, Dennis. I hope I'm not disturbing you. I'd like to talk with you for a few minutes, it that's okay," she said, flashing her trademark smile.

"Sure thing. Make yourself at home." I was always happy to talk with Mary. She walked over and sat down on the edge of my bed.

"I just wanted to speak to you before your test tomorrow. I know you've had it tough lately, but no one would ever know by looking at you. You're a very special young man, Dennis. I know that a lot of people are pulling for you." My cheeks instantly turned a bright crimson shade in an unconscious response to her generous compliment.

"Thank you, Mary. But I think I'm here for a reason. There has to be a good reason why God is making me go through all this. Everything happens for a reason," I said.

"Yes! Yes, you are so right!" I had apparently touched on a subject that was close to her heart. "When my daughter was five years old, she became very sick. Her doctors told me she was going to die. But I refused to accept that." She continued. "I got down on my knees and prayed to God with all my strength, asking him to spare my only child. My prayers were answered. Today, my daughter is a healthy and happy fifteen year-old girl."

"Has Satan ever tricked you?" I asked her, remembering the Redskins game.

"Oh, yes. The beast is tremendously resourceful. He's always trying to keep good people away from God. Tonight, he tried mighty hard to keep me away from this hospital. Now I'm really glad I came. God wanted to here, so we could have this talk." I noticed that her eyes flashed to the top of my dresser.

"Could you hand me your Bible, please, Dennis," she asked hesitantly. "I'm really not supposed to do this, but I can't help myself. I feel like I'm being pulled toward that Bible as if it were a magnet." I handed her the book and watched as she expertly flipped though it. She handed it back, after selecting two verses for me to read. The first verse was Romans 8:28: "And we know that all things work together for good to them that love God, to them who are the called according to his purpose." The second was Timothy 1:7: "For God hath not given us the spirit of fear, but of power, and of love, and of a sound mind."

"Wow. That's good stuff," I said to Mary, grateful that she had taken the time to share her knowledge with me. I found the verse from Timothy particularly illuminating. It made perfect sense. I was a strong man, filled with love. God was going to see to it that there was nothing to be afraid of. Fear was an instrument of the devil, and I was not going to let him use it against me. Mary wished me luck again and left to finish her rounds.

"I'll be praying for you," she said, as she closed the door behind her. Before I fell asleep, I thanked God for sending her to me.

My M.R.I. exam was scheduled for three o'clock at the Freehold Neurological Center, which was located a short block away from the hospital. I would have preferred to walk, but hospital rules mandated that I be escorted to the center. Sean came by at a quarter to three. As we stepped outside the hospital, a cold breeze hit my face. The sky was overcast and threatening. It looked as though heavy rains were on the way.

The Neurological Center was situated in a small brown building that appeared to have at one time been a bank. After I signed in at the reception area, Sean and I sat down in black leather chairs that were placed up against a large, clear picture window. Sean picked up a recent issue of *Sports Illustrated* and began skimming through it. I couldn't concentrate well enough to read anything. I just sat, staring straight ahead, thinking about my past and my future.

The minutes ticked by at an agonizingly slow pace, three-fifteen, three-twenty, three-thirty. Still no movement. I was getting more and more anxious with each passing minute. I wanted to get in there and get it over with. Making me wait like this was pure torture. Please, God. Help me out, will 'ya? Just as my mind was completing this thought, a bright light flashed behind me. I turned around and saw that amidst all the dark clouds, the sun was shining brightly. When I turned back around, there was a large cross on the wall opposite me. It's only a shadow of the window beams, my reason told me. But was that all it was? Where the hell did the sun come from?

I turned to my brother. He was thoroughly engrossed in his magazine and hadn't noticed anything. The sun disappeared as quickly as it had come, taking the cross with it. Had I been given a sign? There was a rational explanation for what I had seen, but I couldn't shake the feeling that the "The Man Upstairs" was trying to tell me something. My faith is weak, God. Show me again, I silently asked.

The cross majestically lit up the wall for just a brief instant, and then was gone. It was as if someone had turned on a movie projector and then pulled the plug a second later. I looked outside the window and saw that the already gray sky was turning black.

"We're ready for you now, Mr. Mulhearn. Come right this way," a woman called from the front desk.

"Good luck, Den," Sean said as he looked up from his magazine.

"Thanks, pal. This will be no sweat," I said nonchalantly. If my brother had bothered to shake my hand, my sweaty palms would have given away my false bravado. I was still thinking about the cross when I walked into a large room to the left of the waiting area. The sign on the white door read, "M.R.I. AUTHORIZED PERSONNEL ONLY."

A thin technician in a white smock was the only person in the room. He greeted me and introduced himself as Steve.

"You're not claustrophobic, are you?" he asked right away.

"No."

"Good. People who are have a hell of a time with this test." I could certainly see why. The M.R.I. machine looked like a miniature ten foot tunnel. Its smooth metal surface was shaped like a half-circle. The opening was only five feet wide and three feet high.

"The test will last forty-five minutes. It will be broken down into one twenty-minute interval and one twenty-five minute interval. You will hear loud noises, so don't be alarmed. I'll put the radio on so you'll have some background music. I'll be able to talk to you through a speaker. Let me know if you're having any problems. All right, hop on," Steve said, pointing to a black rubber platform at the mouth of the machine. When I was positioned correctly, he pulled a lever and the platform began to roll inside the mechanism.

The interior of the M.R.I. machine was cold and dark. I was only submerged a few feet, but it might as well have been a thousand. The light at the opening of the device appeared distant and dim. Behind me, I heard soft music in the background. It didn't comfort me at all.

"You okay in there?" asked Steve.

"Yeah, I'm fine," I lied. I felt as though the cold slabs of metal were going to cave in on me at any moment.

"Keep your head still. I'm going to start the machine," Steve instructed.

Steve had warned me about a loud noise, but I was not prepared for the extent of its loudness. It sounded as if a construction worker were tearing up a cement street just inches away from my head. I lay motionless, fighting back a primal urge to scream. After three or four minutes, the noise stopped. Ten seconds of blissful silence was replaced by another noise. Although different in frequency, it was just as intense as the first one.

I'm going to go crazy! This test would drive the sanest man nuts. I'm losing it. I fought desperately to hold onto what was left of my sanity. My psyche had been dangerously fragile to begin with. The stress of the test was pulling me over the edge. Time had lost all meaning. I would not have been able to differentiate a minute from an hour.

"NAAAAA ... NAAAA   " droned the machine. Stop it! Stop torturing me, my mind cried out. But I said nothing. I knew that I would somehow have to endure this test if I ever wanted to get out of the hospital.

When I was at the brink of losing control, I suddenly remembered the cross and started to pray: "Our father, who art in heaven, hallowed by thy name ..." I completed that Lord's Prayer and then said another, still another. Over and over again, I prayed to God in Heaven. It was working. I was starting to think that I could survive. C'mon, fight! Fight you son of a bitch, fight! "That's it Dennis, the first part is over. I'm bringing you out now," Steve said through the speaker. My relief was tempered with the knowledge that my ordeal was not yet half over.

I sat up on the platform and took a deep breath. Steve left the room for a minute and returned with a youthful doctor. The doctor stuck a needle in my arm and exited quickly.

"Sorry to keep you waiting, Dennis. An M.D. had to do that," Steve said before reentering me into the machine. "Ready? Here goes." Although I was prepared for it this time, the horrible noise still made me shiver. How the hell am I going to survive another twenty-five minutes of this nonsense?

Help me, father. Please, help me fight, I pleaded silently.

The devil is trying to drive you crazy. Don't let him beat you. You have to beat him at his own game. Forget about the noise. Think about something else, I told myself. I closed my eyes and suddenly I was back in Marine Park, in Brooklyn.

I was taking batting practice and sending out one line drive after another. I could almost feel the sweet sensation of my bat connecting perfectly with a hard fastball. In the next instant, I was roaming the outfield, gracefully running down a long fly ball and firing a knee-high peg into second base.

It is not surprising that in one of my darkest times, my mind turned to baseball for comfort. I enjoyed playing football and basketball, but baseball had always been my passion. My father began teaching me the game as a small boy and I instantly became hooked. Throughout childhood, high school, and college, I grew to love the game more and more with each passing season. I always took great pride in being a ballplayer and worked hard at perfecting my skills. For me, a good practice was as much fun as a game.

The frequency of the noise changed again, but I hardly took notice. My mind was busy compiling a personal highlight video of my greatest baseball memories. I remembered every homerun I had ever hit and every great defensive play I had ever made. Then I recalled all the Championship games I had played in and the jubilant feeling that came with victory. My teams won quite a few titles over the years, so there was plenty of material to recollect.

The sandlot team that Kevin and I had played for every summer was called the Cadets. My father coached the team from 1975 until 1981. During those years we won many city, state, and regional championships, and built a reputation for excellence that was known throughout Brooklyn.

My father was a superb coach. He was a keen strategist and an excellent teacher of hitting. Playing for him was fun, but not without its downside. Regardless of how well Kevin and I were performing, as soon as one of us struck out or made an error, some idiot from the stands would invariably accuse our dad of nepotism. As unwarranted as these charges were, they stung just the same. The truth of the matter was that our father was harder on us than he was on the other kids. He expected more out of us because we were his own sons. Fortunately, we didn't disappoint him too often.

I didn't know how long I had been in the M.R.I. machine, but I knew it had been a while. The frequency of the noises had changed at least four of five times. A big smile crept onto my face. Screw you, Satan. Is this the best you've got? I had all I could do to keep from laughing out loud. The devil had taken his best shot and came up short. I was too damn strong for him to break me. Thank you, God. Thank you for helping me. I won't forget this. I thought again about the shadowy cross I had seen on the wall. God is watching over me. Everything is going to be all right.

"So how was it?" Sean asked as I stepped back into the waiting room.

"No problem. It was a piece of cake." There was no need to tell him about the harrowing experience I had just been through. It was over and I had survived. That was all that mattered now. "Take me back to the castle," I joked as I got back into my brother's car. I felt as if I had just climbed Mount Everest. It was impossible to imagine anything worse than that M.R.I. test, or was it? Were there other terrors lurking behind dark, secret doors?

Most of my weekend was spent in the day room, staring blankly at the T.V. set. It looked as though I were watching all the football games but I really wasn't. I was oblivious to the players, the score, and even the teams that were playing. My eyes were riveted to the television screen, but my thoughts drifted back to my own football days at Poly Prep High School, in Bay Ridge, Brooklyn.

Despite being a small prep school, our football program was consistently one of the best in New York City. During my four years there, we compiled a record of 31-2-2. Most of the credit belonged to our coach, a short, fire-hydrant of a man named Phil Foglietta. "Coach," as everybody called him, was a grizzled Army veteran from the "old school." The man instilled instant respect, as well as a certain amount of fear, in each of his players. He drilled us until we executed like a pro team.

Beyond the wins and losses, and the X's and O's of the game, Coach Foglietta taught as many lessons that transcended football. He constantly preached the Three D's of Life: discipline, desire, and dedication. "You've got to have it here!" he would bellow, thumping his right fist into his burly chest.

For me football wasn't fun, it was more like a quest. I learned to reach deep inside myself and find strength I didn't know I had. I approached every practice and every game as a personal challenge to my manhood and character.

My kamikaze attitude and determination eventually made me a favorite of Foglietta's. He singled me out for praise on a number of occasions. "If you guys played the game like number 41, we'd be unstoppable," he said to the rest of the team, during a practice late in my senior year. His glowing words inspired me to play even harder.

In my final game against Maria Regina, I played with a frenzied intensity that surprised even me. My twenty tackles, three sacks, and an interception led Poly to a tight 6-0 victory. A week later at the awards banquet, I won the coveted Leon Wynn trophy given to the outstanding team player. The best part of winning the award was seeing my father strut out of the banquet hall with his head held high and his chest puffed out. I had never seen him more proud of me.

My pleasant daydream was interrupted by a nurse clicking off the T.V. set. Sunday's last game was over. I was rudely forced back to the unpleasant reality of my situation. Waiting for the results of the M.R.I. exam was testing my patience, which had not been one of my strong points to begin with, and my boredom was increasing daily.

Finally late Monday afternoon, a tall, black-haired doctor came by my room to speak with me. He was carrying a large white envelop in his right hand.

"Are those the results of my M.R.I.?"

"Yes, they are. My name is Dr. Katz. I'm one of the neurologists here. I've studied your test and from what I see, there's nothing to worry about. The cyst you have in your brain isn't pushing against anything. It's not affecting your thought processes at all," he said confidently.

I fought back tears of joy. Thank you, God. Thank you. I knew you'd protect me.

"Just make sure you get another Catscan in a year or so to make sure the cyst hasn't grown. Take these, they're yours to keep," Dr. Katz said, handing me the envelope. I raced to the phone, anxious to share my good tidings with my family. Sean picked up the receiver. He listened as I explained the information I had received from Dr. Katz.

"That's great, Dennis. You must be very relieved. I'll call everyone and tell them the news."

When my mother came to visit me that night, I gave her a big bear hug and said, "I'm okay, Mom. There's nothing wrong with my brain. I told you I was completely norma!"

"Is that what Dr. Miller said?"

"No, it's what Dr. Katz, the neurologist said. He's a specialist in his field," I assured her. My mother remained unconvinced. She wanted to see Dr. Miller. We caught him in his office just as he was reaching for his coat and hat.

After my mother explained Dr. Katz's diagnosis, Dr. Miller raised an eyebrow and frowned.

"I don't know about these neurologists. It's my experience as a psychiatrist that a cyst of this nature can cause all sorts of different problems."

"C'mon, Doc. The guy's an expert. He wouldn't make a mistake like that," I retorted. "When can I go home?" Dr. Miller sighed deeply and told me he wasn't sure.

"There are still a few things I want to go over with you. Come to my office at eleven o'clock tomorrow morning," he said before excusing himself for the evening. I turned to my mother and smiled at her. She smiled back at me and squeezed my hand tightly.

I arrived at Dr. Miller's office at ten to eleven. He was already at his desk, going over my file, when I came in.

"Good morning, Dennis. Have a seat. Make yourself comfortable." I was encouraged by his cheerful mood. He began the session by asking me how I was feeling and why I thought I was ready to go home.

"Well, the Haldol you're giving me makes me completely exhausted, but other than that I'm fine. I want to go home because I'm not sick, and I never was sick. I don't belong in a hospital. I want to go home and be with my family."

Dr. Miller studied me carefully with his penetrating eyes. "And how do you feel about The Pines now, Dennis?"

"The same way I did when I got here. They're running a drug operation up there, and I'm going to bring those people down." This was not the answer he was looking for. He scratched his hair nervously.

"Your delusion is so deeply ingrained you might never stop believing it. But your obsessive need to act on it is what really worries me. If you go back to The Pines, you could be in real danger this time. Why don't you just try to let it go?"

"If someone had tried to kill you, could you just forget about it?"

"No. No, I suppose not," he said.

I assured Dr. Miller that I wasn't stupid. I realized that if I went back to The Pines I would either be arrested or thrown back into a funny farm. I didn't intend to subject myself to any more of this nonsense. Therefore, I was going to have to figure out another way to expose the operation.

"All right, Dennis. I'll discharge you tomorrow on the condition that you continue taking the Haldol at home." I started to object, but then quickly thought better of it. I would deal with the medicine when the time came.

"That's great, Doc. Thanks a lot." I reached over and shook his hand. I was grateful to Dr. Miller for again returning my freedom. He could have kept me at Centra-State much longer if he had wanted to.

Before I went to bed that night, the nurse giving me my Haldol referred to me as John. "My name is Dennis. John is my middle name," I corrected her. I didn't think much of it. A new guy named John had been admitted a few days ago. She had obviously made an honest mistake.

The next morning, an African-American nurse named Benjamin woke me up. "Good morning. Time for your meds, John," he said. I looked at him oddly. Benjamin and I had gotten to know each other fairly well during my two stays at the hospital. He knew damn well that my name was Dennis. How could he make a mistake like that?

Again I didn't fret over it too much, though. I was going home. After breakfast, I hurriedly packed my travel bag. I didn't have many clothes with me this time, so that didn't take long. Finally after two more torturous hours of waiting, I saw Sean strutting toward me. I said goodbye to all the patients and nurses, and walked down the hall with my brother. Just before we were about to exit the wing, I bumped into Toni.

"Good luck, Dennis. And God bless you. If you run into trouble, ask God for strength. He will answer your prayers," she said, as her luminous smile nearly hypnotized me. "Read these when you get a chance," she added, as she gave me a handful of Christian tracts. In the past, I had scoffed at literature of this nature, and believed that it was the work of zealous, Bible-thumping fanatics. But this woman was such a kind and loving person, it was impossible to simply dismiss her beliefs. I thanked her and promised to read and evaluate each of the tracts.

7

WAITING FOR
THE LIONS

As soon as I returned home I drove to the local pharmacy and filled my Haldol prescription. I had no intention of taking the drug, but I wanted to appease my mother by having it in the house. My thoughts turned to The Pines. What could I do about the drug operation there? I had an idea. Alert the media. Tell your story to some important people who have the power to do something about it. I bought a pen, looseleaf paper, envelopes, stamps, and all the New York and New Jersey newspapers and headed for the Manalapan Library.

Once inside the library I sat down at a quiet cubicle in the corner and began writing. I wrote a detailed five-page letter outlining my knowledge of the drug operation. I began the letter by candidly revealing my recent hospitalization, explaining that it had been a part of The Pines's plan to discredit me and cover up its actions.

I wrote about their scheme of hiring young men to work for the Activities Department, getting them hooked on crack, and then using them as front men in the drug deals. "Check the whereabouts of Evan Harris, Craig Lawrence, and David Lawson. These are just three of the men they have killed during the past twelve years. They probably hire a new kid every season," I wrote, confident that any competent investigation would turn up a slew of missing persons.

I ended the letter by listing the names of the people who were involved in the operation. Eve Cantor's name headed that list. Although the Richmans owned the hotel, she was in charge of the drug ring.

When I had finished writing the letter, I was left with a difficult decision. To whom do I send it? Who can be trusted? I closed my eyes and asked God for guidance. I randomly selected one name for the editorial page of each newspaper and, remembering the circle Sean had drawn around his name, also included Fred Kerber of the *Post* as a recipient of my letter. I was confident that God had helped me choose wisely.

I made copies of my letter and mailed them at the Englishtown Post Office. When the last envelope dropped through the Out-Of-Town box, I felt tremendously relieved. It was only a matter of time now before the drug operation would be exposed.

My family's attitude toward me was much more cautious than it had been the last time I came home. They were glad to have me back, but were on the lookout for any signs of abnormal behavior. I didn't know what they were so worked up about. I had never felt better.

Later that night, Kevin called for a pickup at the bus stop. Feeling good about my newfound freedom, I happily volunteered.

"Hey, Dennis. How are you doing? Are you feeling all right?" Kevin asked.

"Yeah. I feel great today, why." He looked at me with a troubled expression.

"I'm concerned about you, Den. Your eyes have a far-away glazed look in them. You look really spaced out." I gave my brother a knowing grin.

"The eyes are the window to the soul. I'm not the same person I used to be. I'm better now. There is more love inside of me." These profound words of wisdom did not comfort Kevin. His pained expression remained.

When I pulled into our driveway I saw a large fire engine parked in front of the first house on our left. A small group of people had gathered, and were looking up at the sky. "What's going on?" I asked. Thomas explained that Lisa had called the fire department. Her cat, Summertime, had been stuck up in a tree for four days and she was worried that it would soon starve to death. Lisa was a friend of Deirdre who worked with her at Pizza Hut, and was staying in one of my mother's guest rooms until she found an apartment in the area.

I looked up at the large oak tree just past the dividing line of my mother's property, and saw the outline of a brawny fireman standing on the top rung of a ladder. After a few minutes he came down and asked to speak with the owner of the cat.

"She's my cat," said Lisa.

"I'm sorry, ma'am. We can't get to her. The tree is too high for our ladder to reach." The fireman put the ladder back in the truck and drove off with his partner.

"What a couple of wimps," Sean said disgustedly. "Those guys don't have any balls." I looked at Lisa. She appeared ready to burst into tears at any moment.

"Don't worry, Lisa. If Summertime is still up there tomorrow, I'll go get her down," I promised.

When we all went back inside the house, my mother was in the bathroom washing up. "I'm going to sleep now, Dennis. Make sure you take your medicine before you go to bed," she called out.

"Okay, Mom. No problem." I felt no guilt about lying to her. Why should I take a drug that made me feel awful when there was nothing wrong with me? If I told my family the truth, they would all needlessly worry. My little white lie was just saving everyone a lot of aggravation.

As I laid in bed and stared up at the ceiling I could already feel the effects of the Haldol wearing off. My mind was again starting to think clearly and lucidly. In fact, my brain seemed to be operating on a much higher level of efficiency than ever before. My thoughts raced through my head like a high-tech computer. I had vivid recall of all the intricate details of everything that had happened to me in the past month.

I remembered the conversations I had engaged in, the clothes I had worn, and the food I had eaten. I was amazed and intrigued by the new powers of my mind.

I concluded that I had achieved some sort of enlightenment. God was giving me all the information that the circuits of my brain could handle. I could hardly wait to be further enlightened.

Summertime did not move an inch during the night. She remained perched on a thick branch, high atop our next door neighbor's tree. Since we didn't have a ladder of our own, we had to wait until four o'clock for our next door neighbor to the right, Barbara, to get home from work. She kept an extension ladder in her garage and was always willing to lend it to us.

Sean and I carried the bulky contraption across our front lawn. Deirdre, Lisa, Thomas, Barbara, and her young son, Jonathan, watched us struggle to lean it up against the trunk of the tree. When the ladder was firmly secured, Sean stepped on it to make sure it was sturdy.

"Get down from there. You're way too heavy for that ladder to hold your weight," I yelled. Sean stepped down and looked at me thoughtfully.

"Look, Dennis. I don't think it's such a good idea for you to go up there. You just got out of the hospital for Christ's sake. That branch is at least fifty or sixty feet high. It looks dangerous."

"I'll go up there," Deirdre volunteered. Sean looked at her, then back at me. He was trying to decide which one of us was better suited for the difficult task. I couldn't believe he was actually considering sending my sister up there.

"What's wrong with you? This isn't a job for a woman. I'm the right man for the job and you know it. Don't worry, nothing's going to happen to me."

"Who do you think you are … God?" asked Deirdre. I just smiled at her, gently pushed Sean aside, and began climbing the ladder.

"Be careful!" "Go slower!" yelled concerned voices from below. My family need not have worried. God was certainly not going to let anything happen to me now. He had big plans for me. When I reached the top rung of the ladder, I extended my right hand as far as it could go. I was still a tantalizing foot short of Summertime. "Come here, Kitty. Come to Papa." My words had no effect on the cat. She remained frozen in fear. The poor thing's terrified. That's probably how I looked the night I received Joe's disquieting phone call at The Pines, I thought bitterly.

I could see the problem the firemen had last night. The cat was at least four feet away from the trunk of the tree. It was impossible to reach her from any ladder. Left with no other alternative, I gingerly climbed onto the branch. When I reached Summertime I tried to pick her up, but she did not cooperate. Her sharp claws desperately clung to the branch.

"C'mon cat. Give me a break." I gave Summertime a firm yank and picked her up, barely keeping my balance. I carefully made my way back to the ladder and started down. With my feet safely on the ground, I triumphantly handed the animal to Lisa.

"Oh, thank you, Dennis. Thank you so much. How can I ever repay you?"

"Don't worry about it, Lis. It was my pleasure." She didn't realize it of course, but I had just done something far more important than saving her cat. Summertime represented the entire female population. In my mind, my actions had somehow saved women all over the world.

"Help your brother put the ladder away," I told Thomas. He and Sean, although still concerned about my mental stability, both looked at me admiringly. They had seen what I had done and knew that I feared nothing.

I walked into the house and almost tripped over our other feline friend, Stupid. Stupid was a big, black Persian cat who had earned his unusual name ten years ago by getting himself stuck inside the engine of my father's Oldsmobile, in Brooklyn. My father had to remove the muffler to get him out. Five minutes later, the cat wedged himself into the same place. We removed him again, took him in, and have been calling him "Stupid" ever since.

That night I let Kevin sleep in my bed. I crashed on the floor of Thomas's bedroom. Once I was comfortable, my "computer-brain" switched on again. After I quickly reviewed recent events, I began thinking about my future. What was going to happen to me? To the world? What were God's plans for me? My brain worked frantically, trying to reach some understanding of my destiny, but there were no answers to be found. God doesn't want me to know too much about the future yet. He'll tell me what I need to know when it is time for me to act.

A bolt of lightning flashed across the dark sky. It was immediately followed by a crash of loud thunder and a heavy downpour of rain. I sat up and stared out of one of Thomas's windows. The storm rapidly grew more intense.

Blustery winds banged up against the side of the house and the earth below me felt as if it were moving. I was mesmerized by the sights and sounds of the thunderstorm. This weather is a sign. God is trying to tell me something.

After an indeterminate amount of time had passed, the storm stopped suddenly, as if someone had turned off a faucet. I immediately realized what had happened. A heavenly battle had been waged between God and the devil. Once again, God's incredible power had defeated his rival. I was amazed by my ability to recognize all the signs and comprehend the symbolism of everyday events. God had given me a great gift of perception.

I heard a tapping sound on the windowpane. I walked over to it and saw that Stupid was trying to get inside the house. His blue eyes seemed to be asking for compassion. I had seen those eyes before. They were the eyes of my father!

When I opened the window and pulled Stupid inside, my heart was filled with a feeling of pure happiness. Tears of joy rolled down my cheeks. I wasn't sure of what he had done, but I knew that my father had redeemed himself in the eyes of God. His soul was saved. I was not only thrilled for him, but also for myself. What good was going to heaven if the people you love were not there with you?

On Friday afternoon I drove to a convenience store and bought the *New York Post*. I read through the sports pages hoping to find some messages, but all the articles were ordinary. I skipped the comics and turned to the movie section. *Rocky V* had just been released and, as a big fan of the *Rocky* saga, I was curious to see what the critics thought of the film.

After sports, movies were my second love. Since I was a child, I had loved to escape into the fantasy world of cinema. In a dark theater, all my insecurities and inadequacies were forgotten for a few hours, and temporarily replaced by the valiant characteristics of the hero of the film I was watching.

I particularly loved inspirational movies. Many of these films had a profound impact on my life. When I first saw the original *Rocky*, I became obsessed with developing my scrawny body and began a strict regimen of weight-training. After viewing *Field of Dreams*, I decided to move to Florida to try to become a pro golfer. That movie seemed to be screaming at me to pursue my dreams, no matter how unrealistic they appeared to be.

Roger Ebert's review of *Rocky V* was tepid, but the content of his article caught my attention. He said the film was about betrayal of family and that Sylvester Stallone's young son, Sage, stole the show. The unusual name, Sage, was a most revealing clue. The literal translation of that name is, "wise man of the church."

This movie is about my family! Stallone's son is a prophet. I have to go see *Rocky V* tonight. It will give me invaluable information.

When Kevin returned home from work he was extremely tired, but I cajoled him into accompanying me, Tom, Sean, and Starlight to the nine-thirty show. It didn't take that much effort, as he was a big *Rocky* enthusiast himself.

"This is an important movie, Kev. I'll be able to see things you might not be able to. Pay particular attention to what the boy says," I told him on the drive to the Freehold Cinema Six Theater.

"Just because the kid's name is 'Sage,' Dennis thinks that he's gonna get some kind of divine message," Thomas said with disgust from the back seat. Despite Thomas's pessimism, Kevin was very open-minded.

"I'll do my best to try to see what the hell you're talking about, but I still think that it's only a movie. Try to remember that, Dennis."

Inside the theater, I refrained from my usual snack of popcorn and coke. Tonight I was all business. Ten minutes into the movie I realized that my intuition had been accurate. I looked at Kevin and smiled at him. Surely he could see that this motion picture was about the relationship between me and my father. I couldn't wait for the movie to be over so I could find out what happens next. When the film credits finally flashed across the screen, Thomas informed me that he was going home with Sean and Star. He evidently didn't trust my driving anymore.

"That was a great movie, Den. I think it was the best *Rocky* flick since the first one," Kevin declared as we weaved through a maze of parked cars. While we waited for my car to warm up, I asked him if he understood the real meaning of the film.

"Yeah, sure. The plot was pretty basic."

"Tell me about it. What was it about?" I asked, hoping that he had comprehended at least some of the countless messages.

Kevin cleared his throat and summarized the plot. "Well, Rocky goes broke and he can't fight anymore because of brain damage. He returns to his old Philadelphia gym and starts training a young prospect named Tommy Gunn. In the meantime, he neglects his family.

"After he teaches Tommy all his secrets, the guy turns his back on Rocky and joins up with an unscrupulous, greedy promoter. They both want to get Rocky back in the ring but he refuses their offers. When Tommy decks Paulie in a bar, Rocky leads Tommy into an alley and the two of them start a brutal street brawl.

"Just when it seems as if Rocky is finished, the ghost of his old trainer, Mickey, appears and tells him that he loves him. He gets up, kicks Tommy's ass, and then knocks out the promoter in front of a dozen television cameras. He wins back the love of his family and they all live happily ever after. The end."

I shook my head sadly. It was damn frustrating. I was still the only person who could interpret the raw data that had been made readily available to millions of people.

"You just told me what everybody else saw. You completely missed all the hidden meanings and all the symbolism," I said, trying hard to control my annoyance.

"What the hell are you talking about? What symbolism?" I took a deep breath and tried to educate my brother.

"That movie was about our family. The kid Sage is me, Rocky Balboa is Daddy, Mickey is Poppy, Adrienne is Mommy, Paulie is Deirdre, Tommy Gunn is Willie, the promoter is the devil, and Rocky Marciano is God." Kevin snickered, but I ignored him and continued.

"The movie was about love and family. The golden cufflink that Mickey received from Rocky Marciano and gave to Rocky was symbolic of the gift of love God gave to Poppy, who in turn gave it to Daddy. Daddy was a beaten man. He had given up all hope. But somewhere in heaven, because of his love for his son, Poppy had given him the strength to fight back.

"You see, Kevin? So it's not really Willie's fault. She's weak and Satan uses her weakness against her. But I know that in the end Daddy will find the strength to overcome Willie and defeat Satan. Then he will come to vindicate me."

Kevin looked at me and laughed. "You are one crazy sonofabitch. You know that. You do have a hell of an imagination, though. I'll give you that." I said nothing as I turned onto Route 9. I didn't bother trying to explain any of the other important messages I had derived from the film. I might as well have been speaking to him in Latin.

When we came home, Thomas inserted *The Godfather* into the VCR. "It's kind of late for that, isn't it, Tom?" Sean asked.

"That's all right. We'll watch the first half tonight and the second part tomorrow," he replied. My three brothers and I were *Godfather* aficionados. We considered parts I and II to be two of the greatest cinematic achievements of all time, and were gearing up for *The Godfather III*, due out in December. During the next two weeks we watched both *Godfather* films three or four times. Interestingly, every time we saw one of these movies we were able to understand more of what was really going on.

That night I got my first real sleep in three days. I only slept for a couple of hours, but during that time I had an unusual dream. The dream was broken into two distinct parts.

In the first part, my eyes were blinded by a bright vision of God. I only saw him for a split second because his form was too beautiful for my human eyes to behold. The vision vanished and then a round, lighted machine appeared. I put my hand on it and immediately began receiving knowledge and information. The mysteries of life were being revealed to me. All my questions were being answered.

In the second part of my dream, I was sitting by myself at a large rectangular table. On the top of the table was a roasted turkey. Despite being alone, I was overcome with joy.

I thought this part of my dream was telling me that something very good, perhaps something spiritual, was going to take place on Thanksgiving. I awaited next Thursday with eager anticipation.

When I woke up on Saturday morning I knew exactly what I had to do. I took a fast shower and threw on a pair of navy slacks, a gray sports jacket, and an aqua-blue tie.

"I'm going into the City to see Kevin, Mom. I'll see you later." She told me to make sure I was back in time for dinner. Before I left the house, I took my Bible and put it in a small shopping bag. The book would help protect me in a dangerous city.

I was convinced that New York was a cold city ruled by greed, hatred, and violence. Satan's dark presence lurked behind every street corner and every dark alley. Instead of being afraid, however, I felt invulnerable with or without my Bible. I knew that God was watching over me.

I made it to Gordon's Corner just before the Jersey Transit bus pulled in. When I was comfortably seated I clicked on the overhead light, opened my Bible and reviewed the two verses Mary had shown me.

First I read from Timothy, then turned back to Romans: "And we know that all things work together for good to them that love God, to them who are the Called according to his purpose." I continued reading the next verse: "For whom he did foreknow, he also did predestine to be conformed to the image of his Son, that he might be the first-born among many brethren."

I closed the book and contemplated the meaning of those words. I am the first among many brothers. I must be John The Baptist! Everything was starting to come together. That explained why the nurses at Centra-State had called me John. Subconsciously they already knew my real identity. My mission was becoming quite clear now. I was to spread the word of Jesus Christ. He would soon be giving me the power to perform miracles in his name.

I shut my eyes and drafted off to sleep. I walked up a steep incline towards a huge mansion. Two large lions were guarding a white marble door. When they saw me approaching, they let out a great roar and reverently moved away from the door. I grabbed the golden doorknob and pulled.

"Port Authority," boomed the driver's voice, jolting me rudely awake.

"Damn. I wanted to see what was behind that door."

Kevin's office was in the Pan-Am building on Forty-Second Street and Park Avenue. As I walked along Forty-Second Street I became sick to my stomach. Everywhere I looked there were sleazy porn shops and X-rated movie houses. If Vegas is "Gomorrah West," than this was surely "Gomorrah East." Finally I came to the Pan-Am building and rode the elevator to the fifty-third floor.

An attractive secretary directed me to my brother's office. He was surprised to see me. "What are you doing here, Den? Why are you all dressed up? It's Saturday." He was wearing a sweatshirt and a pair of faded jeans.

I explained that I had something of utmost importance to discuss. He put away his work and patiently listened to what I had to say.

"I know this may be difficult for you to comprehend, Kevin, but God has given me an incredibly important mission. Stopping The Pines operation barely scratches the surface of it."

"What mission? What are you supposed to do?" I pulled my Bible out of the bag and read him the two verses from Romans.

"So? What does that mean? I smiled at him. I didn't want to tell him too much. His mind was not ready to understand. He had not yet been enlightened the way I had been.

"It means we have an exceptional family. Great things are going to happen to all of us."

Kevin nodded. "What do you think of the view? Pretty grand, isn't it?" he said, changing the subject. It certainly was a tremendous sight. I could see the entire city from his window.

"Let's go see Daddy at Chanel," I suggested, "he's working today, right?" Kevin agreed that it was a good idea. We left his office and hailed a cab.

Although my father had been head of security at Chanel for three years, I had never been inside the world famous boutique. I was curious to see the place that charged a thousand dollars for a twenty-five dollar pocketbook with a fancy double "C" embroidered on it. My initial reaction when I walked into Chanel was that it looked like a fancy version of Macy's. The merchandise seemed ordinary enough, but the crystal chandeliers, spiral staircase, and plush carpeting made it clear that it was a store exclusively for the affluent.

My father came over and greeted us immediately. He was exceedingly happy to see us, as I knew he would be. He introduced us to a few of the salesgirls, all of whom wore stylish black skirts and matching blouses. The girls talked with us for a few minutes, and commented on how much our father bragged about his five children. When the girls left and Kevin and I were alone with him, I came right to the point.

I warmed him up by telling him how I had survived my M.R.I. exam. Kevin joined in as we reminisced about our greatest games. I would have loved to have continued talking about baseball, but there was serious business to discuss.

"Come back to Manalapan, Dad," I said calmly.

"I can't do that, son. Willie's got dinner waiting for me at home."

"Don't give me that. You know what I'm talking about. You know what needs to be done. I can't do it alone. I need your help." The distinctive look of fear was back in my father's eyes. "Don't be afraid, Dad. God will give you the courage you need. He has already forgiven all your sins." Kevin stared down at his shoes. My brother was obviously in awe of my tremendous insight.

I reached inside my jacket pocket, pulled out a roll of papers, and handed them to my father. "This is the letter that I sent to all the major newspapers. The story is going to break soon. I want you to come along for the ride."

"C'mon, Den. Let's go. Daddy's got to get back to work," Kevin said, tugging at my arm.

"Come to Manalapan, Dad. You can do it," I said, before turning to leave. My father was still frightened, but I was confident he would find the strength to get to New Jersey.

Outside, it had started to rain. We tried unsuccessfully to hail a cab for ten minutes. A large black limousine pulled up to the curb. Its tinted windows rolled down slowly.

"Need a ride, mister?" boomed a deep voice from inside the limo.

"Yeah." Kevin reached for the handle of the door.

"No! Don't go inside the car!" I shouted. An empty yellow cab appeared directly behind the limousine.

"Okay, whatever," Kevin said, changing his mind and getting into the medallion cab with me. I couldn't fault my brother. He had no way of knowing that the limo driver had been sent by The Pines to kidnap us. That special knowledge was reserved only for me.

We stopped for a quick soda at one of the eateries in the Port Authority. When he went to give us our change, the kid working behind the cash register couldn't get the drawer to open. His boss came over to help him. "Here. Just mark twenty-five," the boss explained. I made a mental note to check Chapter 25 of Mark when I got on the bus. I was picking up helpful clues everywhere.

Although we had both been in the Port Authority countless times, Kevin and I were having difficulty finding our gate. We wandered aimlessly for ten minutes until a young man approached my brother. "Excuse me, sir. You're in the wrong building. To get to New Jersey you have to go across the street, go up the first escalator, make a left, and then go up another escalator." Kevin and I looked at each other for just a brief moment. When we turned back to thank the guy, he was gone.

"That was strange. How did he know we were going to Jersey?" Kevin asked. I just smiled and shrugged my shoulders. He wouldn't understand that God was making sure we returned to Manalapan on time. There was work to be done.

On the bus I discovered that there were only sixteen chapters in the book of Mark. In Chapter six, verse twenty-five, however, there was a specific reference to John the Baptist. Could there be any more definitive proof that he and I were the same man?

By the time our bus pulled into Manalapan it was completely dark outside. On the way home, Kevin stopped into a new video store on Gordon's Corner and emerged with two movies. *Total Recall* and *Rocky*. "Good choices," I said. I was a big fan of Arnold Schwarzenegger, but hadn't seen *Total Recall* yet.

Moreover, after learning so much from *Rocky V* last night, I hoped the original movie would provide additional information.

"What's the score?" Kevin asked as we walked into our house.

"21-7. The Irish are killing them," Sean replied. "The second half just started." He and Tom were flopped on the sofa, enjoying the Notre Dame-Penn State football game. "Penn State is going to win this game," I boldly exclaimed.

"Uh-oh. That sounds like another divine prediction," said Thomas.

"Just watch and learn, Tom. The Nittany Lions will win this game." I knew that the lions were about to roar.

Sure enough, Penn State staged an improbable comeback and won the game 24-21 on a last second field goal that sailed through the middle of the uprights.

"Did you guys see that? Do you still doubt me? Do you doubt the power of God?

"Relax, Den. It was only a game. It doesn't prove anything," said Kevin. He was always so damn judicious. "If your predictions are right, you use them to reinforce your delusion. If they are wrong, you'll come up with a convenient rationalization."

"Got any more big tips for us, Dennis? I might want to place a few bets," Sean joked. I failed to see the humor in his statement.

"Yes, I do. The Detroit Lions are going to beat the Giants tomorrow. You can bet the house on it." I had never been more certain about the outcome of a sporting event, or anything else for that matter.

"Phone call, Dennis. It's Vicki," my mother called down from her bedroom. I picked up the phone expecting to talk with my ex-girlfriend, but it wasn't her. The voice on the line belonged to another Vicky, a girl named Vicky Walsh, who had worked with me at Chi-Chi's.

"Hi, Dennis. I just called to say hello and to see how you were feeling. I talked to Farruk and he told me you look great." I assured her that I was fine and thanked her for her concern. Although I considered her a dear friend, our relationship was strictly platonic. There was another girl who I knew from Chi-Chi's, however, with whom I was completely and hopelessly infatuated. Her name was Cory Malone.

She lived in Manalapan, just a few miles away from my mother's house. Cory was one of the most beautiful girls I had ever seen. She had straight, long brown hair, doll-like features, and a perfect smile. Her obsessive devotion to running gave her a pair of legs a Greek goddess would envy. From a physical standpoint, her only flaw was that she had a mild case of acne. Strangely, her blemishes made her even more attractive to me. They made her seem more human.

In spite of her remarkable looks, Cory was an unassuming and gentle girl. Her warm personality matched the brightness of her beautiful smile. When

I severely burned my face at the beach the previous July, she exhibited tremendous compassion and tenderness towards me. Although my face looked like a swollen tomato, she patiently helped me treat my burn. I did not forget this act of kindness.

It took me the entire summer to work up the courage to ask her to a movie. I was thrilled when she accepted my offer but, unfortunately, the only nights I was free, she was scheduled to work. She returned to James Madison University in Virginia before we had the chance to go on our first date.

I was disgusted with myself for not having the guts to approach her sooner. I had blown a golden opportunity and would have to wait all the way until next summer before I could ask her out again. By then she could have a serious boyfriend.

Later that evening, my family and I gathered in front of the T.V. set to watch *Total Recall*. I had heard that the film was a grim version of the future. In this future, a company called "Recall Incorporated" has developed a program in which they plant memories of a vacation inside people's brains. The company's advertisements assert that the experience is better than an actual trip.

Arnold's character is named Doug Quaid. He desperately wants to go to Mars, but visitation to this warring planet is forbidden. Against the advice of his wife and a friend from work, Quaid makes an appointment with Recall and decides to try the Mars vacation program.

When he is strapped into the recall chair a technician asks him to describe his dream girl, choosing among different characteristics. He selects brunette, athletic, sleazy, and demure. I couldn't believe it; he had just described Cory Malone. Outwardly she was shy and demure, but I had no doubt that she had a sleazy side to her as well. Her body was overflowing with raw sensuality.

I watched the movie with growing interest and excitement. When Quaid's recall program begins, something goes wrong and he reacts violently. Apparently, he has been to Mars before.

"You're having a paranoid delusion," the technician tells him.

"Bullshit," he says, exploding out of his chair and heading off to Mars. Yes! I am Arnold's character. This movie is about me and Cory Malone!

As the movie continued the symbolism became very transparent. Cohagen, the evil ruler of Mars who controlled the supply of air, was really the devil. Quaid worked together with his dream girl, Melina, to try to put an end to Cohagen's reign of terror.

Near the end of the film, Quaid puts his hand inside a machine and activates a nuclear generator. I was dumbfounded. "That was my dream last night. I had put my hand inside a machine exactly like that one!"

After that scene, the rest of the movie was almost anticlimactic. Cohagen was thrown outside the protective cover of the city and into a pit of sand. He breathed the poisonous air and shriveled up and died. Quaid and Malina followed him into the sand. Their eyes popped in and out of their heads, but the air became pure again, and after a minute they were fine. The movie ended with the two lovers holding hands as they watched the sun rise above the newborn city.

What are the implications of all this? Is Cory fighting alongside me? Of course she is. She knows all about the deadly operation at The Pines. Our destinies are somehow intertwined. She must have just been released from a mental institution in Virginia. The poor girl has suffered incredible pain. I couldn't wait to hold her in my arms and tell her I loved her.

I didn't tell anyone in my family about Cory. They would all come to understand her significance soon enough.

After a fifteen minute break, Sean inserted *Rocky* into the VCR. The movie began with the camera panning to a large picture of Jesus Christ, which was hanging from a gym wall. That was all I needed to see. I had forgotten all about that scene but its meaning was clear. It was God who gave Rocky the strength to overcome incredible odds and, likewise, God had empowered me to defeat the people at The Pines. I went upstairs to my bedroom, closed my door, and began reading my Bible.

The words of the New Testament flowed together like never before. I had a keen understanding of all the stories and parables, and saw how they related to me and my family.

At 12:30 a.m. my three brothers, Deirdre, and Starlight were in the living room watching *Saturday Night Live* when they heard a chilling female scream. I bounded down the steps within seconds.

"Stay in the house!" I commanded.

"What are you talking about?" Sean said angrily. "A girl's getting beat up outside. She needs help."

"I know that's what it sounds like, but you have to trust me on this. Do not leave this house." I knew enough now to recognize one of Satan's tricks. He was trying to lure us away from the safety of our home. Despite my warning, Kevin and Sean went outside to investigate. They came back a minute later. "It's okay. The police are here already. They have everything under control," said Kevin.

My mother came downstairs to see what was going on. When everybody had relaxed a little, I asked them to sit down and explained the situation.

"Listen carefully to what I have to say. It is of critical importance that you understand this. Evil people will be coming to this house tonight. They will try to hurt us, but don't be afraid. God will protect us from harm. Daddy will also be coming here tonight. He will come to vindicate me." My prophetic words caused everyone to become very alarmed.

"You're acting and talking real strangely, Dennis. Have you been taking your medicine? Be honest with us," my mother asked. I couldn't lie to her again.

"No, Mom. I haven't taken it all week. I don't need it. There is nothing wrong with me." For the next two hours, my family tried in vain to get me to take the Haldol. They begged, pleaded, and yelled but I remained obstinate. There was no way in hell they were going to get me to change my mind.

Finally at three o'clock in the morning, I decided that everyone needed to get some sleep. "I'll tell you what, if you listen to what I have to say tomorrow morning and still think that I should take the medicine, then I'll take it without putting up a fight. I can't get fairer than that." My family found my deal equitable. They all trudged off to sleep, secure in the knowledge that I would take the Haldol the next morning. I was confident, however, that the Holy Spirit would come to them in their sleep and enlighten them the same way I had been enlightened a few days before.

I returned to my room and again opened my Bible. This time I underlined and highlighted some of the most relevant passages. I wanted to be well prepared for my morning confrontation with my family. Sleep could wait.

My experiences at The Pines were connected to the amazing religious transformation that was happening to me. They were part of God's glorious master plan. I fully expected my father to come bolting through my front door at any moment. Our family restored, we would all join together and defeat the wicked drug lords from The Pines. Good was once again going to triumph over evil.

No one came to our house in Manalapan that night. This indisputable fact did not alter my beliefs at all. I had merely been wrong about the timing. I knew without question that my father was going to come to set things right. It was just a matter of time. My family began waking up at about eleven o'clock on Sunday morning. I took a long, soothing shower and joined them in the kitchen. Sean and Starlight had gone out somewhere, but everyone else was there, anxiously waiting for me.

"Okay, Dennis. It's morning. Now take the medicine," Thomas ordered. I explained that I had agreed to take the medicine only if everyone still thought that I should, after they listened to what I had to say. And boy did I have a lot to say.

"All right, Dennis. We're listening. Go ahead," said Deirdre. I began recounting the events that had occurred at The Pines. This was old news to my family.

"We've heard all this before. What's the point?" Kevin asked. I changed my focus and started discussing all the religious implications. I stopped short of saying I was John the Baptist, though. They would not have understood that. It was beyond their comprehension.

"And we know that all things work together for good to them that love God, to them who are the Called according to his purpose," I quoted Romans from memory. "Not my purpose, not your purpose, but His purpose,

God's purpose. He has a special plan for all of us. The phone rang four or five times late last night. God was sending you a signal that you guys are among 'The Called.' You have all been chosen by God to spread his word throughout the world."

My mother interrupted me there. "Look, Dennis. That's silly. The phone's been ringing like that for months. God had nothing to do with it. We've all listened patiently to you and we still think you're sick. Now, please, take the medicine."

"No. You've heard me talk but you haven't really listened to a word I've said. Open your mind to the possibility that I'm not sick and that I'm speaking the truth."

"That's impossible," Thomas snorted. "We all know you're sick. You've been acting crazier every day." I ignored him and continued trying to enlighten my family.

I preached for more than an hour, explaining that a great war between good and evil was taking place as we spoke. My family tried their best to use reason and logic with me, but even their best arguments were futile. My convictions were etched in stone. There was no way I was going to budge.

My family's growing frustration was beginning to show on their faces and in their voices.

"Why won't you take the medicine?" my mother asked. "What's the big deal? It's just a tiny pill. It will help make you better." I was deeply insulted by her condescending attitude.

"I'll tell you what the big deal is," I answered angrily. "Haldol is a potent anti-psychotic drug given to crazy people. Today is the Sabbath day, it's God's day. I won't desecrate my body on the Sabbath day by swallowing an unneeded drug."

My mother started crying. "You don't love us!" she wailed. "If you loved us, you would take the medicine. I can't take much more of this."

"She's right. You don't love us. You're selfish," Thomas added. They might as well have stabbed me in the heart. Kevin was quick to come to my defense.

"Hey, that's not true! You know he loves us very much. It's not his fault. He's sick. Don't blame him for that," he said with remarkable compassion.

Although he mistakenly believed I was sick, I greatly appreciated him sticking up for me.

"You guys are getting all worked up over nothing," I explained. "Tomorrow, the story about The Pines will be in all the papers and you'll see that I was right all along."

"That's completely irrelevant," Deirdre said. "We don't care about The Pines anymore. We just want you to take the medicine so you can get better."

"Exactly what do we have to do to get you to take the medicine?" my mother asked calmly, having regained her composure. I told her there was nothing anyone could do, but if the Lions lost the football game today, I would take the drugs. "If they lose, I'll take a double dose. Hell, I'll take a triple dose," I said, confident that there was no way this could happen. The Lions were going to roar!

Nobody in my family was particularly pleased that my fate was again being decided by a football game, but they really didn't have any other alternatives. Besides, Kevin and Thomas convinced my mother and sister that the Giants defeating the lowly Lions was almost a sure thing. Nevertheless, my mother was worried that the Lions might pull a big upset. "If they should somehow win, we'll never get him to take the medicine," I overheard her say. She was absolutely right. I had no intention of ever taking the Haldol again.

The Giants dominated the first half of the game, jumping out to a convincing 20-0 halftime lead. This is a test, I thought. God is testing me to see how strong my faith is. Don't worry. The Lions will roar. I was positive that God would not let me defile my body by making me take the Haldol. I was wrong again. The Lions never even got into the endzone. The final score remained 20-0 in favor of the Giants.

As the final seconds ticked off the clock, CBS showed a close-up of the elated Giants coach, Bill Parcells. Seeing the footage nearly made me fall off the sofa. During the course of the game, his hair had changed from a medium shade of gray to pure white. I had never seen a whiter head of hair. What did this mean? Was God trying to send me another sign?

My mother came down a large glass of water and two ten milligram pills of Haldol. I gulped the pills disgustedly.

"You look tired. Why don't you get some sleep? You can sleep on Tommy's bed," she suggested. I reluctantly agreed. My lack of sleep had finally caught up with me. I was exhausted.

"Make sure you wake me up before *It* comes on," I said, before plodding up the stairs. The film adaptation of Stephen King's classic book, *It*, was being shown on T.V. at nine o'clock. Since the day I finished reading that book three years ago, I had been looking forward to viewing the inevitable movie version of the story.

While I laid in my brother's bed I replayed the game in my head. How could the Lions have lost? There were three plays that had really bothered me. In the first half, a rookie wide receiver from the University of Colorado had dropped a sure touchdown pass. I had not forgotten that Steve Richman was also a graduate of Colorado. Later in the game, Barry Sanders had fumbled the ball just as he was breaking into the clear. Most disturbing was a play by Lion's quarterback, Bob Gaglione, in the fourth quarter. On a crucial third down play, he had scrambled out of the pocket and tried to run for the first down. Although he was tackled two yards short of the marker, he came out of the pile with a big smile on his face. What the hell had he been smiling about?

The game had been fixed. There was no other plausible explanation. Gaglione, Sanders, and the kid from Colorado had conspired with the people from The Pines. Since I alone had expected the Lions to win, they were able to throw the contest easily, without the slightest trace of suspicion. This explained the outcome of the game, but I was still trying to ascertain what Parcells's white hair had meant when I lost consciousness.

When I woke up, Kevin and my mother were hovering over my bed.

"Is *It* on yet?" I asked. Kevin smiled warmly.

"*It* is over. No pun intended," he replied. "It's one o'clock in the morning. You slept so soundly, we didn't want to wake you." I nodded.

"The second part comes on Wednesday night. You can watch it with us," my mother reassured me. "You look much better, Dennis. Everything is going to be fine. We'll talk more tomorrow," she said. She turned off the light and quietly left the room with my brother.

Before I drifted back to sleep, I thought about the book *It*. I had been a big Stephen King fan since I was a gangly teenager. Of all his great books, *It* was my favorite. *It* was one of those rare books that was so good that I hadn't wanted it to end. When I had finished reading the last gripping page, I felt as if I had known the main characters all my life.

The theme of the book was very old and very basic. The forces of good battle the dark terror of the ultimate evil. *It*, a powerful creature that can assume many forms and reach inside people's minds, bringing their worst nightmares to life. In the final chapter, the power of love enables five ordinary people to kill the wicked entity.

I pondered the moral of the story for a moment. Wasn't it true? Eventually good overcomes evil and love is much stronger than hate, always, without exception. This belief may have been naïve but, at the time, I considered it one of the truisms of life.

Suddenly I realized the significance of *It* being shown on television. The war between good and evil had been waged since the beginning of time, and the final battle was now being fought. Mercifully, this war was almost over. At the conclusion of the second half of the showing of *It* on Wednesday night, the war would be won once and for all. After thousands of years of a fierce internal struggle, the world would finally be at peace. I was proud to be a part of history. The breakdown of The Pines's drug empire was going to set the wheels of change in motion.

Nothing happened on Monday or Tuesday. None of the papers printed a word about the drug operation at The Pines. I was extremely disappointed by this. What was taking them so long to break the story? At night I was forced to take ten milligrams of Haldol in front of my mother. This experience was humiliating but there wasn't much I could do about it.

By Wednesday night, three days of Haldol had taken its toll on my body. I was back to being my dull, zombie-like self. I watched the second part of *It* without incident. The program wasn't even that good. As usual, the television screen failed to capture the brilliance of King's imagination.

I laughed at myself for thinking that a silly T.V. show could have a profound impact that there was anything wrong with my mind. I had merely misconstrued the facts and made an incorrect assumption.

I woke up on Thanksgiving morning feeling better than I had in months. I was anxious to see if my prophetic dream the week before had any substance to it. Since my parents had gotten divorced, holidays had been difficult for me. I missed having both my mother and father there with us to share the joy of a special day. I grew nostalgic and reflected back on some of the memorable celebrations of the past. For my family, the joy and innocence of those days could never be fully recaptured.

8

SHADOW
BOXING

Despite the turmoil of the past month, my mother was determined to make this Thanksgiving a special one. She prepared a sumptuous twelve course dinner fit for kings. Before we began eating, everyone said a few words of thanks. I was the last to speak. I thanked God for all the great food, my good health, and my wonderful family. I considered myself blessed to be surrounded by so much love. My family was my strength.

The dinner conversation was upbeat and playful. We told jokes, made fun of each other, and laughed quite a bit. Every topic was fair game. Thomas's weight, Kevin's love life, and even my sanity, or lack thereof. An outsider would have thought we were being unusually cruel to each other, but we all understood that everything was said in jest. Deirdre was a little touchy, so we spared her from the harsher insults.

Without warning, Sean started singing, "Na-na-na-na ... Na-na-na-na ... Hey-hey ... Good-bye," he droned in a voice almost as bad as mine. Kevin joined in and the rest of us soon followed. We sounded like a drunken crew of sailors, but we were having a marvelous time. I didn't even know the name of the song but I recognized it as a battle cry of victorious sports fans.

After the racket had died down, Thomas mentioned that today was the twenty-seventh anniversary of John F. Kennedy's assassination. November 22, 1963 was one of the saddest days in the history of the United States. I wondered if it was just a coincidence that this year's Thanksgiving happened to fall on the same date.

Halfway through dinner, my father called to wish everyone a happy holiday. I tried my best to sound friendly and relaxed as I spoke with him, but it wasn't easy. I was still waiting for him to come forward with information about The Pines. His reluctance to do so was trying my patience.

After my father hung up, I quietly walked into my mother's bedroom. I picked up the phone and dialed Cory Malone's number. I really needed to talk to her. Her father answered the phone on the second ring.

"Hello?"

"Hello, Mr. Malone. Happy Thanksgiving. This is Dennis Mulhearn. I'm a friend of Cory's. Can I speak to her please?" There was a pause on the other end of the line.

"Uh … Cory's not here right now. She's at her sister's. I'll tell her you called," he said in a noticeably weary voice. That was strange. I knew that Cory had an excellent relationship with both of her parents and with her older sister, Donna. Why weren't they all spending Thanksgiving together?

The answer hit me like a bolt of lightning. Oh, no. Cory is still in a mental hospital. She knows who I am and has been trying to tell people about me! I tried to imagine what she must be going through. As trying as my own ordeal had been, hers was probably even more difficult. She was a sweet and delicate woman who would not have been prepared for the viciousness of her enemies.

I prayed to God to give her as much strength as she needed. It hurt me deeply to know that she was suffering along with me, but I had no doubt that her extraordinary courage would triumph in the end. Though slight of build, Cory was a person of tremendous moral fortitude.

I walked back into the kitchen and saw that my mother's friend, Frank, had arrived. He was wearing a dark brown sweater that matched the color of his beard. Frank was an amicable man but he had a difficult time matching up to my father. In truth, Ghandi himself would not have matched up to my father in my eyes. I must have been a sexist because it was much harder for me to see my mother with another man than it was to see my father with another woman.

After saying hello to Frank, I went downstairs to join my brothers, Deirdre, and Starlight in the living room.

"Hey, Den, did you hear about Daddy?" Sean asked.

"No, what about him?"

"He gave Chanel his two-weeks notice," Thomas said. "His last day is December 1st."

I didn't know what to say. I was very confused. Although he had somehow managed to save his soul, my father still hadn't done anything to indicate the slightest change in his position. Abruptly quitting a high paying job was definitely not a good sign. Had the Richmans already given him his payoff? What was next? Was he going to announce that he had bought a house on a golf course down in South Carolina?

As the conversation continued I learned that December 1st was going to be a significant day for two of my brothers as well. On that same day, Kevin was moving into a studio apartment on Forty-Second Street and Second Avenue in Manhattan, and Sean was starting a new sales job with the Maxwell Paper Corporation. He was going to Lancaster, Pennsylvania to begin a rigorous, three-month training program. Although I realized these changes were inevitable, I wasn't happy about them. I enjoyed having my brothers around as much as possible and knew that I would miss them dearly.

The time passed quickly, as holidays are wont to do, and when everyone reassembled in the dining room for cookies and cake it was almost nine o'clock. "I don't believe it. We're out of eggnog," my mother said as she walked out of the kitchen holding a homemade pie in each hand. I volunteered to drive to Soda King, a local convenience store that was always open, and buy some more.

As I made a right turn on the corner of my block I reflected on the day. It had been a memorable Thanksgiving but nothing of a spiritual nature had occurred. Maybe my dream had been nothing more than my subconscious mind looking forward to a delicious turkey dinner.

I bought the last two cartons of eggnog on the shelf and drove off. When I came to my corner again my moth opened wide in wonder. The second house on my block was lit up in an ornate spectacle of bright, multi-colored lights. Five minutes ago the house had been void of so much as a candle. Now it looked as though it had been transported from Rockefeller Center. The residents of this home always went overboard with the Christmas lights but they usually didn't start putting them up until the first week of December. I wondered why they had started so early this year.

When I stopped my car to get a better look at the house, the answer came to me. Wasn't Jesus Christ the light of the world? And wasn't John the Baptist the man sent to bear witness to the light? Of course. This impressive display was meant for me. God the Father was trying to show me that his Son was returning to earth very soon. He wanted me to be prepared for the Second Coming. I didn't know exactly when Jesus was coming but I speculated that it might be right around Christmas time. Hell, it might even be Christmas Day. What a day that would be!

Amidst all my excitement, I almost forgot where I was. I had to get going. If I wasn't home in five minutes my mother would probably call the cops. While I drove down the block I turned on the radio, hoping to catch some sports scores. I didn't hear any scores, but I heard something far more meaningful. The disc jockey said a vision of the Virgin Mary had been reported in Central California. Hundreds of people had claimed to see it. My dream was right. Something divine is happening today! I didn't understand the details but I knew that God the Father was preparing the world for something of monumental importance. Jesus was coming!

When I returned to my house no one seemed to notice how long I had been gone, and I kept everything I had seen and heard to myself. Just as He had shown me glimpses of what was to come, I believed God would reveal to me when it was time to share my knowledge. As excited as I was, I didn't think I'd be able to sleep that night, but my nightly ten milligram tablet of Haldol knocked me right out.

When I awoke the next morning, I still remembered the lights on the corner and how they represented the return of the Messiah, but much of my fervor from the previous day was gone. Haldol made it difficult to stay focused on any one idea for too long. Thus, my mind now wandered in many directions with a total lack of discipline.

The rest of the week was boring and uneventful. When I wasn't sleeping, I daydreamed about Cory. Although she dominated my thoughts, I didn't attempt to call her again. Instead, I decided to wait for her to contact me. I was comforted by the knowledge that we would soon be together.

Aside from driving Kevin back and forth from the bus stop, I didn't do anything else of consequence all week. On Thursday, November 29, a full week after Thanksgiving had passed, it finally became apparent that the newspapers were not going to print a word about The Pines. I shared my thoughts with Kevin on the morning drive to Gordon's Corner. "The way I see it, Kev, there are only two possibilities. Either the people who I sent my letter to think I'm a nutcase because I was in a mental hospital, or, after they did some investigating, they were scared off by the powers-that-be at The Pines. I think the latter is the most likely scenario." I assumed my brother's grunt indicated that he did not agree with me.

Later that morning I called my friend, Vicky Walsh. Vicky was extremely supportive. She told me she had called her mom down in Florida and talked to her about me.

"I don't know if it's any consolation," she said, "but my mother and I both believe your story. There are a lot of scary things happening in this world." Her astute words gave me a tremendous boost. At last I had found someone with an open mind!

"My problem is that the story is so bizarre, no one else can believe it. I know they are running a drug operation but I can't prove it," I said excitedly. "The most frustrating aspect of all this is that I can remember every single thing that happened while I was at The Pines. But my credibility is ruined because I was unjustly put into a mental hospital."

"Why don't you write a book?" Vicky suggested. What a terrific idea. I fancied myself as a reasonably skilled writer. Surely I could write a book that would alert the general public to the horrors of The Pines. I thanked Vicky for her understanding and for her excellent idea, and promised to get back to her soon. She was a true friend.

Immediately after I hung up the phone, I sat down at the kitchen table with a Bic pen and an old notebook. By the time my mother came home from work, I had written four pages of notes for each day I had spent at The Pines. I even thought of a clever title: *The Pines Hotel Scandal: You Call It Fiction, I Call It Fact.*

My mother, however, was not pleased with my new project. Like Dr. Miller, she wanted me to just forget about everything and get on with my life. As much as she loved me, she didn't understand me at all. If I lived to be a hundred years old, I would never be able to forget the week I had spent at The Pines.

Unfortunately, despite my best efforts, I was unable to complete page one of my manuscript. The damn Haldol was blocking all my creative juices. I had to rectify this problem right away.

Later in the evening I drove to a drugstore and bought some candy that looked similar to Haldol. I put the candy inside my pill container and swallowed it in front of my mother before I went to bed. She didn't suspect a thing.

I woke up early the next morning with renewed vigor. It felt good to be myself again.

"Hey, Dennis, will you help me check out a car?" Sean asked at the breakfast table. I was anxious to start writing but I agreed to help him. He needed transportation to get him to Lancaster tomorrow. We drove to Toms River to look at the car he was interested in. Sean didn't have time to be too discriminating. If the vehicle had four wheels and a functioning engine, he was going to buy it. My brother wound up purchasing the junk heap for two-hundred dollars. His goal was merely to get three months use out of the well-traveled Chevy.

As soon as I returned home I sat down at my desk and opened my notebook. This time the words came to me easily. It gave me great pleasure to have my brain functioning on all cylinders again. This is going to be a fantastic book, I thought, as I completed one paragraph after another. By the end of the day I had finished the first chapter. I went to bed feeling good about this accomplishment.

I had trouble sleeping that night. Too many thoughts were occupying my brain. I was thinking about The Pines, Cory, and my religious mission all at the same time. However, the sensation was not entirely unpleasant. I felt unbelievably smart and supremely important. My life now had a most definitive purpose. God had chosen me to expose The Pines's drug operation and to prepare the world for the return of his son. I was looking forward to fulfilling my destiny and making Him proud.

At nine o'clock Saturday morning, Kevin and Sean knocked on my door to say goodbye. Sean was dropping Kevin off at the bus stop and then driving to Lancaster. "I'll miss you guys," I said. Kevin promised to try to get home on the weekends, but I wasn't going to see Sean again until Christmas.

After my brothers left, I took a shower and got dressed. I carefully selected my wardrobe for the day, black Bugle Boy pants, black Reebok sneakers, and a bright gold Chi-Chi's uniform shirt. You look just like Captain James T. Kirk, I thought to myself as I admired my reflection in the bathroom mirror.

Lisa passed me in the hallway. "Hi, Dennis. Are you working at Chi-Chi's today?"

"No, Lisa. I just felt like wearing these clothes." That wasn't exactly true. These were the clothes I was supposed to be wearing. I was disappointed to never have been named captain of any of my sports teams, but now I was the captain of a much bigger team, God's team. I wore my uniform with pride.

I spent the rest of the day writing feverishly. The hours flew by as I attempted to recreate my week at The Pines. When I finally took a break to eat my dinner, I had written twenty more pages.

Thomas's best friend, Keith, was a guest for dinner. In addition to being a toothsome kid, Keith was quite bright. His father was a noted psychologist.

"Would you mind if I took a look at your book, Dennis?" he asked after we had finished eating. I gladly obliged him. It only took him fifteen minutes to read my work. "Your story is terrific so far," he said, handing the notebook back to me. "Let me know when you're done. My dad will be very interested to read about you."

"So will a lot of other people," I said, smiling confidently.

To everybody's surprise, Kevin called from Gordon's Corner at eight o'clock. He was cursing like a sailor. The guy he was subleasing his apartment from forgot to leave him a key, so Kevin was stuck in Manalapan for another week. I took the news as an omen. "Everything happens for a reason." God obviously wanted my brother near me for a few more days. Who was I to question why?

On Sunday morning Kevin convinced me to go with him to the gym. We were both members of the Jack LaLanne Super Spa in East Brunswick. Besides having state-of-the-art equipment, the health club was equipped with four racquetball courts, an indoor pool, a running track, and a steam room. With an equal percentage of men and women as members, it was truly a fitness center of the 90s.

Before I took the job at The Pines, I had worked out at the club at least four or five times a week. Although I was still doing my sit-ups and push-ups at home, it had been almost two months since I had lifted any weights.

During the thirty-minute drive to East Brunswick I discussed my book with my brother.

"Did you ever think that you might leave yourself open to a libel suit?" Kevin asked. "Why don't you just change the names and places and try to sell your book as fiction?"

"No, that would defeat the whole purpose of what I'm doing. These people are ruthless and dangerous. I have to put them out of business." Kevin just shook his head. He knew it was pointless to argue with me.

It felt good to be back in the gym. Seeing other people working out always gave me a little extra energy. Despite the abundance of attractive females at Jack LaLanne's, I refrained from socializing with any of them. I was there to sweat, not to pick up women.

After running a mile and riding the stationary bike for fifteen minutes, Kevin and I went downstairs to the free weight room. "This is where the real men train," I joked. To my pleasant surprise, I hadn't lost any strength. Kevin thought I was still taking the Haldol, so he was quite impressed with my performance.

We pumped iron until our arms felt as if they were about to fall off. I had almost forgotten how invigorating it was to push my body beyond normal limits. In college, I became a fanatical weight-lifter, working out for two and a half hours a day, every day. I used my football career as an excuse for my zealousness but, in truth, football wasn't the real reason why I killed myself in the weight room. I just wanted to see how big I could get. I liked the feeling of power and the respect other kids gave me as a result of my size. Also, every semi-serious bodybuilder has a narcissistic streak in him, and I was no exception. Weightlifting was the best thing in the world for building my self-esteem.

I went to the gym again on Monday afternoon. Another intense workout left me with a voracious appetite. I walked into the house just as my mother was serving dinner. "How's the book coming?" Thomas asked me, in between bites of his chicken.

"Fine, thanks. I know exactly what I want to say, now I just have to put my thoughts on paper."

Thomas excused himself and went downstairs to make a phone call. He returned a few minutes later with a frown on his face. "I just talked to Daddy. He sounds really down. Something's bothering him."

It wasn't hard to discern what was on my father's mind. His conscience was clearly gnawing at him. I went into my mother's room and dialed my father's number. Thomas was right, he sounded deeply depressed. When I asked him what he was doing, he told me he was listening to the radio program, *The Shadow*.

Our conversation started out benign enough. I questioned him about how his teeth were feeling.

"They're killing me," he replied. "I have to go to Brooklyn to see Dr. Grayson tomorrow. I've seen him every Tuesday for the past month." In the background, I could hear Willie whispering something into my father's ear. Just once, I would have liked to have talked to him alone, free of her manipulation. She never left his side.

When I eagerly told him about my book, his mood turned even more sour.

"How are you going to support yourself?" he asked dubiously.

"I'll get my old job at Chi-Chi's back. That will give me plenty of time to write." With that answer, he exploded like an erupting volcano.

"That's just great. Go back to your safe, comfortable job at Chi-Chi's. You're going to be talking about The Pines when you're forty years old. Why don't you just put it all behind you and get on with your life?"

Now I was getting angry. "Look, Dad, I know that they're running a drug operation up there and I won't rest until I stop it," I said with just the right amount of righteous indignation.

"I can't believe you still think that. You are really sick!" he screamed. "What do you thing, the phone's bugged? Why don't you call the goddamn FBI or DEA?"

I let him finish his tirade and then exchanged a few choice words of my own. I told him that I thought quitting his job in the midst of my hospitalization was a lousy thing to do. It wasn't fair to place all of the financial burden on Kevin. Although I hadn't meant to be vindictive, my father evidently construed my words as a personal attack. He called me a no good bum and angrily slammed down the phone.

Soon thereafter, Kevin arrived home from work. Before he even had a chance to change out of his suit, he received a phone call from Willie. I was distressed by this because I thought she was going to try to turn him against me. "Don't listen to her!" I said. "She's gonna tell you I'm sick. I'm not sick. I was calm and rational. Daddy was the one who went berserk."

In reality, Willie was worried about her husband. After he hung up on me, he left the house and had not returned. This information revived a previous hope, maybe this was the night my father was finally coming to Manalapan!

I went into my bedroom and waited for him to come. I felt like a young child on Christmas Eve as I anxiously anticipated my father's heroic arrival. The hours passed by slowly with nothing happening. Sleep was not possible, so I decided to record my thoughts on paper. When I found my notebook and a pen, I flicked on the light and began writing:

December 4, 1990 – 1:50 a.m.

"I think Daddy is coming tonight. If he is strong enough, he will come and vindicate me. If not, he'll be coming soon. It's part of God's plan. No one knows the plan except God the Father, so I can only guess and hope exactly when he'll come. Nevertheless, I know without question that he will come to this house in Manalapan."

After I put my notebook away and turned off the light, I began to pray. I prayed for God to give my father the strength to get to our house. He was a strong man, but this was the greatest challenge of his life. I knew the extent of the evil and corruption he was facing. I must have said a hundred Our

Fathers, but my prayers were in vain. My digital clock clicked to 5:04.

Damn, he's not coming tonight. I had to finally accept this dismal reality. I tried to determine what had prevented him from coming. Did he simply lack the courage, or were there other mitigating circumstances? I searched for the answer by replaying our phone conversation in my mind.

Over and over again, I heard his exact words echoing through my brain. My memory was amazingly accurate. Finally, the solution came to me. It had been staring me right in the face all along! My father had given me a coded message. Willie was his "shadow." Her presence prevented him from speaking freely, but he was still trying to help me. His clever idea had worked to perfection. I was smart enough to pick up on everything he had communicated.

In addition to the transparent information that my phone was bugged, and that I should get in touch with the FBI and the DEA immediately, there were other more subtle clues that were equally valuable. Chi-Chi's was safe. I could trust the people there. This knowledge was extraordinarily important because up until this point I really wasn't sure who I could trust.

Also, my father's dental visits were bogus. He and Willie were driving to The Pines every Tuesday to meet with Eve Cantor and the Richmans. Willie was the pipelines to The Pines. My father couldn't make a move without them knowing about it, but maybe he had confided something to Dr. Grayson.

Bernard Grayson had been our family dentist for years. His integrity was beyond reproach. If nothing else, I was confident he would be able to disprove my father's supposed visit on October 28. That would be a good start.

When I dropped Kevin off at the bus stop at 8 a.m., I instructed him to call Dr. Grayson the minute he walked into his office. "Ask him the date of Daddy's last appointment," I said as soon as we were both out of my car. I wasn't sure whether my car had also been bugged, so I had to be cautious.

Although bewildered by my reasoning, Kevin agreed to cooperate with me. "After you talk to Dr. Grayson, I'll be able to tell you more about what's going on," I reassured him.

When I returned home, I went upstairs to my bedroom and took a much needed nap. All those hours of deep thinking had severely drained me. I woke up at eleven o'clock feeling refreshed. The first thing I decided to do was call Vicky Walsh. She was the only person who really believed me and I knew that I could trust her with my life.

I was just about to hang up when Vicky picked up her phone on the fifth ring.

"Boy, I'm glad you're home," I said. "There are some things that I really need to talk to you about." She asked me how the book was going and I explained that I had decided to change the names and write the story as fiction. I had no intention of doing this, but I intended to outsmart the people who were bugging my phone.

"Do you still plan to do anything about The Pines?" she asked. I smiled brightly. She had given me the perfect setup question.

"No. I don't think I'm going to pursue that any further. It's holding me back and I can't do anything by myself anyway. Maybe I can get a job as a teacher, or with another hotel."

Vicky was enthusiastic about my new plans. She should have known me well enough to realize I would never be able to let it go that easily. If nothing else, I was single-mindedly persistent and hard-headed to a fault.

She had to work at Chi-Chi's at five-thirty, so I agreed to meet her at Bennigan's at four o'clock. Bennigan's (at the intersection of Rt. 18 and Rt. 1) was the favorite hangout among Chi-Chi's employees. I had spent many enjoyable evenings there eating, laughing, and talking with my friends. Vicky didn't know it yet, but this meeting was going to be far more than just another social occasion.

I drove to the Manalapan Library and stopped at the reference desk. When I asked the librarian for a book containing the names and addresses of government agencies, an old man seated at the next table looked over towards me. I wasn't positive, but I thought I remembered seeing him at The Pines. Damn. They're watching me closely. I've got to be careful.

Much to my disappointment, the reference book the librarian gave me contained information on every federal agency except the FBI. However, I did find the address of the DEA. I hurriedly copied it on a piece of paper and then began writing a letter to the DE .

This letter was similar to the one I had sent to all the newspapers. I outlined what I knew about the drug operation and gave the names of the key people involved. The only difference was that I mentioned my father's involvement.

I told the DEA that he was working on the inside along with me. "My primary concern is my father's wellbeing. Do not take any action unless you are able to guarantee his safety," I wrote toward the end of the note. I closed by telling them to fax a copy of this correspondence to the FBI, and to await further instructions.

On my way out of the library I looked for the old man I had seen, but he was gone. While this relaxed me somewhat, I was still extremely suspicious and paranoid of every stranger I saw. I was so close to breaking the drug operation, yet I couldn't take anything for granted. The people from The Pines were unusually clever and had a great deal of power behind them. There were no limits to what they would do to prevent me from exposing the horrible truth about what went on in the deceptivly quiet town of South Fallsburg, New York.

I was all set to walk into the Manalapan Post Office, when I saw a police car parked outside. Although I knew that the Manalapan cops had probably never even heard of The Pines, I couldn't risk the miniscule possibility that they were involved. I got back into my car and decided to let Vicky mail the letter for me. Yes. That's a good idea. No one will ever suspect an innocent girl like Vicky. She'll be a perfect carrier.

During the drive to Bennigan's, I spent more time looking in my rear view mirror than I did at the road in front of me. If someone was tailing me, he was doing a damn good job of remaining inconspicuous. I arrived at the restaurant at five minutes before four. Vicky was already waiting for me by the front door. She greeted me with a warm hug and a big smile.

It was great to see her but I hoped she was not expecting a romantic date. She had no idea about my relationship with Cory and, as far as she knew, I was single and available.

Immediately upon going inside, I saw an old friend working behind the bar. I quietly sauntered over to him. "Hey, Roger. I see you finally found someone who would hire you. I didn't know Bennigan's was so desperate." He laughed heartily and pumped my hand. Roger was a tall, African-American young man who had worked at Chi-Chi's for three years. We quickly became friends because in addition to being a helluva nice guy, he was a sports junkie who had the misfortune of being a Philadelphia fan. I enjoyed mocking him about his teams' failures at every opportunity.

Unfortunately, our reunion was short-lived. After saying hello to Vicky, he had to get back to work. The bar was rapidly filling up with thirsty customers. "God, he's so thin," Vicky observed when he had moved to the other end of the bar. She was right. He had lost about thirty pounds since the last time I had seen him.

I had heard a rumor that Roger had become heavily involved with drugs. At the time I angrily dismissed it as a vicious lie, but now I wasn't so sure. Could my friend be involved with The Pines? I didn't think so, but anything was possible. Drugs make people do some crazy things sometimes.

A hostess came over and tried to seat us at a deuce in the middle of the restaurant. Nobody looked particularly suspicious, but the sheer volume of people made me uncomfortable. I told the hostess that my friend was allergic to smoke and requested a table in the back. The section was closed but, since we were friends of Roger's, she made an exception for us. We were seated at a table in the corner, far away from the earshot of any of the other patrons.

I ordered a New York strip steak and Vicky selected a pasta dish. The food came within ten minutes. I waited until after the waitress had checked on our meals before I told Vicky anything of relevance.

"I've got those bastards right where I want them. I'm finally going to bring down the people from The Pines." Vicky's mouth dropped to the floor. After our conversation in the morning, she certainly had not expected to hear a statement like that.

"What do you mean? I thought that was over." I patiently explained how my phone had been bugged and why it was so important for me not to divulge any of my knowledge.

"If they found out my father was helping me, they'd kill him in a second." Vicky gulped hard and took a big swig of her Diet Coke.

"Why are you telling me all this? You're starting to scare me."

"I'm really sorry about getting you involved, but I didn't have any other choice. You're the only person who believes me, and I know I can trust you."

I reached inside my jacket pocket and slowly pulled out the letter. "Can I count on your help, Vicky?"

"Yes, of course. What can I do for you?" I knew that was the answer she was going to give me. She was one of my loyal friends.

"As soon as you get to Chi-Chi's, call Federal Express and send this letter to the address I have written down. Don't discuss this conversation or what is in the package with anyone. Can you do that, kid?"

"No problem. You can count on me, Dennis." Evidently Vicky was moved by the magnitude of what she was about to do. She insisted on leaving the restaurant immediately.

"I'll call you as soon as it's safe. Thank you, Vicky. You don't know how much I appreciate this." I kissed her softly on the cheek and said goodbye. When she was gone, I sat back down to finish my steak and then proceeded to eat whatever was left on her plate as well. Roger saw me do this and grinned at me from behind the bar. I grinned back at him. It was a relief to realize that he was not involved with The Pines.

Kevin came home from work at nine o'clock. I immediately interrogated him about his phone call to Dr. Grayson. "I called just like you told me," he said. "Daddy was already there. I talked to him for a few minutes before he had to go."

It was tremendously disappointing to realize that my theory had been incorrect. Perhaps a new wrinkle that I was not aware of had been thrown into the equation. I asked Kevin exactly what our father had told him. He paused for a moment in an attempt to recall the conversation.

"He really didn't say anything important, Den. He just talked about a story he had written regarding his experiences at Chanel. He ridiculed his bosses for their inability to deal with the problems of the real world." When prodded further, Kevin remembered the last line in my father's story, "If you want fantasy, go watch *The Wizard of Oz*."

I had to think for a minute before I understood what my father was trying to tell me. *The Wizard of Oz* was a classic tale of good versus evil. He knew that I would grasp the meaning of this information.

I drove to the new video store on Gordon's Corner and rented *The Wizard of Oz*. I knew it was no coincidence that the store had opened in October. It was clearly part of the undercover operation in which my father was involved. Renting that movie was just my way of letting them know we were on the same page. The cat and mouse game had begun.

9

IN SEARCH OF EDEN

I wasn't able to sleep at all that night. I was too excited. My long battle was finally coming to a glorious conclusion. I was very grateful to God and to all the people who had been working with me. Throughout the night and into the next day, I laid in bed, stared at the ceiling and did some heavy thinking.

By the time my mother came home from work I had reached some startling new conclusions. After she changed her clothes, she joined me in the kitchen for what she thought would be a light-hearted chat.

"I've figured out a lot of things," I said. "All the guys that I played baseball with when I was a kid are really undercover cops. They have been working for years to try to stop the drug ring at The Pines.

"Uncle Harry is in charge of everything. He's heading the operation."

Technically, my great-uncle, "Uncle" Harry Mulhearn was my grandfather's only living brother. He was a former New York City Police Captain who had built a legendary reputation on the streets of New York. My grandfather used to delight in telling us stories detailing some of his heroics. Following his retirement from the force, he wrote a number of books on police procedure, and also ran a very successful police school for many years.

Uncle Harry was certainly a person worthy of my admiration. He combined a keen intellect with a terrific sense of humor and a superbly conditioned body. Despite all his achievements, he never forgot his humble beginnings and never put anyone or anything before his family. Nevertheless, he immediately became the focal point whenever he walked into a room. His commanding presence demanded respect from everyone who had the pleasure of meeting him.

"Uncle Harry's the best cop around. We'll be hearing from him soon," I assured my mother.

"That's ridiculous, Dennis. There is no police operation. Uncle Harry is almost eighty years old now. He's been living in Virginia for the past two years. Don't you see what's happening? The circle is getting bigger and bigger. Dr. Miller explained that this is one of the symptoms of your illness. You think the whole world revolves around you."

I gave my mother a compassionate smile. She obviously didn't understand the scope of what I was involved in. "First of all, I am not ill. Secondly, your mind is incapable of comprehending the forces that are at work here. The circle is getting bigger, it is bigger than you can even imagine."

"What the hell are you talking about?" asked my mother. Her confusion did not surprise me. I was talking about an extraordinarily complex subject.

"A circle has no beginning and no end. Most people think that life is a straight line, marked by various events along the way. They are wrong. Life is one continuous circle, void of time and space. Time is only for man. For God, there is no time.

"God has created a magic circle, upon which each person has a specific role to fulfill. I am no better than anyone else, but my role happens to be particularly significant. Yes, Mom, the circle is getting bigger. The magic circle is bigger than the universe itself."

My mother stared at me blankly. She not only failed to understand the metaphysical concept I was discussing, but seemed wary of it as well.

"I'm concerned about you, Dennis. You're not speaking rationally. I'm going to call the hospital," she announced. I listened amusedly as she described my so-called "irrational" behavior to one of the nurses.

"Dr. Miller is on vacation now," my mother said. "When he gets back, I want you to talk to him."

"Okay, Mom. Whatever you say. But do you really think he'll be able to understand me any better than you do?" Not waiting for an answer, I left the kitchen and started up the stairs. I had planned on telling my mother about Cory but decided that there was no need to alarm her any further. The secret was going to have to remain with me for a little while longer.

I walked into my bedroom and sat down on the edge of my bed. My thoughts drifted back to one of the most memorable events of my childhood.

Bryan Adams once wrote a song about the summer of '69. My memories of that block of time were filled with a mixture of nostalgia and loss. We had moved into a new house on Kimball Street, just two blocks away from Flatbush Avenue, at the end of May. My brothers and I soon discovered, to our delight, that there were many children on our new block for us to play with.

One of these playmates was a little girl who lived only three doors away. Her name was Eileen Baker and although I had not yet turned five, I was instantly smitten by her. As the summer progressed, I began to spend more and more time with my little friend. Kevin and Sean made fun of me for playing so much with a girl but I really didn't care what they thought. While I was too young to fully grasp the concept of love, I was old enough to know that I felt good whenever I was with Eileen, there was something special about her.

When my parents questioned me about her one evening, I proudly declared my intention to marry the girl as soon as we both grew up. They reacted to this announcement with convulsive fits of laughter. Their incredulous laughter was embarrassing, but it didn't deter me at all. I looked forward to growing up with Eileen and learning about the wonders of the world with her. To my five year-old brain, the future seemed as bright as the sun.

All my plans changed on one fateful Saturday in late August. Unbeknownst to me, Mr. Baker had brought home his guard dog from the gas station he owned. As we had done a hundred times before, Sean and I walked innocently into the Bakers's backyard.

I stopped to tie my shoes while Sean continued walking toward the back door. When I looked up, I was horrified to see a German Shepard pouncing on my brother and snapping at his face. The dog was tied to a tree but the leash was far too long. Poor Sean was completely defenseless against the vicious attack.

"Help! Somebody, help!" I screamed with all my might. Mrs. Baker came running out of the house and quickly subdued the dog, but the damage had already been done. Sean's face had been chewed to a bloody pulp. I watched my father hold Sean's protruding skin to his face as he rushed him to the hospital.

Later that night Sean came home with his face wrapped in bandages like a miniature mummy. He handled himself with tremendous courage, but behind the bandages I could see the fear in my younger brother's eyes.

Through a small miracle, Sean was spared the agony of permanent disfigurement. His plastic surgeon did a masterful job. When his bandages were finally removed, he was left with a slightly noticeable scar under his eye and across his cheek. It could very easily have been so much worse. Had the bite been only a few inches higher, he could have lost his nose or his right eye, or both.

Unfortunately, this terrible incident had other painful consequences. A few months later, the Baker family moved out of the neighborhood. Although I was only a child, the realization that I would probably never see Eileen again hurt me deeply. I can still remember seeing her waving to me from the backseat of her father's station wagon as the car rolled down Kimball Street for the last time.

All these memories had come flooding back to me in precise detail last night as I lay awake contemplating my existence. In order to fully understand my present situation, it was important to examine and evaluate my past. For some inexplicable reason, I could not shake loose the memory of the German Shepard attacking Sean. A vision of the dog hovering menacingly over my brother kept repeating in my mind again and again. This must have gone on for ten minutes before I realized there was something disturbingly wrong with the mental image my brain was receiving. The defenseless little boy lying on the ground wasn't Sean, it was me!

Even after all these years, it had never occurred to me that if I hadn't stopped to tie my shoelaces, the dog would have gone for me. It would have gone directly for my throat and killed me instantly! Why was death so important? Why was I spared? The answers came to me almost instantaneously.

The German Shepard was no ordinary guard dog. It was a ruthless, evil force with one specific purpose, the extermination of my life. I wasn't sure whether the dog was actually an agent of Satan or the embodiment of the beast himself, but that really didn't matter. In either case, God had protected me from danger the same way he had saved me from certain doom at The Pines. Only He knew how important it was for me to fulfill my destiny.

While this realization about my past provided me with crucial insight, it also opened up a whole new can of worms. What was little Eileen's role in all of this? Was someone or something trying to keep us apart? I pondered these questions for quite a while, carefully poring over all of the possibilities. A big smile crept onto my face as I reached what I thought was a logical conclusion.

Mr. Baker was a shrewd man. He hadn't moved because of embarrassment or guilt about the attack, as I had previously believed all these years. No. His motive had been far more complicated than that. He abruptly left Brooklyn because he feared for the life of his daughter. Somehow, he had become aware of the demonic forces that were desperately trying to keep me away from her.

Although it could have been interpreted as a cowardly act, I didn't blame him for leaving. He did what any loving father would have done. At that time, I was only a small boy. I did not yet have the strength, knowledge, or courage to fight back against the unholy power of pure evil.

Knowing all this, Mr. Baker took his wife and two daughters and moved to the rural town of Manalapan, New Jersey.

Undoubtedly, in an effort to begin a new life, one of the first things he had done was change the family name. That is how Eileen Baker became Cory Malone! My childhood sweetheart had grown up to become a breathtakingly beautiful woman.

This new theory, of which I was ninety-nine percent sure was accurate, created another series of intriguing questions. Why did Mr. Baker choose Manalapan? Did he know that I would come to live there one day? When would I be reunited with Cory? I didn't have any concrete answers to any of these questions, but that didn't prevent me from making some educated guesses.

Like many townships in Central New Jersey, Manalapan was an Indian name. I did not have the exact translation but I inherently knew that the name meant "where man began." This knowledge had a potentially startling implication. Our quiet, suburban community might very well be the original Eden!

Thinking along those lines, I surmised that God had directed Mr. Baker/Malone to Manalapan, knowing full well that my family and I would come there many years later. I didn't think Mr. Malone knew anything about God's plans for me, so it must have shocked the hell out of him to hear my name again after all this time. Don't worry, Mr. Malone. I won't put Cory in any danger. I'll wait until I take care of this drug business before I see her again.

I had reached all these conclusions and more last night during my marathon brainstorming session. As I continued sitting on my bed, more thoughts kept surfacing with amazing speed. Previous memories and new ideas popped in and out of my head with equal abandon. I was anxious to give my mind a much needed rest, so I threw some clothes in a bag and left for the gym.

It was nearly six o'clock when I arrived at Jack LaLanne's. I could hardly wait to get inside the building. Despite my lack of sleep, my body was charged with adrenaline. I knew that this was not going to be an ordinary workout. But then again, I was no ordinary man. God had given me the unique power to overcome all obstacles.

Just as I reached the top step of the main gym floor, the song *I've Got The Power* came blaring through the speakers. I chuckled softly, realizing that this was not merely a coincidence. After stretching briefly, I began jogging around the track that surrounded all the workout equipment with the exception of a row of twelve stationary bikes in the back of the gym.

During my third lap I noticed something peculiar. Three of the girls riding the bikes had worked at Chi-Chi's at one time or another. Each of them smiled and waved to me as I ran by them. Their presence inspired me to push my body harder. I increased my speed until I was at a full sprint. I don't think I've ever run faster. I felt like an untamed eagle soaring through the clouds as I passed a plethora of slow-moving runners.

I finally stopped after completing what seemed like a sub four-minute mile. Everybody in the gym was staring at me, but I didn't care. I had never felt so robust. My physical prowess was living, breathing testimony to the power of God. I hurriedly walked down to the free-weight room, anxious to display my strength.

The room was surprisingly empty for that time of night. Just four or five guys were spread throughout the workout area. I immediately walked over to the bench press and did a couple of warm-ups sets. "C'mon, you pans. Is that all the weight you can do?" said a familiar voice while I was in the middle of my second set.

After completing the set, I looked up and saw the smiling face of a man named Lenny Wolf. Lenny had a body that looked as if it were chiseled out of marble, and a large tattoo of a beautiful woman stenciled into the upper part of his right arm. He was married to a waitress at Chi-Chi's, and although he was probably more crude than Dice Clay, I couldn't help but like the guy. He always made me laugh.

After trading insults for a minute, we returned to our work-outs. "Let's go. Let's lift some fucking weight," he said, while putting three forty-five pound plates on each side of the bar. With a great deal of grunting and groaning, Lenny did two solid repetitions.

"How much do you want me to take off?" he asked smugly.

"Nothing. Put a quarter on please," I replied. He gave me a startled look, but did as he was told.

The added weight made the bar three-hundred and sixty-five pounds. Although this was sixty pounds heavier than my maximum press, I was confident of my ability to lift it. Everyone in the room stopped what they were doing and turned their attention towards me.

Show them the power, God, I prayed silently. Show them the power! When I placed my back against the bench and carefully took my grip I was almost in a trance. One thought permeated through my mind: Power, Power, Power!

"No way he can do it, he only weights about a hundred seventy-five pounds," said a voice I didn't recognize. The voice was wrong. I lifted the weight above my head three times. Lenny stared at me with an open mouth as I gently returned the bar back to the rack. "That's it for me, pal. I gotta get going," I said to my friend.

"Okay. Good to see you, Dennis. I'll see you soon." As I walked out of the room I saw a couple of the guys huddling quietly with Lenny. They were undoubtedly trying to ascertain how an average sized guy like me could lift so much weight. He scratched his head in bewilderment and appeared to be as dumbfounded as they were. None of them could have ever imagined that the source of my incredible power was Almighty God!

While I was in the shower I reached some more astounding conclusions about what as going on. Seeing the three girls and Lenny here was no accident. Chi-Chi's is not just a popular Mexican restaurant; it's really one of the headquarters of the undercover police operation. Burt Lewis, all the managers, and many of the staff, are undercover narcotics agents who knew that it was necessary for me to infiltrate The Pines's operation.

I wondered why I hadn't realized this sooner. Burt Lewis was the General Manager at Chi-Chi's who ran the restaurant with an iron fist. He was tough and demanding, but also very fair. His broad shoulders and wide back made him appear even taller than his 6'3" inches, and a dark beard made him a menacing figure when he was angry. Many of the employees were intimidated by him, but he and I always got along extremely well. We shared a mutual respect for each other.

Two things tipped me off about Burt's involvement in the drug operation. First, he was a "retired" New York City police officer who still looked, acted, and talked like a cop. Indeed, he ran Chi-Chi's with the autocratic style of a police commissioner. Second, his best friend was Mr. Matthew Malone, Cory's father. I was quite sure that he and Mr. Malone had been keeping close tabs on me. They knew about everything I had done.

My hair was still wet when I walked past the live cacti and opened the thick wooden doors at the entrance of Chi-Chi's. The lobby area, as well as the dining room, was beautifully decorated with Christmas ornaments and multi-colored streamers. Resonating through the building was the melodic sound of Bing Crosby singing *White Christmas*.

A new hostess greeted me enthusiastically. "Good evening, Sir. Welcome to Chi-Chi's. How many are in your party?"

"That's all right, I'm not eating. I used to work here. I just came to visit some friends."

She nodded and moved back behind the hostess stand. I felt like a victorious soldier returning from an historic battle as I triumphantly strode through the floor of the main dining room. When I reached the bus stand, seven or eight people were hanging out and talking. Their collective reaction was not what I had anticipated. Two good friends of mine, Brian and James, greeted me warmly and appeared pleased to see me. The rest of the people, all of whom knew me well, said hello, but scattered quickly without even managing to make eye contact.

The significance of this was clear. Not everybody at Chi-Chi's was a cop. Some of the employees were part of the drug ring at The Pines. The criterion I used to make this determination was remarkably simple. All the people who had the courage to look me in the eyes were with me. Those who could not were against me. No amount of trickery or deception could alter this fact. Indeed, anyone involved in a drug operation was at least indirectly worshipping Satan and had good reason to fear me, and thus did not dare look into my eyes.

As I walked through the kitchen on my way to the main office, the kitchen crew's response was much more positive. Although none of the guys could leave the line, they all exuberantly welcomed me back to "The Chi." Their nervous anticipation and excitement was quite evident. I went behind the line and began shaking hands like a politician running for office. "Thanks. Thank you Danny. Thanks a lot, Jeff. Great job, Sean."

No one said a word about the drug operation, so I assumed they were still careful to not blow their cover. I didn't need any reassurances, however, their big smiles and subtle nods spoke volumes. I gave the boys a friendly wink before walking over to the office door and knocking on it firmly. The door was slowly opened by the service manager, Angela.

"Hi! Come on in. What a nice surprise. We miss you here, Dennis," she said, smiling warmly.

Although I had hoped to speak directly with Burt, Angela was an acceptable substitute. She was a tall, attractive single mother who was originally from Colorado. Her down-to-earth personality and low-key approach made her by far the most popular manager at Chi-Chi's. She was definitely someone I could trust. "Have a seat, I'll be right with you, Dennis. I'm just finishing up Renee's checkout."

Renee, a cocktail waitress, said hello but carefully avoided looking at me. She had been talking with the bar manager, Geri. Geri also said hi and then hurriedly left the office. My presence seemed to unnerve her. She must be in on the drug operation, too. Why else would she be afraid of me? When Renee's checkout was completed, she bolted out of the office as well.

When we were finally alone, I asked Angela to lock the door so we would not be disturbed. She did so, and then sat down in a black leather chair next to mine.

"What's on your mind?"

"It's okay, Angela. You don't have to pretend anymore. I know what's been going on here."

"Tell me, what do you know?"

"You're a cop aren't you? You've been a cop for a long time. I know that this place is just a front for the undercover police operation led by Burt Lewis." After a long, awkward pause, Angela finally spoke, "Yes. I'm a cop. What else do you know."

Her answer gave me a tremendous high. After all this time, my persistence had finally paid off. I had been right all along! "I know just about everything." I said arrogantly. "My father was an undercover narcotics agent in the mid-seventies. He told us he left that detail, but he never really did. He's been working undercover for years. Do you know my father?"

"No. But I know of him."

"Of course you do. How much else do you know?"

"Not too much. I just do my job."

I believed her. Burt had apparently spared her from any knowledge that would have placed her in danger. Turning away from Angela, I quickly surveyed the office. In the right corner, the bright red lights of the electronic safe blinked on and off. "Pretty smart, Burt. No one would ever suspect the safe," I said out loud. "Burt has this office bugged doesn't he, Angela? He and Mr. Malone are listening to us right now, aren't they?" She didn't say a word, but her bright smile was a sufficient answer to my question.

"Do you mind if I talk to Burt for a minute, Angela?"

"Uh … no. G-Go right ahead," she squeaked in a barely audible voice. I was not alarmed by her loss of composure. The woman was understandably humbled by my greatness. I stared directly at the blank wall in front of me, and began to speak.

"Thank you, Burt. Thanks for doing a great job here. I could never have done it without you. Thank you, too, Mr. Malone or Mr. Baker, whatever you want to call yourself. Don't worry, Cory is safe. Her courage has helped me win this fight. You should be very proud of her. Thank my Uncle Harry for me. Tell him I'm looking forward to seeing him."

My monologue was interrupted by a knock on the door. I stopped talking and watched Angela let Brian in. "I just need you to sign this," he said, handing her a credit card slip. "Are you coming back to work here, pal?" he asked me.

"No. It's over. It's all over. You're a helluva cop, Brian." He gave me a confused, uncertain look.

"I'm not a cop. My father's a cop."

"Yeah, sure. Whatever you say." To his credit, Brian remained unwaveringly cool.

"Hey, go for it, man," he said before leaving the office. "He's a great guy, isn't he?"

"Yes, he is," Angela agreed.

"I'm going to fill you in on some of the missing pieces of the puzzle," I said. "Burt and Mr. Malone already know this. This restaurant was started up twelve years ago, in 1978. The whole purpose of the restaurant was to stop the drug ring at The Pines Hotel. I'm sure you already know what a brilliant man my Uncle Harry is. What you don't know is that he is also an astute biblical scholar. After many years of diligent study, he discovered that I was the only person who could break the drug ring. Personally, I don't know that much about the Scriptures, but I do know that what I am doing has all been foretold."

At this point, the belief that I was John the Baptist had all but disappeared from my consciousness. I was still well aware of the spiritual significance of my mission, but the details now completed eluded me. It seemed as if all my knowledge were jumping into my brain through the process of osmosis. In reality, I was taking little tidbits of factual information and expanding upon these facts in whatever direction suited my fancy. This freed my imagination from any boundaries whatsoever.

Angela listened patiently as I continued to enlighten her. I went down the Chi-Chi's roster sheet and named all the double agents for her. Using nothing but my instincts, I was able to expose twenty people who had been trying to undermine Burt Lewis's operation. When she asked me how I knew a certain person was involved, I gave her a logical and reasonable explanation.

"Did you see the movie *Total Recall?*" I asked.

"No, not yet."

"Well, I'm the guy in the movie. I know more and more each day. Very soon, I'll be able to remember everything. I'll have complete and total recall!" I noticed Angela's lower lip start to tremble ever so slightly. She was beginning to fear me.

"My grandfather's still alive, isn't he?" Again, she did not respond, but I interpreted her silence as a positive affirmation. His death had been staged by his brother Harry. He had been doing valuable research all these years to try to help me successfully fulfill my destiny. I was in awe of the great sacrifice he had made for me. The thought of seeing him again was remarkably exciting. I was about to live a dream.

Sensing Angela's discomfort, I clasped her hand in an attempt to calm her. "Don't worry, Angela. All the work has already been done. It's all going to be over soon," I said. "Tell Burt I want the story broken right away. My family has suffered through this with me. It's time to put an end to their pain." I looked away from Angela and spoke to the wall again. "Burt, make sure my father is safe and then finish taking care of business. You know what to do. Send some camera crews to my house as soon as possible."

I strutted through the restaurant with a euphoric grin on my face. My friends waved goodbye and wished me well. Just as I was ready to exit the restaurant, I saw Vicky Walsh out of the corner of my eye. She was earnestly polishing the top of one of her tables. I understood why she had not bothered to look up. "Good night, Vicky," I said, stopping in my tracks. She responded with a weak smile and a feeble wave. Even though she had betrayed me by not mailing my letter to the DEA, I did not have any animosity toward her. She was an extraordinarily good person who must have been seized by a moment of weakness.

When I came home I went upstairs to make myself a sandwich. My mother was sitting at the kitchen table, munching on a tossed salad.

"Hi, Dennis. Jim Freeman called right after you left. He set up an appointment with Dr. Schwartzman tomorrow at six o'clock. I'm leaving work early so make sure you're ready by four-thirty."

"All right, Mom, I'll be ready," I said wearily.

I thought that seeing another doctor would be a colossal waste of time, but went along with it to give my mother some peace of mind. From the very beginning, she had not been satisfied with Dr. Katz's evaluation of my M.R.I. exam and Dr. Miller's skepticism had not done wonders for her confidence.

Fortunately for her, Jim knew a doctor at Jefferson, who would be able to provide a conclusive second opinion. Dr. Robert J. Schwartzman was widely known as one of the leading neurologists on the East oast. I was certain that his expertise would alleviate all of my mother's unwarranted fears.

"What are you watching, Tom?" I asked my brother as I sat down on the couch.

"*Back to the Future III*. I just put it in."

I was pleased with his selection. The concept of time travel fascinated me. I had greatly enjoyed both the original *Back to the Future* and its sequel. In light of all the new information I had recently acquired, I looked forward to a relaxing diversion. Unfortunately, the film only confused me further.

Everything was fine until I saw the date Marty (Michael J. Fox) was taking the Delorean time machine back into the past: October 20, 1888. Thomas spoke before I could say a word. "Don't go making any connections. It's just a coincidence. A lot of people have birthdays on October 20."

True. But how many people just happen to get involved in a drug ring on that same day? I said to myself. It's no coincidence. God must be trying to tell me something.

Any enjoyment I might have garnered from the movie was replaced by a burning desire to learn something of value from it. More and more pieces of the puzzle were becoming available, but I was having a difficult time putting any of them together. Instead of giving me answers, the sequel to the sequel was creating additional questions. Was I supposed to be Marty or Doc Brown (Christopher Lloyd)? Was Clara Clayton really Cory Malone? Did I have to go back and change the past in order to stop the drug ring?

The ending of the movie helped abate my confusion. Marty takes the Delorean back to October 27, 1989. If October 20 was just a coincidence, what the hell was this? Clearly, my visit to The Pines on the 27th had altered history forever!

The film concludes with Doc Brown triumphantly appearing with Clara and their two young sons. When Marty asks him about the future, he replies, "There is no future! Every man determines his own destiny."

"That was pretty good, huh?" Thomas commented.

"Yeah, it was real good."

I was excited about the message I had received in the last line of the film. God had told me that mankind's future was still unknown. Each man and woman had the power within himself or herself to change the inevitable path of destruction we seem headed for. There is hope. We can still choose life and peace over violence and death.

After yet another sleepless night, I approached the next day with eager anticipation. There was no question in my mind that my Uncle Harry, Burt Lewis, and thousands of other brave policemen, were working around-the-clock to wrap up their case against The Pines's drug empire. I expected the story to break at any moment.

I spent the day lying on the sofa and reminiscing about Poppy. One of my fondest recollections of him occurred just a few months before his supposed death. Kevin and I were attending our graduation ceremony at St. Thomas Aquinas Elementary School. The moderator announced our names as recipients of scholarships to Poly Prep High School. When I stood up to accept my applause, I stole a look back at my family. Poppy's enormous smile could have lit up the entire church.

It warmed my heart to know that Kevin and I had given him so much pleasure. His goofy smile remained with him all day. He was so damn proud of his grandsons, one would have thought we had developed the cure for cancer instead of just finishing the lousy eighth grade. My high school and college graduations were both exceptionally happy occasions, but in neither of those events did I approach the unmitigated joy I felt on that warm June day.

My mother didn't get home until a quarter of five. She quickly washed up, and hurriedly rushed me into the passenger seat of her black Dodge Shadow. As she started the car, I opened my white M.R.I. envelope and glanced at the X-rays. My cyst centered my brain the way a well-placed cherry sits on top of a hot fudge sundae, yet I was unworried about my forthcoming examination. There were other far more pressing matters to be concerned with.

I was looking forward to going into Philadelphia. The "City of Brotherly Love" had many of the same urban problems as New York City but I chose to ignore this fact. One Gomorrah on the East oast was more than enough, so it was easy to romanticize Philly and think of only the rich history of the city.

When my mother turned onto Interstate 95, the combination of traffic volume and narrow lanes sent her into a bit of a panic. "Oh, God, this road is terrible," she said nervously. I could see the white of her knuckles as she squeezed the steering wheel with both hands.

"Don't worry, Mom. I have confidence in you. You can do it." My supportive words helped her relax. We were both relieved when we finally reached the Broad Street exit.

I pointed out Veterans Stadium and The Spectrum to her as we made our way up South Philadelphia. Broad Street was already regally adorned with lights, bells, and a variety of Christmas decorations. "This display could get the biggest scrooge into the holiday spirit," said my mother.

"Why don't you let me take the wheel, Mom? I know this city much better than you do," I suggested. She pulled over to the side of the road and exchanged places with me.

I was happy to be driving the car. It wasn't that I didn't trust my mother, but I worked in this city for a while and knew how bad the streets were. In addition to the roads being in terrible condition, there were an inordinate number of blind spots that could sneak up on an unsuspecting driver. I did not want to take any chances.

After driving for a few more minutes I finally came to the street on which the hospital was located. "You can't go down this block, the sign says 'No Left Turns'," my mother shrieked. Ignoring her, I made a sharp turn the instant the light turned green. Mundane traffic laws no longer applied to me. I didn't have to answer to any form of authority anymore.

Before I drove halfway down the block, however, I was pulled over by a large police van. A portly, Irish-looking patrolman stepped out of the van and asked me if I had seen the sign.

"Yes, officer, I saw it, but I'm late for an appointment at the Jefferson Medical Center. I was just trying to make some time."

"Yes, he's right. We have to go see one of the doctors. It's a medical emergency," my mother added.

Not only did the cop let me off with just a warning, he also directed us to the closest parking lot. "You see, Mom. Some cops out there are pretty nice guys," I said, while wondering whether he had been part of the undercover operation. Just how far did the operation extend? Was the entire Philadelphia Police Department being mobilized to protect me? I didn't know for certain, but with Harry Mulhearn in charge anything was possible. His circle of influence was vast.

I pulled into the Five-Star Parking Garage and parked in the first available spot. A young attendant walked over to my car.

"Excuse me, sir. You can't park here. This spot's reserved. Bring your car over to the other side and put it in number twelve." I did as I was instructed and then paid the attendant. On the way out of the lot I noticed that my original parking spot had been number twenty-five.

The two numbers struck me as more than just an eerie coincidence. 12-25 was Christmas Day and the name Five Star must have represented the Star of David. The spirit of Jesus was following me wherever I went.

This knowledge was very comforting, yet I still couldn't shake the feeling that God the Father was trying to tell me something else. As excited as I was about the immediate future, I was equally intrigued by what God would choose to reveal to me.

I didn't say a word to my mother during the two-block walk to the hospital. Instead, all my energy was used to try to figure out what was going to happen next. I imagined my father, Uncle Harry, Burt Lewis, Mr. Malone, and Poppy all greeting me upon my arrival at the hospital. After I was briefed on some of the facts, we would hold a major press conference announcing the overthrow of The Pines drug ring. By tomorrow morning the entire free world would know of our heroism.

I was disappointed, but not disheartened, when no one greeted us at the hospital. I was just going to have to be patient for a little while longer. Everything was going to break soon enough. It was pointless to try to ascertain my Uncle Harry's strategy. So, instead, I focused my attention on my medical appointment.

My mother stopped at the security desk in the main lobby and asked a female guard for directions. I noticed the woman's hat, which was placed sideways on top of the desk. Inside the hat was a little index card that read: "Jesus Loves You" in bold. I stored this message away for future reference.

Jim Freeman was already waiting for us when we walked into the waiting room of Dr. Schwartzman's office. Dressed in a white jacket, white shirt, tan slacks, and brown loafers, he looked like a junior Marcus Welby. I was pleasantly surprised to see him there.

After we all said hello, the three of us sat down on the sofa while we waited for Dr. Schwartzman. Jim explained that he was on-call all evening.

"What does that mean?" my mother asked.

"Well, unless an emergency situation arises, I'll be able to assist with Dennis's evaluation. If that's all right with you, of course," he said turning towards me.

"By all means, Doctor Jim. Join the party."

The conversation turned to my compulsive behavior. Jim chuckled as he listened to my mother describe some of the quirks of my obsessive personality. "My dad's the same way. Last spring, on a whim, he decided to plant Christmas trees in our backyard. He must have planted a hundred of them."

Outwardly I smiled politely, but internally my brain was working overtime to try to grasp the meaning of yet another religious symbol. First the parking lot, then the hat, and now the Christmas trees. What was going to be next?

These thoughts were put on hold for a while with the appearance of Dr. Schwartzman. He was a slim, gray-haired middle-aged man who looked pretty much as I had anticipated. After brief introductions, I followed the doctor and Jim into an examining room.

"Take your shirt off and hop up on that table please, Dennis," Dr. Schwartzman instructed. I liked this guy's style. He remained friendly without sacrificing any of his professionalism.

The doctor took me through a routine physical with impressive alacrity. He then proceeded to administer a series of motor function tests. I winked at Jim as I effortlessly breezed through the tests.

When we were finished, Dr. Schwartzman pinned my M.R.I. images to a glass fixture placed against a wall, and then scrutinized them closely under an intense light.

"That's all I need to see. You can send your mom in here now," he said after just a couple of minutes.

"Well, Doctor. What do you think?"

"Mrs. Mulhearn, your son is in perfect health. He is a superb physical specimen. He exhibits no evidence of even the slightest amount of neurological damage." As always, my mother took this positive news cautiously.

"What about the cyst? Is that a problem?"

"Take a look for your self," Dr. Schwartzman said, pointing to one of the images that had an overhead view of my brain. "As you can see, there is a small cyst located in an area called the Pineal Lobe. The surrounding brain tissue, however, remains completely unaffected. This indicates that the cyst had been there for many years, probably since birth. It is definitely not the cause of any psychiatric problems Dennis may have experienced."

It was not just what Dr. Schwartzman said, but the certitude with which he expressed his findings that eased my mother's worried mind. Prior to leaving the office, I made sure to thank the doctor personally.

Jim convinced me and my mother to stop at an Italian restaurant with him before we drove back to Jersey. We sat down at a checkered table, and I ordered two large cheese-steaks. When the food came, I ate my sandwiches slowly, savoring the distinctive flavor of a Philadelphia specialty.

10

JUDGMENT DAY

It was nearly ten o'clock when I pulled into our driveway. Kevin was waiting up to find out the results of my examination. He was relieved when our mother told him Dr. Schwartzman's diagnosis.

"Don't act so surprised. I've been telling you guys the same thing for weeks," I said.

"You're right, Den. Just don't go making any more predictions for us," Kevin replied.

Before he trudged off to bed he showed me and my mother a *New York Times* article about a new drug for mental illness. Since I knew I wasn't ill, I wasn't interested in the article until I heard the name of the drug. This new so-called wonder drug was called Clozapine. Either this was yet another coincidence, or someone was sending me a not too subtle message to "Close The Pines."

I was deeply troubled by this new revelation. It was now clear that Uncle Harry, Burt Lewis, and all the other police, did not have the ability to combat the supernatural forces that controlled the drug empire. I was the one person with the power to stop The Pines. Everyone was standing by, waiting for me to fulfill my destiny. The only problem was that I had no idea what I was supposed to do next.

My mother called down from her bedroom and asked me to bring in a movie from the backseat of her car. When I returned to the house, I saw that that film was *The Hunt for Red October*. I found it odd that she had selected this particular movie. My ordeal had started in October, was "Red October" a metaphor for the week I had spent at The Pines? Hoping to find some clues, I popped the video into the VCR.

To my dismay, I was unable to follow the plot. My mind was spinning dangerously out of control in a desperate attempt to solve the mystery of my life. Who was I? What was my purpose? I stared blankly at the T.V. set, trying hard to put all the elusive pieces of the puzzle together. The puzzle was expanding exponentially at a rate that was beginning to overwhelm me. It took a tremendous amount of energy just to keep all my thoughts straight.

I blocked out my rambling thoughts long enough to watch the last few minutes of the movie. After narrowly averting a nuclear disaster, the Russian submarine captain (Sean Connery) speaks to his American counterpart about "a new dawn." Was that it? Was I supposed to usher in a "new dawn?" If so, how was I going to accomplish this?

My confusion remained with me throughout the night and into the early morning. The pressure to come up with a workable solution was almost unbearable. I felt as if I had the entire weight of the world on my shoulders. I needed to find some answers fast.

I was still searching for these answers when Thomas knocked on my door at about 7:30 a.m. He told me had had missed his bus and would need a ride to school. "No problem, Tom. Tell Kevin to hustle up. I have to drop him off first."

The frigid air stung my face as I followed my two brothers out the front door. Winter had finally asserted itself.

"Turn on the FAN," Thomas said from the back seat, while we waited for my car to warm up. I flicked on the radio in time to hear the end of Don Imus' (WFAN's morning disc jockey) scathing critique of *The Today Show*. I found the piece amusing, but Kevin and Thomas both carried on as though it were the funniest comedy routine they had ever heard.

They continued laughing and joking all the way to Gordon's Corner. Kevin was especially exuberant. I hadn't seen him this happy and relaxed since the day before I had first started at The Pines.

"Have a real good day, Den," he said before getting out of the car. I knew my twin well enough to recognize there was something he wasn't telling me. Why was he so happy?

Thomas remained in the back seat while I backtracked to Manalapan High School. He didn't say much, and I was grateful for the chance to piece my thoughts together. Something strange was going on here, and I was very close to unraveling the mystery. I stopped at a red light two blocks away from the high school.

"Take your time, it's a long light," said Thomas. The light turned green in less than five seconds. I turned my head around, raised an eyebrow at my brother, and then shared a good laugh with him. "Don't think so much, Den. You might hurt yourself," he said.

After I dropped him off, I stopped to watch Thomas walk into the front entrance of his school. He moved with an aura of self-confidence and maturity I had not seen before. My kid brother was growing into a fine young man. Out of the corner of my eye, I noticed a girl staring at me from a second floor window. She quickly moved away from the window as soon as she saw that I had observed her.

As I drove though the parking lot I wondered why the girl had been staring at me. "Do these kids know who I am and what I'm supposed to do? If they do, how many other people know about me?"

On the radio, Imus was talking about the historical significance of today's date. December 7, 1990 marked the 49th anniversary of the bombing of Pearl Harbor. In addition to this infamous event that propelled the United States into World War II, tomorrow was going to be the anniversary of John Lennon's murder.

I turned the radio off and pondered what all this meant. I had known that today was going to be an important day even before I had heard of its historical perspective. Kevin and Tom had all they could do to contain their excitement. They both knew I was going to do something great today but were not permitted to say anything about it. It was entirely up to me to search inside my soul and discover the secret of my ultimate destiny.

The urgency I had felt all night was gone now and replaced by the inspirational knowledge that this was the day I would finally have all the answers. As I turned down Tarrytown Road the blurry picture was finally coming into focus. I knew exactly who I was and what I needed to do. By the stroke of midnight I would be blessed with the gift of total recall.

Imus's mention of John Lennon's death provided the final clue. Lennon was a brilliant artist who spread the message of peace in many of his songs. His wonderful music was secondary, however, to his bold social vision of a world ruled by love and humanity, instead of by hatred and greed. Mark Chapman may have squeezed the trigger of the gun that ended his life, but I believed that it was the devil who had really killed him. Satan had every reason to fear one of the greatest men of our time.

God had inspired Don Imus to talk about Lennon's assassination, knowing that it would help me reach an understanding of my destiny. It started me thinking about all the injustices that occur every day. Although I was an eternal optimist, it was impossible to ignore the ever-increasing violence, racial tensions, and unadulterated hatred that were spreading through society like blazing forest fires.

Fortunately, I had the ability to reverse this horrible trend and finally end Satan's brutal reign. God had granted me the power to stop Satan before he destroyed the earth. Regardless of how blatantly clear it had become by this time, the realization of my true identity was mind-boggling.

I was the Second Coming of Jesus Christ!

My body trembled with excitement. While I was aware that it was quite common for mental patients to develop the belief they are God (known as a "Messianic Complex" by mental health professionals), I had never been more sure of my sanity. From the day I was first admitted to the hospital, I had received countless signs designed to help me discover my true self. Of all the signs, the cross on the wall was the most important. The Father had shown me the cross to trigger the memory that I had once made the ultimate sacrifice for my fellow man.

Had a devil's advocate been present, he would have asked me some questions such as: Why did it take more than twenty-six years to learn you are Jesus? If you are the true Christ, aren't you supposed to be completely free of sin? Why can't you perform miracles?

If I had stopped to consider any one of these questions, I might have chosen a different course of action. However, I had no time to concern myself with inconsequential details. I was the savior and I had a job to do.

I left my car running in the driveway and walked over to the curb. I took off my gray suede jacket and threw it on top of a pile of garbage bags. The jacket had been a birthday gift from Vicki. Discarding it among the trash was my way of erasing my memories of her. I had always thought she was a great girl, but now I realized that she must have been very tainted to reject a union with the Son of God. Her failure to contact me since my release from the hospital reinforced these beliefs.

I ran inside the house and quickly retrieved my Sony tape player from Thomas's room and a blue windbreaker from my closet. As I slammed my car door and began backing out of the driveway, I surveyed my house one last time. I wasn't sure if I was ever going to see it again. I couldn't see anyone, but I could feel scores of eyes peeking out their windowsills, hoping to catch a glimpse of me as I drove down the block. I couldn't resist giving a confident "thumbs up" sign to my admirers before I turned the corner.

Once on the highway, I drove slowly, keeping my speed between forty-five and fifty-five miles per hour. I had all day to close The Pines. I no longer feared any possible consequences of returning to South Fallsburg. Re-hospitalization, imprisonment, or even death, could not prevent me from fulfilling the prophesies that had been recorded long ago in the Holy Scriptures.

I zipped along the Garden State Parkway without bothering to stop and pay any of the tolls. After today money would be as obsolete as the horse and buggy. My thoughts were getting increasingly clear with each passing minute. I understood what Thomas had meant when he mentioned the "long light." The light he had referred to was the new way of life I was going to usher in. I had the power to break through the darkness and change the harsh realities of life, ending Satan's legacy of evil, hatred, and pain.

In order to accomplish this lofty goal, I was going to have to confront Satan and banish him from the earth forever. Along with my divinity came the knowledge of the devil's most guarded secret. I knew who he was. Throughout history he had taken the form of so-called "people" such as Genghis Kahn and Adolf Hitler. This time he had cleverly selected a female body to hide in. He arrogantly took the name of God's first woman. As sure as I was that I was the true Christ, I was equally certain that the woman known as Eve Cantor harbored the flesh of Satan!

This knowledge caused me to rethink many of my previous conclusions about The Pines. Steve Richman, Bruce Smythe, and many of the others were not bad people. They were simply too terrified of Eve's power to do anything to try to stop her. Before the day ended I would give them all a chance to redeem themselves.

After I drove past the last New Jersey exit I turned on the radio with the hope of garnering more information. The D.J. spoke of a major conference today at the United Nations in New York. The leaders of the world know what is going to take place today. Uncle Harry and other biblical scholars have prepared them for my final conquest against Satan.

They were all gathered not to deal with problems of the Middle East, but to hear my holy message and to share in my victory. The cyst inside my brain was not there by accident, nor was it a meaningless physical aberration. It was a complex biological transmitter, given to me at birth by God the Father for the sole purpose of communicating with every nation of the earth on this monumental day. Every person in the world would be able to hear my message, and then have the same opportunity to renounce Satan and come follow me.

When I entered the New York State Thruway I decided that it was time to procure more spiritual knowledge. I pressed the play button on my Sony, expecting to hear the majestic voice of my Heavenly Father. Instead of receiving a divine message, I was treated to a rendition of Bing Crosby singing "White Christmas." Thomas had replaced my blank tape with an old Christmas tape I hadn't heard in years.

While I was enjoying the music, the first snowflake fell from the sky. The brief flurry that followed only lasted a few minutes, but its profundity was apparent. It was not yet time to hear the voice of my Father or see his image, but he had expressed his supreme confidence in my ability to carry out his will.

I was not going to get any detailed instructions or advice about what to do. But that was fine with me. As the son of God, I trusted that my instincts alone would be enough to carry me through any situation I might come across. I was ready for anything.

As I grew nearer and nearer to my final destination, I took some time to review my life, knowing that everything I had experienced had been meant to prepare me for this moment in time. After I had finished reexamining my adult and teenage years, I recalled two significant events from my early childhood.

At age five, I had my tonsils and adenoids removed. There was nothing uncommon about this except that I had remained hospitalized for a full week. Only now did I stop to wonder why I had stayed there for so long. The answer to this question was obvious. The doctors who had performed the operation had detected something unusual about me. When I was asleep at night, they had anesthetized me and studied my intricate brain in great detail. I was released from the hospital only after all their efforts had failed to produce any conclusive results.

Three years later, when I was in the third grade, I wrote a play called *The Christmas Without a Santa Claus.* The plot focused on Santa's refusal to deliver any presents to the children of the world. He felt that all the commercialism and greed had caused people to forget the true meaning of Christmas.

Things looked gloomy until Jesus himself comes down to earth and visits Santa on Christmas Eve. He convinces the jolly fellow that most people are basically good at heart. They just need to be reminded of what is really important from time to time. After Jesus's pep talk, Santa dusts his sleigh off, makes his appointed rounds, and saves the day for the children.

When I showed my teacher the story, she was astounded by the depth of my writing. She was impressed enough to cancel the traditional Christmas pageant and have my class perform my original play in front of the entire school. Inspired by this surprising recognition, I completed a New Year's play with the same moralistic theme a few weeks later.

The memories of my earliest writings made me break into a wide smile. Even at that tender age, I had a subconscious inkling of my true essence. The Christmas play in particular was a powerful omen of the future. I had written a semi-autobiographical story with a unique plot twist. The fictional character called Santa Claus represented me. It was my spirit that traveled the earth to touch the heart of every child and bring him or her the gift of love.

This gift was what made Christmas such a great day. Long after the fire trucks are broken and the Barbie dolls discarded, the special feeling of being loved by those closest to him or her remains with each child forever. In our unabashedly materialistic society, many people had lost sight of this simple fact. The problem had magnified tenfold in the eighteen years since I had written my play. Now it was time to get back to the basics.

I finally arrived in South Fallsburg. Although it was approaching noon, the streets were deserted. The townspeople must have been aware of my omniscience. As I drove through town, my feelings of excitement were mingled with a certain amount of trepidation. The knowledge of the ultimate outcome did not relieve my anxiety about facing the unknown. Only God the Father knew what was going to happen. I didn't have a clue.

Father, make me worthy to be your son, I prayed silently, while I pulled into The Pines's parking lot. Since there were only two cars parked there, I assumed Eve had been aware of my coming and had orchestrated a last minute evacuation of the hotel. What other tricks did she have up her sleeve?

I stepped out of my car into the cold South Fallsburg air. A brisk wind dropped the wind-chill factor down into the single digits. Ignoring the elements, I strode confidently through the open front gates and approached the main entrance to the lobby. I stopped a few feet short of the steps and scanned the area. There was not a soul in sight but I could feel Satan's ominous heart surrounding me. Surprisingly, I felt no fear.

"Eve Cantor, Satan, Devil, Lucifer, or whatever you wish to call yourself, your time is up. I know who you are and what you've done. I have come to carry out the will of your creator," I said with the boldness of a deity. "Show yourself. Let me see your true form."

The sing-song whistle of the swirling wind set the stage for a dramatic showdown. When nothing happened, I began to taunt my adversary. "C'mon, let's see what you got. Try some of that evil power on me." Still no response. It was just as I had thought. The ultimate bully lacked a pair of gonads. He was cowering behind a tree, terrified by the mere sound of my voice.

"Get off my earth. In the name of my Father in Heaven, I command you to leave this world right now. Go inside the ground and crawl back to the center of the earth where you came from and where you belong, you miserable, vile, deceitful excuse of a creature," I shouted above the wind. I had wanted to call him a few more colorful names but refrained from doing so. It would have been inappropriate for the incarnation of Jesus Christ to use street language.

My words were met by a foreboding silence. After a couple of minutes, the roaring wind died down to a light breeze. The battle was over. Satan had fled without even trying to fight. He was totally intimidated by my strength. The surge of pride I felt from my victory was tempered by my knowledge that my mission was only half complete. The other half of the mission was equally important.

I was to give a great speech in which I would share my infinite wisdom with the entire world. I realized now that the cyst inside my brain not only had telepathic powers, but also had electronic capabilities as well. People could see and hear me on television sets and radios all over the world. They had already witnessed my confrontation with the beast and were now waiting anxiously to hear my vision of our new future.

I decided that my old room would be a good place to begin my oration. I walked around the side of the hotel past a deserted security office and entered the main building through the side entrance. The low hum of a Coke machine next to the elevator was the only sound that could be heard.

The sight of room number 261 filled me with mixed emotions. This was the room where my journey to discover the great secret locked inside my mind had all begun. Nevertheless, I could not forget the dreadful fear that had immobilized me on that same night. I was embarrassed by my weakness but rationalized that I had not yet been made aware of the power I possessed.

I shouldn't have been surprised when my old key no longer worked, but it hadn't occurred to me that they would have changed the lock the day after I was fired. I hesitated momentarily and considered where I should go next. I wanted everything to be perfect. Wait a minute. I know exactly where to go. I smiled as I walked back inside the elevator.

I stepped outside again, made a sharp right and headed directly for the baseball field, which was located behind the tennis courts. The magical allure of the game of baseball had captivated me since I was a little boy. I could not have chosen a more poetic site to deliver the words mankind had been anticipating for almost two thousand years.

I hardly noticed the bare spots and knee-high weeds that sprouted up sporadically through The Pines's infield. As seen through my glazed eyes, the field was as beautiful as Yankee Stadium itself. I was very conscious of the symbolism of what I was doing. Thanks to me, humanity had come full circle. Now it was time to take one last homerun trot. I circled the bases as slowly as possible, and savored the sensation of the soft earth beneath my feet. As I rounded second base and headed for third, I cleared my throat and began to talk.

"Hello, my name is Dennis Mulhearn. As many of you know by now, I am the person who was known as Jesus Christ in my first life. Today is the Day of Atonement. I will do my best to explain what lies ahead for us, and I'll try to answer all the questions I'm sure you have.

"First of all, don't worry if you are not a Christian. I don't care if you're a Jew, Buddhist, Mormon, Jehovah's Witness, or even an atheist for that matter. There is a certain amount of truth in every religion, but each of them is flawed in one way or another. I have found that the world's religions have some markedly different belief systems but they all share the common theme of living life as virtuously as possible.

"That is all I care about. If you have made a genuine effort to be a person of good character, and more often than not have treated your fellow man with respect, kindness, and compassion, then you have unknowingly worshipped me and my Father. All religions originate from man's basic need to find spiritual truth. You can stop searching. I am the truth. Believe in me and trust in me."

While I was enlightening the masses, I continued walking around the bases over and over again. Life was going to be one never-ending homerun trot from here on in.

"Christianity is the true religion, of course, but it too has been distorted by man over many centuries. The Catholic Church is the most egregious culprit in this matter. The wickedness and corruption of the Pre-Reformation era produced a whiplash effect, which is largely responsible for making modern Catholicism a religion of guilt and denial.

"The Church has subtly and sometimes not too subtly perpetrated the myth that sex is a dirty, sinful act. They have perverted the most natural and greatest gift that my Father has bestowed upon the human race. Furthermore, the practice of prohibiting clergy from marrying is no less inane than the ancient custom of self-flagellation. To all the priests listening to me, let me say this. I respect your devotion but now it is time to go out and find yourself a good woman. My Father would never deny anyone the joy of raising a family."

I was on a roll now, enjoying this tremendous forum in which I could espouse my erudite views on the misconceptions of organized religion. "Most Protestant denominations are more modern than Catholicism, but they also have some fundamental beliefs that are erroneous. As I stated before, you don't have to believe in the Christian faith to join my kingdom.

"I realize that if you are born in India or Israel, you will likely be raised in the prevalent religion of your culture. I will not penalize anyone for not having proper access to Christianity. I can't do that because religion is not a personal choice. You are all impressionable children when your parents teach you that their spiritual beliefs are undeniable facts. Thus, regardless of your religion, you are all subject to this 'generational brainwashing.'

"I'm sure many of you have questions about the Holy Bible. The Bible is the greatest book ever written. It was designed to educate and enlighten you about my past and future, and help you live your life with the purity in which I lived mine. The New Testament is supposed to help you understand that the love you share for each other is all that really matters.

"Unfortunately, many Christians have decided that every word in the Bible needs to be taken literally. Not only is this incorrect, it is also impossible to do. Aside from the infinite possible interpretations, there are quite a few conflicting theorems presented in the Book as well. If you want to translate each paragraph, you can prove any number of statements that contradict each other. No, my friends, the Bible was meant to be a guide, not a manual. The discrepancies are there because the words were written by men, many of whom wrote of stories their fathers and grandfathers had told them."

By this time I had circled the bases at least eight or nine times and was beginning to get a little dizzy. I decided that the golf course would be the right place to continue my historic discourse. On my way over there, I examined our most pressing social issue: drugs.

"As some of you know, Satan has been running a drug operation from this hotel. Sadly, some of the richest men in this country and in the world are bloodsucking drug dealers. They are the generals in Satan's army, but all the money in the world will not be able to save them from my wrath. Thankfully, the drug dealers no longer rule the earth. I do. The rules are going to change.

"Your body is the temple in which you house your soul. Don't abuse it with drugs, alcohol, cigarettes, or any other foreign substance. Every time you take drugs, you weaken your spirit, and leave yourself vulnerable to the lure of one of Satan's cunning traps. In order for your mind and soul to be strong, you must first cleanse your body of all its impurities."

I stood on the first tee and marveled at the raw beauty of the green landscape before me. The Pines's golf course was designed by the famous architect, Robert Trent Jones, and although I never had the chance to play it, I could recognize a work of art when I saw one. As I started down the lush fairway, I felt like Jack Nicklaus walking the 18th at Augusta. I was the champion of champions.

Switching topics once more, I turned my attention to something else I felt strongly about: my patriotism.

"It should not be surprising to anyone that I have come from the United States of America. The U.S. is the greatest country in the history of civilization. At the turn of this century, men and women emigrated here from all nations with nothing but the hope of building a better life for their families in the 'land of opportunity.' Today, every living American is a fortunate recipient of the dreams of those courageous pioneers.

"Unfortunately, many Americans have forgotten their heritage and their roots. It is all too easy to take for granted the freedom and the liberties our ancestors risked their lives for. As of this day, all of our cities, suburbs, and small towns will be restored to their former greatness. Today will mark the beginning of the return of the old values that made us the world's leading democracy."

Feeling sheepish about the extent of my provincialism, I sung the praises of other cultures and promised a merger of the best ideas and principles. Indeed, countries and states were now just meaningless names on a map.

As I plodded through the first green and toward the second tee, I realized that my own background was very relevant. Since I was justifiably proud of my Irish-Italian heritage, it was a great pleasure to share my genealogy with the world. After I had finished recounting my family tree as thoroughly as possible, I began a longwinded monologue that was roughly the equivalent of twenty consecutive Academy Award acceptance speeches.

"I'd like to thank my father, Thomas Lee Mulhearn, my mother, Mary Ann Michaela Mulhearn, my brothers Kevin, Sean and Thomas, and my sister Deirdre, for their indomitable strength, courage, and love that helped me to survive an arduous battle against evil. Without their help, I would not have been able to fulfill my destiny."

I proceeded to thank my friends from Chi-Chi's, ex-teammates, teachers, coaches, and anyone who had touched my life in a meaningful and positive way. I was grateful for all the kindness and wisdom I had received throughout my life, from peers and authority figures alike.

Now I was giving these individuals the highest honor, naming each of them personally in my address to the world. I put my memory bank into overdrive, and made sure I left no one out. About halfway through the process, I realized just how many friends I had helping me along my journey. Psychotic or not, it was an uplifting experience to recall all the people who had unselfishly given of themselves. When I was finished, I had recited close to three hundred names.

I was standing on the fourth green now and the inclement weather was starting to bother me. Hey, I'm God. I don't have to stay out here in the cold if I don't want to, I reasoned. I took a shortcut through the hotel grounds and returned to the warmth of my car, from where I began discussing the concept of salvation.

"For those of you not familiar with Christianity, although my Father is the creator of the universe, he has given me the responsibility of judging each man and woman. Don't be afraid my brothers and sisters. Many of you will be quite surprised by my leniency. Look inside your heart; if you can honestly say that you have tried your best to model your life after me, then you may begin celebrating. You will join me in what I can best describe as a great party that will last for all eternity. After fifty years of paradise on this earth, my Father will take us up to Heaven in chariots driven by angels. There, he will show us new treasures beyond our wildest imagination.

"For those of you with cold hearts hardened by your wicked deeds, I give you this final warning. This Day of Atonement will be your last chance to repudiate Satan and grasp the gift of everlasting life. No matter how repugnant your sins are, I will forgive you and welcome you into my kingdom with open arms if you sincerely choose to come follow me. You are running perilously short of time, however. Unless you can free yourself from Satan's bondage, you are doomed to miss the party. When your physical body eventually dies, your soul will disintegrate along with it."

I was interrupted by a security guard rapping on my window. I had been so immersed in my speech I hadn't noticed the security van pull up beside me. I rolled down my window, curious to hear what this guy would have to say. The security force was the one department of the hotel that I was certain Eve had absolute control over.

"Can I help you, Dennis?" he asked timidly.

"No. May I help you?" I replied, amazed at his audacity to question me.

"Yes, you can. The hotel is closed this week. You are trespassing here. Please leave, or I'm gonna have to call the cops." The fear in his voice was unmistakable. I felt sorry for this weak pawn of Eve Cantor's.

"No problem. I'll leave. My work here is finished. It's not too late for you, but unless you stop believing your bosses' lies, you're going to miss the party." The look of confusion in his face gave me hope that he was seriously considering my offer. I drove off, confident that his interaction with me had saved his soul.

Immediately after I turned onto the New York State Thruway, I noticed that the needle on my fuel gauge was below the "E." This posed an interesting question. Could I simply will the car to run, or was I going to have to stop and get some gas? Since I was not sure of the extent of my powers, I took the next exit and pulled into a gas station.

That I didn't have a dime in my pocket was completely immaterial. I filled up my tank in the self-service aisle and waved to the man working the cash register. He pretended not to notice me but I knew that he knew who I was. He was simply too humbled by the force of my personality to turn away from the counter. The experience didn't hurt my ego but I didn't feel an overwhelming need to be worshipped. Seeing everyone come together was what was going to bring me immeasurable joy.

When I got back on the highway, I sensed something was wrong. Three miles down the road, I realized that I was again headed toward The Pines. How was this possible? I was positive that I had turned back onto the southbound Thruway. Don't try to figure it out. God wants me to return to The Pines. He has something planned for me there.

My excitement grew substantially when I realized exactly what was awaiting me at the hotel. My reign as the ruler of the world was going to officially begin with a private party in the lobby of The Pines. My family, friends, and closest relatives were now assembling there to help me celebrate our wondrous victory. Cory was going to be there as well. It was finally safe for us to be reunited. There were so many things I wanted to tell her, I didn't know where to start.

The parking lot of the hotel was as empty as it had been before. I wondered where everybody had parked their cars. Maybe they had all been transported by helicopter. When I reached the front gate, I saw Bruce Smythe, bundled up in a blue parka, walking toward the side door. I smiled at him, happy to see him released from Eve's powerful stronghold. He smiled back at me and ducked inside the door.

I gave Bruce a few minutes to alert everyone of my arrival and then followed him through the door. I wasn't fooled by the misleading silence that enveloped the hotel. The place was going to erupt as soon as I entered the lobby. On the elevator ride up, I couldn't decide what I was looking forward to more, seeing my mother and father dancing together again, or seeing Poppy for the first time in twelve years.

The elevator door slid open and I was again greeted with more deafening silence. Two girls working innocuously behind the front desk were the only people in the room. Oh, of course. They must all be upstairs in the upper lobby and fining room area.

To my disappointment, the upper lobby was equally abandoned. I noticed that the doors of the dining room were locked shut, and walked over to investigate. I pressed my face against the glass doors and peered closely inside the dark room but I still couldn't see any signs of life. My attention was diverted by the sound of the elevator door opening again. I turned around in time to see six uniformed guards, each of whom wore a scowl on his face, emerge from the elevator. They ran at me with the fury of a pack of wild dogs in heat.

Although I gave them no resistance, they roughly pushed and shoved me toward the elevator. "Hey Mothafucka, get the fuck out of here before you get hurt," said one of the more educated guards. Their callous treatment infuriated me. After everything I had said and done, these assholes were still running around like scared little mice. I didn't like being treated with such a lack of respect, but reminded myself that persecution by the ignorant was part of the package.

One of the guards held the side door open, while two others attempted to throw me out on my face. Fortunately, I grabbed hold of a railing just before I hit the hard pavement. I regained my balance, and proudly walked back to the parking lot without a scratch on my body. The guards' efforts to hurt me were pathetic. Had I been so inclined, I could have knocked each of them to the moon. But I didn't use my physical strength because violence was no longer the solution to all of mankind's problems. If I was going to preach peace and love, I needed to set an impeccable example for others to follow.

I put my divine mission aside for a moment, and wondered what six uniformed guards were doing in a "closed" hotel. How did they get to the lobby so fast? They must have been preparing for a drug transaction of some kind. I pitied them for their stupidity in following Eve's antiquated orders. If only they knew the price they would pay for their blind loyalty.

This minor setback did not dampen my enthusiasm. I was wrong about the party being at The Pines, but so what. I had the unique ability to look into the future and see a perfect world, so who cared if I missed a few of the details. Despite being the Messiah, I had to keep reminding myself that only God the Father had the blueprint for everything that was going to occur. It's not quite time yet. Soon, very soon. Be a little more patient. The party could very well be at my house in Manalapan.

During the first half of my long drive home, I shared my exhilaration with my worldwide audience. When I came to the New York Thruway again, I broke into my victory song: "Na-na-na-na, na-na-na-na, Hey-hey, Good-bye," I screeched repeatedly for more than thirty miles. Following that, I led a somber rendition of The Lord's Prayer, clearly ennunciating each and every word. It was a great thrill to introduce millions of people to this prayer for the first time.

By the time I had reached New Jersey, my throat was extremely hoarse. I shut up for the first time all day and relaxed into a deep state of meditation. My unrestricted imagination explored new tangents. Night had fallen but I wasn't even sure it was still December 7. Had God the Father propelled me into a time warp? Was it Christmas Eve already, or was I now somewhere in the year 2000?

As I entered Old Bridge, I was pulled back into reality by the sight of a hitchhiker on the side of Route 9. The young man looked to be about my age, and must have been freezing standing out there in the cold. I pulled off the highway and opened up my passenger door.

"Thanks a lot, buddy. My name's Jim."

"Nice to meet you, Jim. I'm Dennis Mulhearn. Where you headed?"

"Manalapan."

In the course of my conversation with Jim, I learned that he had lost his license due to an insurance screw-up.

"Don't worry about that," I said, "starting tomorrow you'll be able to drive anywhere you want to go."

Remarkably, he lived right around the corner from us on Old Queens Road. He was appreciative of the door-to-door service, but I didn't mind. I wanted to see exactly where he lived.

"Right there," he said, "the house with the circular driveway and the American flag in the window."

"I'll see you again sometime," I said, certain that the circle and the flag were both symbols of my eternal spirit.

My mother's house was not going to be the site of the great celebration party. Not on this night, anyway. Only her car and Frank's Buick were parked in the driveway. I walked inside and found them both upstairs in the kitchen drinking coffee. My mother was relieved to see me.

"Jeez Dennis. You had me so worried. Why'd you go back up there?" she asked.

"I did what I had to do. How did you know where I was?"

"The people from The Pines called, but I already knew something was wrong when I saw your good jacket outside in front of the house."

While I was talking to my mom, Frank made a conscious effort to avoid looking anywhere near me. His reaction proved what I had suspected as soon as I saw his car. He was a soldier in Satan's army who had been sent into my home to extract information about my thoughts and my general condition. I had to admit that it was a clever ploy on Satan's part, but his trickery was no match for my brilliant mind.

"Let me give you your medicine," said my mother, leading me into the bathroom. "Have you been taking the medicine?" Mindful of Frank's ever-so-attentive ears, I feigned disorientation.

"Uh   yeah, I've taken it … I think I took it. Maybe … I don't know. Did I take it?"

"I don't think so. It's very important that you take the medicine every night."

"I know. I'm sick, mom. I need help," I said, making sure I spoke loud enough for Frank to hear every word.

"That's good, hon. Coming to terms with your illness is the first step to recovery." She smiled and gently kissed me on the cheek. It bothered me that she thought I was nuts but I had to continue playing the game. She was a trusting and kind-hearted soul who would have never believed Frank's real motive for coming to see her.

I had forgotten to put my candy in the container, so the two pills my mother gave me were actually Haldol. I swallowed them without hesitation, anyway. This was part of my Father's plan. The intense internal struggle to reach an understanding of my destiny had prevented me from sleeping for an entire week. Now my exhausted body welcomed the chance to shut down for a few hours. I went to sleep expecting to wake up next to Cory Malone, just as in the movie *Total Recall*. When the sun came up tomorrow, there would be a new world order.

11
TEMPTATION

I slept until one o'clock the next afternoon. When I woke up, Cory was not by my side and nothing else had changed. Although nothing apocalyptic had happened, I remained completely sure of myself. The devil was on the run. He was exerting all his remaining power to postpone his impending doom. It was just a matter of time before I assumed my rightful position as King of Kings.

On Sunday morning my mother and Kevin called me into the kitchen for a discussion. My mother said she had spoken with Dr. Miller, and he wanted to readmit me into Centra-State so he could try a new drug on me.

"Fine. I don't need any new drugs, there's nothing wrong with me, but if that's what you want, I'll cooperate fully." My mother and brother looked at each other quizzically. They had both expected a long, bitter fight.

It wasn't difficult to read their minds. Why is he being so receptive? He hates the hospital, they were surely thinking. How could I explain that I accepted the suffering I was going to endure in the hospital. The humiliation of again being treated as a common mental patient was going to be worse than the numbing effects of the anti-psychotic drugs I would be forced to ingest. But as the savior, I gladly sacrificed my pride for the good of humanity. In a twisted form of machoism, I anticipated the psychological pain I would be subjected to with a certain amount of masochistic pleasure.

Deirdre drove me to Centra-State on Monday afternoon. The admitting procedure had become depressingly familiar. I was moved into the same room once again, now occupied by an older gentleman named Henry.

Henry and I hit if off right away. I learned that he suffered from a disorder which prevented him from leaving his home. After more than eight years as a prisoner in his own house, he was finally seeking medical assistance.

I didn't see Dr. Miller until the following morning. If he was annoyed at seeing my ugly mug again, he certainly didn't show it. He began the session by asking me why I went back to The Pines. I explained that it was something I had to do to fulfill my destiny.

"Do you think you're God?" he asked in a challenging tone of voice.

"No, of course not," I smiled, feigning incredulity. "I'm just on a very important mission from God." I was smart enough to realize that I could not divulge my true identity to anyone, especially not a psychiatrist. I hadn't lied to him, either. I didn't merely think I was God, I knew that I was the Second Coming of Jesus Christ.

"What about this cyst of yours. Your mother tells me you think it has some kind of powers. Do you still think that?"

"Yes. I'm not exactly sure who can hear me, but I know it's an electronic bugging device." Try as he might, the doctor couldn't refrain from smiling.

"You're a smart guy, Dennis. Don't you realize how ridiculous that statement is? I mean, really, it sounds like something right out of *The Twilight Zone*."

"I know it makes me sound crazy, but it's true nevertheless. I can't prove it, but you can't disprove it either."

Before I left his office, Dr. Miller assured me that I was back at Centra-State solely for therapeutic reasons. The new drug he was prescribing for me, in addition to the Haldol, was called Tegritol. It was an anti-seizure medication found to be effective for a large percentage of patients with neurological damage. I found Dr. Miller's proposed treatment plan laughable. Despite Dr. Schwartzman's expert opinion, he still thought my cyst was the cause of my supposed problems.

I was comforted by Dr. Miller's promise that I would be released in about a week, but time moved by at a snail's pace during my first few days back in the hospital. The side effects of the Tegritol were terrible. The drug made me dizzy, uncoordinated, and threw my balance off. I couldn't even walk without wobbling noticeably. Although I still believed I was Jesus Christ, I despised putting these damaging drugs inside my body, which was obviously not immune from the laws of biology.

I dealt with my boredom and impatience by escaping into unconsciousness whenever possible. My daily dose of Haldol made it easy to fall asleep at will. Henry began calling me "Rip," in reference to Rip Van Winkle. The moniker was well-earned. If not for meals and the mandatory group therapy in the mornings, I would have gladly stayed in bed all day.

Dr. Miller interpreted my excessive sleeping as a clear-cut sign of serious depression. He questioned me about my behavior on Sunday night. I explained that I wasn't depressed at all. In fact, I was extremely happy considering my circumstances. Sleep was just the most effective way to pass the time. The doctor wasn't satisfied with my answer.

"I'm going to start you on some Lithium. It will help treat your depression," he said, ignoring everything I had just told him. I'm not sure why, but I thought Lithium was a drug for seriously disturbed people. Actually, it was far less potent than the drugs I was already taking.

"No, Doc. I'm not taking anything for depression, because like I already told you, I'm not depressed. As a matter of fact, I'm not sick at all. I shouldn't even be taking the crap you're giving me now."

Dr. Miller persisted in trying to get me to change my mind but I remained stubborn. I had to draw the line somewhere.

He made it clear that my obstinate attitude was not going to be conducive to an early release from the hospital, but I didn't give a damn. The Haldol and Tegritol had already done enough damage. I wasn't going to be bullied into taking another drug. Furthermore, I had read that sometimes anti-depressants actually cause people to become even more depressed. No one had the right to ask me to treat my body as if it were a roulette wheel.

I lay awake in bed that night and tried to analyze my thoughts in the few minutes I had before I dozed off. A full week of Haldol had slowed my brain considerably, but it hadn't altered my beliefs that much. The only idea I was willing to reconsider was that my grandfather's death had been faked. It didn't matter that I had been wrong about that. Death was just an illusion anyway. Poppy was in Heaven, proudly watching my every move. It wouldn't be long before I saw him again.

On Monday morning two new patients were admitted onto the unit. A nineteen year-old girl named Katrina, and a twenty-four year-old man named Richie. Katrina was a shy, delicately built girl with straight, golden blond hair. In sharp contrast, Richie was loud, boisterous, and vulgar. He made a grand entrance onto our peaceful ward, spewing a stream of obscenities as he was escorted to his room. Well above average in height, he would have had an impressive physique were it not for a large beer gut. Along with his formidable size, his angry demeanor kept the orderlies alert.

My initial impression of Richie was negative. But when I got to know him better, I found that beneath his pompous exterior was a kind-hearted person struggling to escape from a wretched past. This young man had experienced one bad break after another. Many years of abuse and neglect were responsible for him being in Centra-State. I vowed to give him a place of honor in my new kingdom.

Katrina really didn't belong in the hospital. Her father had suffered a heart attack the night before, so she faked a panic attack to be near him. However unorthodox her strategy was, I admired her devotion to her father. I was delighted to hear that he had stabilized by early afternoon. When she returned from her visit with him, her radiant face told me that he was going to be fine.

Kevin had moved into his midtown apartment, so I was impressed when I saw that he had come with my mother to visit me. I was further pleased when he handed me a book called *The Iowa Baseball Confederacy* by W.P. Kinsella.

"It's about an epic game between a local Iowa team and the 1908 Chicago Cubs. It should help you kill some time," he said. I grabbed my brother's hand and thanked him ostensibly for the book. I was really thanking him for caring so much about me. Kevin knew me better than anyone. He could not have selected a more suitable book.

W.P. Kinsella was the author of *Shoeless Joe*, the book upon which *Field of Dreams* was based. I had read *Shoeless Joe* the weekend after Thanksgiving and loved every page. Kinsella wrote with a uniquely religious slant. He had insight into my divinity and understood that baseball wasn't just a game, it was man's most beautiful and highest art form. He intrinsically knew that baseball, God, and Life itself were woven together like the stitches of a brand new ball.

After Kevin and my mother left, I wanted to stay in my room and read my new book, but decided that I needed to show my face to the nursing staff. I shuffled into the dayroom and planted myself in front of the television set. Richie, Katrina, and a few other patients were watching a classic Christmas cartoon.

Although I had seen it at least twenty times and knew the dialogue almost word-for-word, I enjoyed the show as much as everyone else. The nurses looked pleased to see me interacting with other people. I knew that they thought I was an enigma. During my first two stays at the hospital, I had been garrulous and outgoing. This third time around, however, I had retreated far into myself, alone with only my thoughts and dreams. How could they account for such an abrupt change in my personality? They had no way of knowing about my spiritual awakening, which had transformed me from a grounded caterpillar into an omnipotent butterfly.

As I watched the end of the cartoon, I was reminded of the two plays I had written as an eight-year-old. My childhood stories were far more important than I had previously believed. They weren't merely symbolic harbingers of the future. They were revelations about what was going to take place as soon as I discovered my true identity. The future was now. And I was the future. In a way, Christmas Day was going to be my first birthday. Something wonderful was going to happen on that day, and on New Year's Eve as well. I was going to have to bide my time until then.

I met with Dr. Miller again on Wednesday evening. Katrina had been discharged in the morning, and Richie had spent the entire day bitching and moaning about being released as well. I could empathize with my friend's boredom and frustration, but could also see how annoying his incessant whining must have been to Dr. Miller. If anything, it was probably counter-productive.

In light of this, I didn't press the doctor about my own discharge. I would be better served by showing him, rather than telling him that I was ready to go home. I answered each of his questions with succinct, lucid answers.

Our talk was interrupted by a phone call. When his attention was diverted, I strained my neck to take a look at my chart. What I saw shocked me.

On the bottom of the page he had listed his clinical diagnosis: schizophrenia. Schizophrenia! The word itself denotes the harsh ugliness of the disease. I hardly knew anything about it, but knew enough to realize that I was being grouped with the likes of David Berkowitz and John Hinckley, Jr.

While Dr. Miller's diagnosis was unbelievably demeaning, I didn't bother to confront him about it. What was the point? For all its wondrous achievements and incredibly advanced technology, modern medicine was still sorely lacking in one important respect: it never failed to underestimate the power of the human spirit.

The entire spectrum of knowledge accumulated about the human body does not bring us any closer to answering the esoteric questions of how we came into being and what is the real purpose of our existence. Some things cannot be explained by science, yet the scientific community arrogantly chooses to dismiss or ignore anything that does not have tangible, physical properties. This oversight prevents us from achieving a true understanding of ourselves.

In their quest to conquer our physical bodies, doctors have lost sight of the fact that we are first and foremost spiritual beings. Life is not a biochemical equation. It is a mysterious adventure that each man and woman experiences in his or her own way.

Because of his inability to comprehend my unique mind, Dr. Miller labeled me "schizophrenic." I wasn't suicidal, depressed, or dangerous, so what else could he possibly call me? It was a horribly unfair label, but one that would soon disappear. At one time or another, all the great prophets in history had been accused of sorcery, witchcraft, or madness. Why should I be any different?

Dr. Miller hung up his phone and concluded our session shortly thereafter. I was so distracted, I didn't even remember to ask him when I could go home.

Over the next few days, I continued to make a concerted effort to spend more time in the day room. It was important to play the part of a socially adaptable, cooperative mental patient. I was watching T.V. there on Friday night, when a nurse informed me that I had a visitor. My mother had only stayed for fifteen minutes, so I assumed that she had forgotten to tell me something. I was very surprised to see Katrina standing in the hallway.

I almost didn't recognize the girl. In her two days at Centra-State, she had worn a raggedy old sweat-suit. Now she stood before me wearing a white Angora sweater, tight blue jeans, and high-heeled boots. She looked positively beautiful. As I moved closer to say hello, I smelled the sweet fragrance of her perfume. As much as I tried to fight it, I couldn't deny the sexual attraction that I felt toward her.

Normally it was against hospital policy for ex-patients to come back and visit, but since she had brought me a present, the nurses didn't have the heart to turn her away. We sat down in the Visitor's Room, and she handed me a neatly-wrapped box and said, "Merry Christmas, Dennis. I wanted to give this to you before you went home." Her gift was a black cashmere sweater that appeared to have been purchased at an expensive men's shop.

"Thank you, Katrina. That was really sweet of you. You didn't have to do that." I was touched by her generosity but a little confused by it as well. During her brief stay at the hospital, I had talked to her a few times and tried to be friendly, but she was only on the unit for two and a half days, so I had not had the time to get to know her all that well.

"Oh, that's all right. I just hope you like it," she said. "I was going to come here last night but I got into a car accident in East Brunswick."

"Were you anywhere near Chi-Chi's?" I asked.

"Yes, as a matter of fact, the girl I hit worked at Chi-Chi's." Katrina pulled the accident report out of her purse and showed it to me. The name of the other driver was Victoria Walsh, better known as "Vicky."

Under ordinary circumstances, I might have been spooked by this information. But these were no ordinary circumstances. I didn't attempt to compute the odds of these two strangers banging their cars into each other, nor did I try to understand the cosmic significance of this event. I just chalked it up as another example of the Father's intriguing plan. He must have had his reasons.

Katrina and I engaged in a sociable conversation. She talked about her eight month-old baby girl, and her husband, from whom she was separated. She edged closer to me and placed her hand on my forearm.

"Dennis, I have to be honest with you. I haven't been able to stop thinking about you since I left Wednesday. I really like you a lot." I didn't know what to say.

"Uh … thanks, Katrina. I like you, too," I blurted out. She leaned over and kissed me softly on the mouth. I could have turned away, but I didn't. Her wet lips were impossible to resist. Unfortunately, a nurse saw what we were doing and politely asked Katrina to leave.

"Man, oh man! That's some piece of ass," Richie remarked as she glided down the hallway.

I felt guilty about succumbing to her feminine charms. It was wrong. Cory was patiently waiting for me to be with her. She certainly wasn't running around kissing other men. The worst part of the whole experience was that my earthly desires had been violently unleashed. Had Katrina and I been given a little more privacy …

Later that night I wondered if Satan had sent her to tempt me with pleasures of the flesh. "Nah. She just couldn't resist me—I'm God. Every woman wants me, it's only natural." I had to be strong enough to exhibit some self control. If Cory could wait, so could I.

Dr. Miller finally gave me my discharge on the morning of Sunday, December 23. He did so with great reluctance. I sensed that he felt there was still something very wrong with me, but that he believed there was nothing further he could do for me in the hospital. The Tegritol experiment had failed miserably, and I had been adept at hiding my true thoughts from him. I told him only what I thought he wanted to hear.

When I called Kevin to tell him to pick me up at eleven o'clock, I asked him to dig up a couple of old sweatshirts.

Richie had worn the same dingy gray sweatshirt all week long and was badly in need of some clothes. Kevin couldn't find any sweatshirts in the house, so on his way to Centra-State he stopped at The Freehold Mall and bought two new ones.

Richie was so pleased with the gifts he insisted on carrying my bags to the lobby. It made me feel good to see how much my brother's generosity had cheered him. It was probably the nicest thing anyone had done for him in a long time. Before I said goodbye, I asked him what his last name was. "Pines. My full name is Richard Pines."

12

HOME FOR THE HOLIDAYS

I arrived home in the middle of a family argument. My mother and sister were screaming at each other. They were bickering about me. My mom had made plans months ago to go on a trip to San Francisco but, because of the circumstances, was having second thoughts. Deirdre was trying to persuade her to not cancel the trip. Kevin and I knew how much she had been looking forward to seeing California for the first time, so we tried to assuage her concerns.

"Don't worry about me. If it makes you feel better, I'll give Kevin my car keys while you're away. Hurry up. Get out of here. You're going to miss your flight," I said. "Bring us back some souvenirs."

"He'll be fine, Mom. There's no reason for you not to go," Kevin added.

As much as we were going to miss her for Christmas, we realized how much she loved to travel. This was too good an opportunity for her to pass up. Moreover, I believed that she was supposed to go to San Francisco. The vision of the Virgin Mary had been seen in California. Something special was going to happen in the Golden State and my mother was going to be there to witness it. Deirdre drove her to the airport.

A few hours later, I received an unexpected phone call from Vicki Stevens. I was thrilled to hear from her. Despite my preoccupation with Cory, Vicki sometimes drifted into my thoughts. Any remaining doubts that she might still be involved in a conspiracy against me dissipated as soon as I heard her soft, feminine voice. I wondered if she still loved me as much as I loved her.

When she said she wanted to come visit me right away, I nearly lost my breath. "Sure, kid. I'd love to see you. Put some gas in your car and c'mon over." It had been so long since she had been to Manalapan, I had to give her a new set of directions. When we were dating, the distance between our homes had prevented us from seeing each other as often we would have liked. But, nevertheless, we had each made the three hour drive many times.

Vicki knocked on my front door, looking as pretty as she had on the first day I met her at Albright. She wore a Kelly green blouse, tan slacks, and black heels that highlighted the curves of her lithe body. No words needed to be spoken. I let her in, and we hugged each other tightly for a long time. I didn't want to release her from my grasp.

"Damn, it's good to see you, kid."

"I know. I'm so glad I came. You look terrific, Dennis." She reached inside her purse for a Kleenex and wiped a stray tear from one of her eyes.

Deirdre, Sean, and Starlight were out doing some last minute shopping, while Kevin and Tom stayed home to observe me. "Don't hog her all to yourself, Den. Bring the girl up here so we can say hello," Kevin called from the dining room. Everyone in my family loved Vicki. They were all disappointed when things hadn't work out between us.

The four of us sat down at the dining room table and ate one of the dinners my mother had pre-cooked before she left. When all the dishes were cleared, Kevin and Thomas excused themselves and went downstairs to watch T.V. I took Vicki's hand and led her into the family room. We sat down and talked about many things. The good old days, the reasons for our breakup, our families, her career, et cetera.

I took a quick glance at the microwave clock in the kitchen. "It's getting late. Do you have to go home?" I asked.

"That depends."

"On what?"

"Do you want me to go?"

Her flirtatious smile got me instantly aroused. "No. There are a lot of maniacs on the road after eleven. You better stay until the morning," I said, with a devilish smile of my own.

While Vicki was washing up in the bathroom, I experienced a mental tug-of-war. Should I or shouldn't I? What about Cory? My raging hormones made the decision easy. I rationalized that there was nothing wrong with one last night of passion with someone for whom I cared deeply. As judge and jury, I ruled in favor of sex.

I gently placed her head on my pillow and slowly began removing her clothing, working from top to bottom. Although we had made love hundreds of times before, I felt as though I were a virgin on prom night. The chemistry between us was strong enough to light up a city.

It was all over in an embarrassing short amount of time, but she didn't seem to mind.

"I love you, Dennis," she whispered tenderly in my ear.

"Thank you. I love you too, kid. Always have and always will." I stroked the nape of her neck with my fingers.

"Things are going to be different, kid. I'm going to end the suffering. I have the gift to make the world a perfect place again. You won't believe how happy you're going to be. Your whole family, too."

Vicki sat up and looked at me apprehensively. "You think you're God, don't you?" she said in a way that implied a question rather than a statement.

"Is it that obvious?"

"Oh Jesus, Dennis!"

"Yup, that's me—Dennis/Jesus. Same thing. I am the true Christ."

She lowered her head and fought back tears. "Don't be sad, kid. I can do some great things now," I said. I told her of all the signs that had helped me reach an understanding of who I was. As far as I was concerned, the evidence was indisputable.

After recovering from the initial shock, Vicki used her knowledge of psychology to try to convince me that my beliefs were unfounded. She was extremely bright and asked all the right questions, but I had an excellent answer for every one of them.

"Prove you are Jesus!"

"I can't. You have to have faith."

"How can you account for the Holocaust, Vietnam, and all the senseless brutality in the world?"

"It's Satan's work. War, famine, violence, disease and every other negative thing you can thing of are all caused directly by the devil. He has undermined my Father's plan of perfection, but I have the power to end his rule."

"When?" When is all this going to happen?" she asked.

"I'm not exactly sure, either Christmas or New Year's Eve. By then everyone will know who I am." I was curious myself about what my Father had planned, but not knowing the details was going to make my inevitable coronation that much more fun.

"What about me. Am I going to be your woman?" It broke my heart to have to tell her no, but I had to be honest.

"No, Vicki. Another woman has been chosen for me. You are going to marry Kevin. He was known as John the Baptist in the Holy Bible. There is not a better man alive."

"That's silly, Den. Kevin's a great guy but he's not the man I love."

"In time you will come to love him even more than you love me. Your destiny has already been mapped out. Don't question it."

We didn't talk any more after that. What could she possibly say to me? Vicki fell asleep in my arms, as she had done so many times before. I ran my fingers through her thick hair, and enjoyed the feel of her soft skin for the last time. My time with this young lady was almost over, so I decided to stay up all night and memorize the contours of her face. It was a face I will not soon forget.

She woke up at eight o'clock in the morning. Remarkably, the sky was still black.

"That's really strange," she said, when I opened the blinds for her inspection.

"Do you still doubt that I am who I say I am?"

She mumbled something into her sweater and then quickly got dressed.

"Do me one favor, Dennis. If nothing happens by New Year's, will you admit that you have a problem and get some help?"

"Sure, kid. But don't worry. Something will happen." I held her close and kissed her goodbye.

I spent the rest of the day writing a letter of appreciation to each member of my family. The letters were corny and shamelessly sentimental but they came from the heart. My family had all done so much for me. I wanted to give each of them a gift that could not be bought at any department store.

I selected each word with great care and consideration. It was important to express my feelings as eloquently as possible. By the time I completed my work, it was approaching six o'clock. When I emerged from the solitude of my room, my brothers and sister gave me a derisive ovation. I hadn't told them anything, so they could only guess what I had been doing.

"Connie and Mark called. They invited all of us over to their house for dinner. Do you guys want to go?" Deirdre asked me, my brothers, and Starlight. Since we hadn't made any other plans, we decided to take them up on their offer. Connie and Mark were the proud parents of Andrew Wilson, the three year-old boy whom Deirdre cared for four days a week. They owned an expensive home in Colts Neck, an upper middle-class town near Freehold.

Sean put on a strikingly realistic Santa Claus costume and walked through the front door toting a bag full of toys. Andy didn't show the slightest trace of shyness or fear. He hopped right up on Sean's lap and flashed a wide toothless smile.

I don't know about everyone else, but I felt privileged to see Andy's wide-eyed innocence firsthand. His excitement continued to increase as he moved from one toy to the next.

"Take it easy, little man. Santa's running out of presents," Sean joked.

Connie's mother and father had come all the way from Pennsylvania to be with her and her family. They watched their grandson with delight as he tore through the gift wrapping paper with dazzling speed. Connie introduced us to them while Sean continued to hand Andy his gifts.

When Santa's bag was finally emptied, Connie put her son to bed and then served us a chicken-ala-king dinner. Soon after dessert, I began to experience an episode of inexplicable mental anguish. It came suddenly, without warning, but its impact was staggering.

I felt as if my whole body were being engulfed by a dark cloud, which carried the cumulative suffering of man with it. I was powerless to fight against the wave of depression that overcame me. I would have much preferred a large dose of physical pain to this psychological torture. My head felt as though it were going to explode.

Deirdre was the first to notice that something was wrong with me. "Do you feel all right, Dennis? Do you want to go upstairs and lie down in my bed?" she asked. I heartily welcomed the idea. As I looked up at her pink ceiling, I understood exactly what was happening. In order to save the world, I first had to take away every man's and woman's pain. My body was now absorbing this pain.

Because of my sorry condition, we cut our visit short and left a short while later. When we returned home, Deirdre assumed my mother's nurturing role and immediately gave me a Haldol pill. I swallowed it without debate and fell into a sound sleep. The pain was finally gone.

The pain was still gone when I awoke on Christmas morning. In contrast to the previous night, I was filled with a sense of well-being and peacefulness. This was the day I had anticipating for so long. I doubted if even little Andy was more excited than I was.

Deirdre and my brothers had let me sleep until 11:30. They had already opened all their presents and were now patiently waiting for me to open mine. It took me quite a while. There were enough presents underneath the tree to start a department store. After I opened the last box, I went upstairs and returned with my letters. When I finished reading them out loud, there wasn't a dry eye in the house.

Despite protests from Kevin and Deirdre, I insisted on driving to New City. We needed to take two cars, and I was perfectly capable of driving my own vehicle. Kevin and Tom rode with me, while Deirdre rode shotgun with Starlight and Sean. None of us liked to fight the holiday traffic, but since the divorce, it was a sacrifice we gladly made every year to see our father.

Christmas had always been a special day for our family. My father used to disappear right after Thanksgiving, not to show his face again until Christmas Eve. He moonlighted as a cab driver, bouncer, and delivery man, and took any other job he could find to earn extra cash. Thanks to him and my mother, we always had some wonderful surprises waiting for us on Christmas morning.

The traffic was dense, but not as bad as we had expected. We moved steadily along the Garden State Parkway at forty-five miles per hour. Thomas had brought *The Godfather III* soundtrack, and Paul Simon's *Rhythm of the Saints* cassette tape with him to help pass the time. His selections could not have been more appropriate than if he had chosen a collection of church hymns. The music moved me deeply.

When we finally arrived at my father's home, he chided us for being so late. "I'm glad you guys found the house before it got dark," he said. Both he and Willie were upbeat. They seemed excited to have us all there with them to help celebrate the holiday.

On the living room coffee table was a recent issue of *Life* magazine. The cover read, "Who Is God?" I smiled. The world would learn the answer to that question very soon. "Take a look at the mantelpiece, guys. Your father is trying to give you a hint," Willie said, pointing to a picture frame next to the T.V. The frame was blank, with the inscription, RESERVED FOR MY FIRST GRANDCHILD, written inside it. We all had a good chuckle over that.

Neither my hospitalization nor my mental health was discussed. As far as my father was concerned, the entire episode was over and best forgotten. From my perspective, The Pines's drug scandal was hidden away in the outer realm of my consciousness. I never actually absolved my father or Willie, but I didn't even think about The Pines anymore. All I was concerned with was my divinity. Everything else was going to fall into place.

When we exchanged our presents, my father was rendered speechless by the letter I gave him. I think it meant more to him than any other gift he received.

I was considerably impressed by Willie's gifts to Star and Deirdre. She had made each of them a homemade doll, which had obviously entailed many hours of delicate work. The dolls were definitely not the product of an evil devil-worshipper. I was more than happy to admit that I had been very wrong about Willie.

The day was living up to all my expectations. I didn't say too much. I was content to just absorb all the love that was flowing through the living room. My father was in rare form telling jokes and talking about some of the zany characters we had known in Brooklyn. It was the happiest I had seen him since his divorce from my mother.

We left New City at eight o'clock and drove straight to Freehold, getting there just in time to catch the late showing of *The Godfather III*. The film's release had supposedly been pushed back a few weeks, but I knew that it was really right on schedule. Three hours later we stood in the parking lot and critiqued the final chapter of *The Godfather* saga.

"It was good, but not in the same league as the first two," Kevin said with an air of authority.

"All I know is that's the first time I ever saw Sean cry at a movie," said Star.

"I had something in my eye," Sean protested.

After everyone had offered their opinions, I gave my review: "That was the greatest movie of all time." Everybody burst out laughing.

"There he goes again, Mr. Hyperbole," said Thomas. No one would have laughed if they had known what was going through my mind. The connections I had made from the film were too numerous to count. Every scene was laced with symbolism and double meanings. The entire movie had been a birthday present to me from God the Father.

The Christmas lights on the house on the corner of my block were another reminder of what I had accomplished, and what was yet to come. I was the light of the world. I took the Haldol before going to bed and continued taking it all week. I assumed that since I was God, I could overcome the side effects of the drug by willing them away. I was right. Even with the drugs in my system, my energy level had never been higher.

My mother came home on Saturday, December 29. It was good to see her again. "So, how was San Francisco?" I asked, as I carried her luggage into her bedroom.

"Oh, it was wonderful. I've never seen such a beautiful city. I didn't like being away from you kids during Christmas, though. I won't do that again."

We sat down on the family room couch and she showed me the photographs she had taken. The city was indeed breathtaking. "It's amazing how fast they rebuilt the area after that earthquake," I remarked.

"Yeah, you're right. You would never even know that it had happened," she agreed.

Back in 1989, I had been in Chi-Chi's lounge in Kissimmee, Florida when I saw the earthquake on T.V. At the time, I found it strange that such a calamity should occur on the eve of the third World Series Game, but now it made perfect sense. God had used baseball to get the world's attention. He then performed a miracle rebuilding the city as suddenly as he had destroyed it.

When the people of California saw what He had done, they banded together and carefully guarded this secret. The commissioner of baseball, Fay Vincent, was a key figure in this movement. As a biblical scholar, he knew the danger of this information falling into the wrong hands. The miracle was a sign that Jesus was again walking the earth. But no one knew where he was living, or what his new name was.

I waited excitedly for New Year's Eve to arrive. On the stroke of midnight, everything was going to change. I didn't know exactly how, but I knew that the world was finally going to learn about me. With my secret revealed, the human race was going to come together and live as one. Racism, sexism, and discrimination of any kind would no longer exist. Drugs, alcohol, and even tobacco products were going to be impossible to find. All our social ills were going to vanish instantly. Every day was going to be like Christmas. I couldn't wait to get started.

My brothers and sister had a small New Year's Eve party at our house in Manalapan. They invited a few close friends over and bought some champagne and wine. I chose not to participate in the festivities. Instead, I rested in my mother's bed and waited for my impending glory. The digital clock clicked to 11:59. One more minute 'til Utopia!

I closed my eyes and listened for the countdown that would be coming from my living room at any moment: "10 … 9 … 8 … 7 … 6 … 5 … 4 … 3 … 2 … One! Happy New Year!" There was nothing happy about it for me. My stomach became nauseated and my head started spinning as I heard my brothers and their friends celebrating loudly.

Another year was over and nothing had happened. Life was continuing just as it always had. I felt as if I were a balloon and someone had simultaneously stuck a dozen needles in me. It was a big joke. All my dreams and plans were the foolish ravings of a deranged mind.

I'm a really sick bastard. I had to be out of my fucking mind to think that I was God! Who the hell am I? I'm nobody, a complete nothing, I thought miserably, alone in the dark room. Reality was painfully cruel. Instead of being the savior, I was an unemployed, mentally ill man, not exactly a prize catch.

I stayed in bed for the next few days and tried to make some sense out of what had happened to me. The letdown was so great, I might have seriously considered suicide if I hadn't known what that would do to my family. Suicide was a coward's solution. I was going to have to try and fight my way out of the depression in which I was mired.

By the second week in January my spirits had improved. I stopped feeling sorry for myself and tried to be thankful for everything I still had going for me. My delusions were gone but I hadn't stopped dreaming. I continued to imagine myself doing great things some day.

As a very mortal human being, however, the effects of the Haldol were starting to wear me down. I fought to maintain a minimal energy level but was clearly losing the battle against constant fatigue. I tried consuming large doses of caffeine, but even that didn't help much. I didn't know what else I could do about my situation, other than learn to accept it, and I was having a difficult time doing that.

Over the weekend, I visited Sean in Lancaster and then drove ten miles to see Vicki in West Chester. Her apartment was spacious and comfortable. It was tastefully furnished with a four-piece living room set, an oak coffee table, and a Sony entertainment center. My ex-girlfriend was doing well for herself.

Although Vicki was polite and friendly, I detected a certain aloofness from her. She tried to hide it, but her emotional detachment was painfully obvious. Tonight was definitely not going to be a repeat of the last night we had spent together. I couldn't really blame her. I wouldn't want to have sex with a psycho, either.

We sat down in the living room and talked about everything except my current status. I desperately wanted to talk about my Messianic delusion, but decided against subjecting her to that. It was too damn weird.

"What do you think of this Middle East deal, Den. It looks pretty bad. Bush set a deadline for Iraq to pull out of Kuwait by the 15th. That's only four days away," she said.

"To be honest with you, Vicki, I haven't followed it too closely. I thought I'd be able to put an end to war."

I thought it was ironic that the President had chosen Martin Luther King Day to give Saddam Hussein his ultimatum. I had always greatly admired King. He was a man who stood for the true Christian ideals in which I believed. His call for the brotherhood of all men, regardless of race, creed, or color, was a far cry from the racial and religious polarity that exists today. It angered me that instead of making progress, in many ways we had gone backwards since the time of the Civil Rights movement. Martin Luther King's noble dream was dying a slow death.

Vicki made some popcorn and inserted *The Little Mermaid* into her VCR. I wasn't surprised to see her get a big kick out of the film. She had always loved those goofy, animated cartoons. I was enjoying the movie also, but had to struggle to remain awake for the ending. I was glad I was able to hold on. The fairytale ending helped me forget my troubles for a while. The movie concluded at 9:30, and I was sound asleep on the couch by ten o'clock.

I drove back to New Jersey on Sunday morning and moped around the house for the next few days. I bought all the newspapers and tried to catch up on what was happening in the world. From everything I read, Saddam Hussein was a dangerous sadist. He was a ruthless, cold-blooded murderer who had the gall to talk about fighting a "Holy War" against the United States. This heresy was the ultimate abomination. I hoped a disaster could be averted before it was too late.

13

THE FINAL
FRONTIER

I woke up on Wednesday, January 16 with a horrible toothache. I called the nearest Manalapan dentist and scheduled an emergency appointment. The receptionist told me that an early evening slot was the best she could do on such short notice, so I suffered through the rest of the day and waited for the designated time to arrive.

My dentist, Dr. Edward Faktor, was a thin young man with curly brown hair. He looked as though he could have been a classmate of my brother Thomas's, but he handled himself with a great deal of professionalism and confidence. Despite his youth, I had no doubts about his competence.

After thoroughly examining my teeth, he took a set of preliminary X-rays that revealed my problem.

"You have an impacted wisdom tooth, Mr. Mulhearn. Since you're my last patient today, I'll be able to do the work right now if that's all right with you," Dr. Faktor said. "I'd also like to pull your other wisdom tooth, before that one gives you any problems."

"Go ahead, Doc. You're the boss, do whatever you think needs to be done."

He shot me full of Novacaine until my lips dropped somewhere below my chin. When I observed that I had drooled all over the bib and onto my sweater, I knew it was time to proceed with the extractions. The first tooth came out easily, with hardly any pain or discomfort. That wasn't too bad. Maybe I'm gonna catch a break today. I wasn't that lucky.

The impacted wisdom tooth was not nearly as cooperative. Dr. Faktor pulled, yanked, and poked at it, but the damn thing wasn't budging.

"Am I hurting you, Dennis?" he asked with sincerity. I had to laugh.

"Yeah, I guess you could say that. My tooth hurts like hell. I think you found the nerve." I had experienced nearly every dental procedure known to man and this was the most excruciating pain I had ever felt in a dentist's chair. Dr. Faktor injected me with a few more shots of novacaine and then began attacking my mouth again.

He was still fighting my stubborn tooth when one of his assistants popped her head inside the door. "Excuse me, Doctor. You might want to turn on the radio. Something's going on in the Persian Gulf," she said. The radio announcer spoke in a low, somber voice. Our air force had begun a full-fledged attack against Iraq. The United States was officially at war.

I made the sign of the cross and prayed for a quick ending to the bloodshed. It sickened me that kids not much older than my youngest brother were going to lose their lives over there. What a waste. Was this going to be another Vietnam? Dr. Faktor and I listened to the radio for another few minutes, and then he glumly finished extracting my tooth. It was a sad day for every American.

Before I left his office, Dr. Faktor gave me detailed instructions on how to care for my tender gums, which were bleeding profusely. I was feeling groggy and probably should not have driven home, but I stubbornly refused to call for a ride. I didn't want to leave my car in the parking lot all night.

When I came home, I watched a few different news reports and then saw President Bush's speech to the nation. After listening to him, I reluctantly agreed with his decision to deploy our troops. Although I was a pacifist at heart and hated the very idea of war, it seemed imperative that we stop Saddam Hussein. Hussein was a threat to every civilized society, a madman without a conscience. If left unchecked, there were no limits to the destruction he could cause.

I took my Haldol pill and tried to go to sleep. Maybe when I woke up, the chaos in the Middle East would all be just a bad dream. Unfortunately, the Novacaine soon wore off and left my mouth throbbing. Despite taking a double does of Tylenol, I was still in agony. Not even Haldol was going to help me sleep on this night.

I couldn't help wonder if my suffering had anything to do with the war. Was the senseless death and destruction responsible for my pain? I quickly dismissed that thought. You're not God. You can't take away everyone's pain, I told myself, fully aware of how dangerous it was to think that I had any control over world events.

By Friday morning my mouth was back to normal, but the gloominess I felt from the war lingered. Day and night, the American public was bombarded with a play-by-play account of every SCUD missile launched and every retaliatory measure taken. The electronic age brought the war right into everyone's living room, providing images that would leave an indelible imprint in our brains.

I had finally resigned myself to the fact that I couldn't do anything about the war, so I set about the business of getting my own life in order. Lying around the house all day was getting boring beyond belief, and I was itching to get back to work. After I ate a bowl of cereal and a donut, I drove to the library and looked up the names and addresses of every hotel in New York City and New Jersey. A hundred resumes and cover letters were in the mail in time for the late afternoon pickup.

Despite my desire to rejoin the "real world," I still could not accept all the random events that had occurred in the past three months as merely coincidental. Being in a dentist chair when the war broke out was yet another "coincidence" that created more doubt in my mind. The burning question of whether or not I had a divine purpose remained unanswered.

I could not put my illness completely behind me. The realization that I was mentally ill was so odious, it made me hold onto a small glimmer of hope that my Messianic fantasy was, indeed, fact. As nonsensical as this belief was, I actively sought evidence that might confirm it. I looked, without success, for any revealing signs from newspaper articles, songs on the radio, T.V. shows, the spoken words of my loved ones, and every other form of communication imaginable.

Since I hadn't told anybody in my family that I had thought I was God, no one aside from Vicki knew how sick I had been. Therefore, it was up to me, and me alone, to try to work things out.

Starlight stopped by to visit me and Deirdre on Saturday night. The three of us sat down in the kitchen and began talking. The usual small talk gradually evolved into an intellectual exchange of ideas, in which we examined an interesting topic, the occult. We discussed religion, death, reincarnation and ghosts. Deirdre claimed to have heard the distinctive sound of our grandfather limping up the steps that led to her room, three days after his death!

"I'm sure I wasn't sleeping, and the noise suddenly stopped when he reached the top of the stairs. I was so scared," she said.

It probably was not wise of my sister to talk about this subject matter in front of me, but I was unperturbed by the conversation.

"That's very interesting," I said. "Either your mind was playing tricks on you or you heard Poppy's spirit. Maybe he was trying to tell you something."

"I believe you, Deirdre," Star added. "Just because you can't comprehend something doesn't mean that it doesn't exist."

"You're right, Star. It's the same way with a phenomenon like 'dejavu.' Vicki once dreamed she was in a beautiful bell-shaped dining room. Two months later she went on a cruise for the first time and the ship's dining room was exactly the same as the one she had seen in her dream. She said even the smallest details matched perfectly. How do you explain that?" I asked.

The girls didn't say anything for a minute. "Go ahead, Deirdre. Tell your brother about your dream," Starlight urged her.

"What dream?" Deirdre looked at me and smiled.

"I don't know if I should tell you this, Dennis. I don't want you to get weird on us again." I assured her that there was no need to worry anymore. I was fine now.

"All right. I had this dream on the night you wouldn't take your medicine until the Lions lost the football game. We didn't mention it to you afterward because we didn't know how you'd react. It was the strangest and most vivid dream I've ever had." Deirdre's dramatic buildup titillated my curiosity. I was on the edge of my chair.

"Sean, Starlight, and I are walking down a street, and we come to a triangular staircase. We walk down the steps to investigate. At the bottom of the steps in a large platform, we walk a little farther and discover that in the middle of the platform there is a square chasm which looks like a Black Hole leading to outer space. Star leans over to get a better look at it and accidentally falls into the hole. Sean dives in to get her out but he is trapped also.

"You, Kevin, and Thomas materialize out of thin air and try to help us. A tall, gorgeous man, dressed in a black suit, is suddenly guarding the hole. He tells us we can't go in and that there is no way out. But you don't believe him, Dennis.

"You walk around the side of the platform and look for a hidden entrance to the hole. When you discover a back door and walk through it, the beautiful guard is transformed into a gigantic, demonic creature with no physical substance. The entity is now pure energy and illuminates a blinding orange and white light. However, it is not the good light that you're supposed to see at the end of a tunnel when you die. This light is violent and evil. I'm terrified by the presence of this shapeless monster.

"The creature emits a blood curdling screech that jars me to the bone, and then vanishes. Then you walk out of the hole with Sean and Star. The six of us are so excited we can hardly contain our emotions. We start laughing and hugging each other.

"Finally, we all walk into another building and join a large gathering of people. I can't make out any faces but everyone there seems benevolent and kind. In the corner of the room are two huge buffet tables loaded with food. There is a cake on one of these tables, so I assume we're at a party of some kind, but I don't know if it's a wedding, birthday, or what, and I don't know who the party is for. As we walk over to the buffet we are approached by Aunt Frances.

"The woman doesn't look like Aunt Frances but we all know it's her anyway, you know how it is with dreams sometimes. She's wearing a blue dress and has bright white hair. She hands you a beautiful, golden golf club with the inscription, 'To Dennis, Love, Patrick Mulhearn.' Then I woke up. Strange dream, huh?"

Strange, indeed. Aunt Frances was my Uncle Harry's wife, who had died three years ago. Patrick Mulhearn was my Uncle Packy, my grandfather's youngest brother, who had passed away about a year and a half ago. They were both wonderful people. Was it a coincidence that they were my two relatives who had most recently died? I didn't think so.

The most fascinating aspect of the dream was Aunt Frances's appearance. Her white hair had something to do with Bill Parcells's hair turning white on that same day! In life, her hair had been grayish-brown. There had to be a significant reason for this discrepancy. The color white must have been symbolic for purity and righteousness.

If I had had the same dream, I would have dismissed it as a grandiose delusion, but it wasn't mine, it was Deirdre's. She was completely sane and didn't even know that I thought I was Jesus. At the time of her dream, I didn't even know yet. Her dream was definitive proof that I was truly the Messiah.

The next day, Tom and I went to New City to watch the NFC Championship game between the Giants and 49ers with our father. I hadn't been to New City since Christmas, so the visit was long overdue. While I was looking forward to spending some quality time with my dad, I was even more excited about the football game. I hadn't seen the Giants play since they had shut out the Lions, and was curious to see if Parcells's hair was again going to turn white, or if something different was going to happen this time.

Kevin also decided to pay our father a surprise visit. He was already at my dad's house when Thomas and I arrived there. During the first half of the game, my father switched to CNN at every commercial break. It's so depressing seeing our boys over there," Willie said. I couldn't have agreed with her more. Is there anything I can do to stop the war? I wondered.

At halftime, Dan Rather came on the air and gave a report for CBS. I immediately noticed that something was wrong. For someone who had supposedly been working non-stop for five straight days, Rather looked too damn good. Why wasn't he showing the slightest signs of strain or fatigue? How could he possibly have so much energy left?

I concluded that the war was being faked. It was all an elaborate hoax perpetrated by the government and the media to make the American people forget their economic woes. The war footage had probably been shot months ago in a remote location. As frightening as the images appeared to be, they were not real. The soldiers were a bunch of obscure actors, dressed in military garb and armed with unloaded rifles; the sounds of gunfire and exploding bombs were produced by a special effects machine; scenes of destruction and fire had been colorized and then spliced from old war movies. The aircrafts and missiles were magnified models filmed in a Hollywood studio.

Greatly relieved, I focused my attention on the football game. The 49ers dominated the action but couldn't put the pesky Giants away. Things looked bleak for New York, however, when their quarterback, Jeff Hostetler, left the game with an injury late in the fourth quarter. "That's it. They can't win with a third-string QB," Kevin lamented.

I said nothing, but attempted to deliver a long-distance, telepathic message: "Get back in there, Jeff. Your team needs you. You can do it." Hostetler returned on the next series and courageously marched the Giants into field goal position. With seconds left on the clock, the game was going to be decided by the right foot of Matt Bahr, the Giants one-hundred-and-fifty pound place-kicker.

Bahr stepped into the ball, and appeared to have hooked it. Miraculously, the ball straightened out and squeaked just inside the left upright. The New York Giants were the NFC Champions. Amidst my brothers' and father's exuberance, I questioned my role in the win. Did I will Hostetler back onto the field, and did I control the flight of the game winning field goal? Or had my Father provided the divine intervention?

In the victorious locker room, Jeff Hostetler dropped to his knee in prayer. You're welcome, Jeff. It was my pleasure. You played with a lot of guts out there. I'm proud of you. At that moment I knew that the Giants were going all the way. It didn't matter how impressive the Buffalo Bills had been in their AFC victory. The outcome of the Super Bowl had already been decided.

Before I drove home to Manalapan, Kevin gave me a book that Jim Freeman had recommended. It was titled *The Eden Express* and was written by Mark Vonnegut, the son of Kurt. Supposedly, the book was one of the best accounts of a person experiencing mental illness. Kevin said he had already read it and found it to be quite illuminating.

"I'm going to bed now, Dennis. Come in here and take your medicine," my mother called out from her bedroom.

"All right, Mom. Just a minute." She was already lying in her bed when I entered the room. I slipped the Haldol underneath my tongue and tilted my head back convincingly. Then I went into the bathroom, spit the pill into the toilet bowl, and flushed.

Again, I felt no guilt in having deceived my mother. The drug was messing with the chemicals in my brain, and I needed to be at my absolute best for my confrontation with Satan. Only God the Father knew the exact date, but I was certain that Judgment Day was right around the corner. I could not afford to be at less than full strength.

I turned on the nightlight in my bedroom and read *The Eden Express* from cover to cover. Although Mark Vonnegut was a drug-using hippie of the seventies, some of his schizophrenic thoughts were remarkably similar to mine. Unfortunately, I was unable to see this the first time I read his book. I was too concerned with looking for clues.

Kevin and Jim had given me the book hoping that it would help me see I was ill, but there were some strange facts in it that only reinforced my delusions. For starters, Vonnegut's dog, which he described as noble, loyal, and courageous, was named Zeke. Zeke had been my nickname in college. Several of the guys on my baseball team hadn't even known that my real name was Dennis.

Secondly, his last doctor was a man by the name of Dr. Miller. I knew there were a million Dr. Millers in the world, but I had a funny feeling that this was the same one who had treated me. Fate was crisscrossing all over the place.

Finally, and most interestingly, was the story of Mark Vonnegut's roommate's father. When the roommate had been a young boy, his father fell from a six-story building, and subsequently walked with a limp because one leg became shorter than the other, just like my grandfather! What were the odds of this happening to one man, let alone two?

If these coincidences had not been there, I'm sure I would have found others. Everything pertained directly to me. I was the center of the universe. In any event, the coincidences drove me deeper into my Messianic delusion. I was completely functional, but any semblance of reality was gradually slipping away and my true personality was slowly disintegrating.

When the video store opened on Monday morning, I rented two of my all-time favorite movies: *Field of Dreams* and *Chariots of Fire*. Both were stories about hope and believing in your dreams. Vicki had always teased me about being the world's biggest dreamer and I never argued with her on this point. I believed anything was possible if a person worked hard enough and maintained a positive mental attitude.

As terrific a baseball fantasy as *Field of Dreams* was, *Chariots of Fire* inspired me even more. It was a true story of two 1924 Olympic runners from Britain. One was a devout Christian missionary who ran for God, the other a Jew who would settle for nothing less than being the best. The film perfectly captured the symbiotic interrelationship of mind, body, and soul, which is so often overlooked in athletics.

Chariots of Fire contained one of my favorite scenes, the athletes running on the beach to the beat of the Vangelis theme song, while a distinguished gentleman looks on with his young son. The movie starts and ends with this same wonderful scene. I believed that the filmmakers had intentionally done this in an attempt to reveal the true essence of God, Alpha and Omega, the beginning and the end. Likewise, the man and boy on the beach represented God the Father and Jesus Christ.

I watched both movies repeatedly throughout the week, whenever the T.V. was available. Besides being highly entertaining, every time I viewed one of these films I uncovered new secrets that had previously eluded me. They provided a smorgasbord of spiritual information that could prove to be quite useful. I was eager to learn more.

On Tuesday afternoon I received a phone call from the secretary of The Hilton at Short Hills Hotel. She said her general manager had been impressed by my cover letter and resume and wanted to interview me this Saturday. If I had had the slightest bit of rational thought left, I would have been excited about the career opportunity, but I didn't see the phone call for what it was. Instead, I immediately assumed that The Hilton was going to be the site of my long awaited victory party.

These suspicions were confirmed when the secretary gave me directions and told me the hotel's address, 41 JFK Boulevard. 41 was the high school football number I had worn with tremendous pride and I attached great importance to this unremarkable coincidence. In my delusional state, I felt that all names and numbers had a deep meaning. Sometimes, as in this case, the meanings were decidedly transparent. In other circumstances I had to dig deep to find them, but they were always there.

Thomas brought the *New York Post* home from school. I read the paper uninterestedly until I came across an article about a man name Corey. Cory Malone was still never too far from my thoughts. She was being protected while I did what I had to do. When everything was all over, she would join me at my side. As I read through the article, I learned that the name "Cory" means Rabbi. Of course, Cory is a teacher. She is teaching people about me right now!

That evening, my mother detected something unusual about me. "Are you taking your medicine?" she inquired.

"Yes, of course. I take it in front of you every night," I said. "Why do you ask?"

"I don't know. I can't put my finger on it, but something is not quite right. Are you sure you're taking the medicine?" Do you swear?"

"I swear. I swear on Poppy's grave."

This answer satisfied her completely. She knew I would never blaspheme my grandfather's memory. I was able to make that statement because I truly believed I was taking the medicine. The real medicine wasn't Haldol; it was love. All the people in the world who were praying (millions were praying for a quick end to the Gulf War) were making me stronger each day. They were helping me heal my wounds.

On Thursday morning I began feeling tense and anxious. To help soothe my worn out nerves and relax my body, I listened to my *Godfather III* and *Rocky* cassette tapes. The stirring music worked wonders, but as Jesus Christ, I still had some monumental decisions to make.

All day long I agonized over who I should save and who should be subjected to eternal damnation. The lack of any guidelines for me to follow made the responsibility a heavy burden. Finally, I figured out what to do. I can't send anyone to hell, I want them all, Father, I decided. Believing that my cyst was indeed a transmitter, I gave another great speech to the world.

"My friends, your pain is almost over. Thank you for hanging in there and accepting the pain that you have had to endure. I have been absorbing much of your pain for you, and will continue to do so. I am getting stronger and stronger. The love inside each of you has given me the strength to finish the work of my Father and rid the world of everything that is not good and loving.

"This is all very difficult for your minds to comprehend. I am the Son of God and have existed since the beginning of time. Almost two-thousand years ago, I was called Jesus. I came to this earth having been sent by my Father. I lived and taught, and made many disciples. My word was recorded by these disciples, and, through my inspiration, they wrote about me in the Holy Bible.

"There is truth in the words of the Bible, but some people have misinterpreted many of these words. Although some of you have heard me more than others, there is a part of me in each man and woman. I am one of you, so I know how difficult life can be sometimes. The temptations of Satan are very enticing, he preys on your weaknesses and your most vulnerable areas.

"I am not afraid of Satan, though, fear is not in me. My Father has not given me the spirit of fear, but instead, has filled me with love and has bestowed upon me the power to take away all the pain that Satan fills your hearts with. The Angel of Death is no match for me. I forgive all men and women for all their sins. Together, we will begin a new way of life devoid of hatred and violence.

"My new name is Dennis Mulhearn. I was born in Brooklyn, New York on October 20, 1964. I am now twenty-six years old and live in Manalapan, New Jersey. During this second life, I have again endured many trials and tribulations, but I didn't mind. My suffering was necessary to fulfill my destiny.

"I am drained but very happy. The Day of Atonement is near. We are going to live in peace, harmony, love, and incredible happiness. Take the best moment of your life and remember the joy you felt, that joy will be multiplied to the infinite degree. All the people who have died will return to live with us in utter bliss. This feeling won't ever go away."

Later in the evening I drove three blocks to the Acme supermarket and bought a gallon of milk. On the way back, I heard Mike Francesa interviewing Giants coach Bill Parcells on WFAN. Parcells seemed to know that his team was going to win the big game. I thought about him for a moment. He and his buddy, Bobby Knight, were the same age as my father, and had both started their careers at West Point. They had undoubtedly been students of my old high school coach, Phil Foglietta.

The night before I had first left for The Pines, my dad had shown me his senior yearbook. In it was a picture of Coach Foglietta, taken when he was just starting out as an assistant at Saint Francis Prep. Why hadn't I seen this connection before?

Coach was a lifelong bachelor who lived in a modest Bay Ridge apartment. I had discovered his secret. The man was a Catholic High Priest in the guise of football coach. He knew of my identity and had been preparing people for my coming for many years. I had always chalked up Coach's wisdom to his vast experience, but now I clearly saw that he was one of the great prophets of the twentieth century!

After all these years, I finally understood the special aura about Foglietta that made him such a remarkable man. Through the sport of football, he was able to reach the hearts of thousands of young boys. The men that these boys had become were now working behind the scenes, helping me fulfill my destiny. The lessons they had learned on the football field were far more valuable to them than anything taught in a classroom.

By Friday, January 25, 1991 all hell had broken loose inside my mind. I started the day by watching my movies, and then began reading from the Bible. After reading the verse, "the Father and the Son are one," I stopped and pondered the meaning of those words. Wait a minute. I'm not Jesus Christ, I'm God the Father! Who is the Son?

This question posed some semantic problems but my fertile imagination quickly provided a solution. Cory and I had conceived a son eight years ago, when I was eighteen and she was just fourteen. For safety precautions, the incident had been blocked from both our memories. Our son was being reared by my Uncle Harry in Virginia and was helping me in my fierce battle against Satan.

Although I was God the Father, and every person was my child, I was not the highest form of life, in spite of what the Bible said. I, too, had a spiritual mother and father. My paternal grandmother and grandfather were my true parents! They lived on a higher plane of existence, in a galaxy light years away.

There was no mention of this fact in the Bible because Poppy knew that Satan would have access to the Holy Book and would use some of its secrets against humanity. My grandfather/father had ingeniously chosen not to divulge the most important secret of all. In this poker game that had been played since the beginning of creation, it was finally time to show the cards. My son was the trump card that Satan could not match.

I sat up in my bed and seemed to remember every movie and T.V. show I had ever seen and every book I had ever read. My mind was the most brilliant in history. All information was meant for my assimilation. I made William Shakespeare look like an illiterate dimwit.

The movie *Superman* popped into my brain. I was receiving the crystals of knowledge at a lightning quick pace. The Haldol I had been forced to take was the equivalent of kryptonite it robbed me of all my amazing powers. The best part was that I wasn't just Superman. I was also Batman, the Lone Ranger, and the Incredible Hulk all rolled into one.

In addition to the communicative powers of my cyst, I discovered that I had telepathic abilities as well. I concentrated with all my energy and sent out a message: Call someone you love and let him or her know that you care. Kevin, Sean, my father, and my friend Bob all called me within the hour. It was pure magic. My message to Jeff Hostetler had not been an isolated fluke. What other powers did I possess that I didn't yet know about?

Thomas came home from school and asked me if I could take him to the barber shop. "Sure, Tom. I could use a trim myself." My driving was erratic. I barely avoided crashing into a school bus that had stopped to drop off a passenger. I was so wrapped up in my thoughts, it was extremely difficult to concentrate on the road. On the car radio, we heard a commercial for tomorrow's Super Saturday fifty-million dollar lottery.

"That's a nice chunk of change, huh Den?" Thomas said wistfully.

"Yeah. We sure could do a lot of things with all that money."

I let my brother get his haircut first. While I sat in the waiting area, I telepathically instructed Kevin to purchase a lottery ticket, and then gave him the winning numbers: 23, 41, 14, 18, 25, 28, and 5. Those were the numbers I had worn during various stages of my athletic career, and I was certain they would be the winners. I just hoped Kevin received my message without any interference.

The song that began with the verse, "I've been through the desert on a horse with no name," came over the radio. The music was clearly relevant. It told me that the movie I had watched at Vicki's apartment, *The Little Mermaid*, was an apocalyptic film. Man comes from the sea, we need to drink large quantities of water and to frequently bathe and wash. The oceans and rivers are the life blood of our planet.

I thought about the war and the role America was playing in the world. My belief that the Persian Gulf crisis was not real magically disappeared. George Bush was a hero who knew about what was happening inside my mind. He was a modern day Moses … Moses—George Bush—burning bush … it all fit together nicely.

As I continued to wait, I picked up a recent issue of *Rolling Stone* magazine and began reading a Francis Ford Coppola interview. The article was fascinating. In it, Coppola says he considers the three *Godfather* movies to be stories more about the balance of power than about the inner workings of a mafia family. His subjugation of the mafia storyline proved my theory that the movies were really metaphorical religious films, each containing important spiritual truths.

Finally, I was told that I could go to the back sink and get washed. An older, gray-haired woman did the honors. After she finished rinsing my locks, she lit up a cigarette and inhaled deeply. She looked very serene. The pleasure of touching my hair must have been better than sex.

It only took the barber a few minutes to trim my already short hair. Before I left the shop, I asked the owner if I could buy the magazine I had been reading. "Go ahead and take it," he told me. "Don't worry about it." I thought back to one of the wedding scenes from *The Godfather*, "There may come a day and that day may never come, when you will be asked to perform a service for the Don." I was the Don, and it was collection time!

As Thomas and I walked to my car, it was just starting to get dark outside. "Oh, great! You left your headlights on, way to go," my brother informed me. How was that possible? The sun had been shining brightly when we went inside the barber shop. Thomas evidently was thinking the same thought. "You must have accidentally turned them on while you were driving," he said.

"No. That's impossible. It takes a good yank to turn them on and I never even went near the light-switch," I said. "Don't worry, Tom. I'll get the car going." My Chevy turned over on the first try, much to my brother's surprise. He was confused by what had happened, but I wasn't. The lights had been turned on for me by my son. The true light of the world was in Manalapan, probably with Cory somewhere. He wanted to show me that he was ready to stand by my side. The moment of truth was getting closer.

We arrived home just as Kevin was leaving the house. He was borrowing Deirdre's car to go on a hot date in Devon, Pennsylvania. Perfect. My enemies will think that Kevin is me. They'll follow him all the way to Pennsylvania and give me a free reign to finish my work here. Brilliant strategy, Poppy.

I went into my room and continued reading the *Rolling Stone* article. I read slowly, making sure I understood the significance of every word. Time and time again Coppola talked about power. His obsession with it was extremely interesting. As I read further, I saw that many of his thoughts mirrored mine. This was a man with remarkable insight. I looked forward to speaking with him soon.

I felt like staying in my room and reading my Bible, but I had already promised to take Thomas and his friend Keith to the movies. "So what do you want to see?" I asked the boys, after Keith's mom had dropped him off at our house. They chose Arnold Schwarzenegger's new hit, *Kindergarten Cop*. With my mother a kindergarten teacher and my father an ex-cop, I didn't have to stretch too far to conclude that it was important for me to go see this movie. I began to get excited.

My excitement soon turned to panic, however, when my dependable car refused to start. The devil was trying to keep me away from the theater! "It's the battery," Thomas said. "The lights must have drained it."

"That's okay, Dennis. We can go some other time," Keith added innocently.

"No, Keith. We'll go tonight. I'll find a way," I vowed. I shut my eyes and placed a telepathic distress call. I did not have to wait more than thirty seconds for assistance.

My sister's boyfriend, Dave, came outside and graciously offered to give us a lift. "Thanks a lot, Dave. I really appreciate this," I said, as I hopped into the backseat of his Firebird. Ha! My power is far greater than yours, Satan. You have no chance against me.

The Pond Road theater was unusually crowded. We had to stand in line for fifteen minutes before going inside. The girl behind the ticket window handed me a black and gold 777-Film card along with my three ticket stubs. "What's this?" I asked. "It's a promotion for a new telephone movie service that just came out," she replied.

I put the card in my jacket pocket and got on the popcorn line. "We'll meet you inside," Thomas said, as he and Keith impatiently scrambled to find some good seats. While I stood there enjoying the aroma of freshly baked popcorn, I recognized someone who had worked with me at Chi-Chi's standing a few people in front of me. He was a tall, muscular guy also named Dave, who could have easily been mistaken for a soap opera actor.

Although I had only worked with him a handful of times, he greeted me as if I were a long lost brother. I was pleased with the unexpected reception. He spoke to me with reverence, as though he were aware of who I was.

I found my brother and Keith and sat down next to them. The movie meshed beautifully into my delusion. Schwarzenegger, his love interest, and her small boy, were the central characters of the story. They, of course, represented me, Cory, and our son. The film's villains were easily identifiable caricatures void of any redeeming qualities. They were evil personifiedTowards the end of the movie, I delivered another telepathic message to all my children: "I trust that you have all learned your lessons well. Tonight I need your help. My mother and father are ready to take us to the far limits of outer space and show us a perfect world, but first we must win the battle against evil on this planet. I am very strong and getting stronger, but I can't do it alone. I need a lot of help. If we all band together, we have unlimited power.

"You can help me fight the powers of darkness by loving each other a little more. Love is our most potent weapon. Give me everything you've got if we are successful, we will break through the boundaries of our physical limitations and reach new heights. Heaven is at our fingertips. Take your best grip and don't let go."

When the crowd started filing out the exits, I saw couple after couple holdings hands or putting their arms around each other. They had heard me. My army was mobilizing into an insurmountable force.

On my way out of the theater, I bumped into a girl I had known at Albright. Karen had been a freshman when I was a senior, and I had always found her extremely attractive. She had a girl-next-door wholesomeness that was engaging.

"So what are you up to these days, Dennis?"

"Well, I'm starting a new job at The Hilton Hotel. I have to go there tomorrow. How 'bout you?" She told me she worked for an insurance company in New Jersey.

We chatted for another five minutes before going our separate ways. In addition to being beautiful, Karen was a warm and friendly young lady.

Under normal circumstance, it would have taken me about ten seconds to ask her for her phone number. But the thought never ever crossed my mind. My psychotic obsession with Cory was quite powerful. After all, I believed she was the mother of my child.

We waited outside in the cold for Dave to come pick us up. Thomas and Keith were in high spirits. To pass the time, they broke into loose dialogue from one of their favorite movies.

"Kirk, I will chase you around the moons of Nebula to get my revenge. I will have it," said Keith.

"I'm right here Khan. If you want me, you're gonna have to come down and get me," Thomas replied in a brilliant impersonation of William Shatner.

I immediately recognized the film, *Star Trek II: The Wrath of Khan*. My entire family couldn't get enough of Star Trek. We all watched endless reruns of the classic T.V. shows, the movies, and even the new *Star Trek: The Next Generation* episodes. We were, undeniably, a family of "Trekkies."

In the backseat of Dave's car, I reached an understanding of why I had run into two old friends at the theater. Dave and Karen were not who they appeared to be. They were the spirits of my grandfather/father and grandmother/mother. They had both taken physical forms to safeguard the success of my mission and to provide a foolproof "insurance" policy.

My mother confronted me as soon as I walked through the front door.

"I counted five pills yesterday, and there are still five pills left in your container. How long haven't you been taking your medicine?" she asked.

"I've taken the medicine every single night," I told her. "You know I would never lie to you."

"You're right. Normally you wouldn't lie," she agreed. "But why are there still five pills left?"

I saw what was really going on here. I was engaged in psychological warfare against Satan. He was trying to use my family's love for me as a weapon. I had to be stronger than they were, the fate of the world depended on it. Under no circumstances could I let their unwarranted fears prompt me to take the Haldol. I knew I was in for the fight of my life.

Conscious of the hidden cameras observing this historic battle, a battle I could not lose, I began with a simple mathematics lesson: "4 + 1 = 5, 2 + 3 = 5, 5 + 0 = 5, 1 + 4 = 5. Do those numbers mean anything to you?" I asked my mother.

"No."

"They are all numbers I have worn in my life, and they all add up to five. Now, what is 5 − 1?"

"Four," Thomas answered testily.

"No. You are wrong. 5 − 1 = 5," I corrected.

"What the hell do you call that?"

"New math."

"Don't try to argue with him, Tom, it's useless. Just take the medicine now, Dennis. In front of me," my mother said, handing me a pill.

"No. This is not medicine." I put the pill back into the container. "Haldol is a very harmful drug. The real medicine is love."

My mom began sobbing and Thomas screamed at me: "You're not my brother anymore. I only have two brothers now." His words stung but I remained obstinate. As the Godfather, I had to be strong for my family, which consisted of the entire human population.

I can only imagine my mother's and Thomas's frustration in dealing with me. As much as they loved me, I was becoming a tremendous nuisance. I'm surprised my kid brother didn't cold-cock me and shove the pill down my throat. That was probably what he felt like doing. His restraint was admirable.

I held my ground for hours. When I was confronted with sensible logic and reason, I responded with an equal dose of anti-logic.

"I don't need the Haldol. It makes me weak," I explained. "Like I told you, the real medicine is love. That's all I need."

"Look. It's almost four o'clock in the morning. Please take the medicine. If you won't do it for yourself, then do it for us," my mother pleaded.

"No, I can't do that. I need to be strong," I replied. "I am doing this for you."

Thomas continued screaming and yelling and my mother started getting hysterical herself. She didn't know what to do. "How To Care For A Psychotic Child" was not one of the lessons offered in any Lamaze class. I wanted to cooperate but I knew that I couldn't, the stakes were far too high.

Nevertheless, seeing my family suffering this way was no picnic for me, either. I had never experienced such a stressful ordeal. I went into my room to find my Bible, hoping that the Book would provide some added strength. I was sidetracked, however, by the sight of my 777-Film card lying on top of my bed. The card must have fallen out of my jacket pocket.

I recognized at once what I was supposed to do with it. In *The Wrath of Khan*, Kirk and Spock punch in a defense code that immediately drops Khan's shields and leaves him vulnerable to an attack. The 777-Film card held the correct sequence of numbers that would enable me to break through Satan's formidable defense system. I hurriedly reached for the telephone.

My mother and Thomas didn't know what I was doing but, considering the circumstances, they were less than enthralled to see me dial a movie service. Thomas tried to take the phone out of my hands, but I angrily shoved him away.

"Don't try to stop me from doing this. It's too important?" I yelled, as I finished dialing the number.

A computerized voice asked me to punch in my zip code and then gave me additional instructions. Finally, the voice asked for the first three digits of my movie selection. I keyed in G-O-D, hoping to hear a message from Poppy. Instead, "*Godfather III* is now playing at Loews Cinema Six in Freehold," was the only message I received.

The instant I hung up the phone, Kevin came barging through the front door. His timing was remarkable. He was quickly briefed about the crisis, and implored me to take the Haldol.

"C'mon, Den. You need the medicine. Stop giving us such a hard time," he said, while my mother and Thomas looked on in hopeful anticipation. They both knew that Kevin had the best chance of reaching me.

I carefully analyzed all my options, and then charted a course of action. "Use this and I'll take the drug," I said to Kevin, handing my First Officer the magical movie card. He responded with an incredulous laugh. "This is completely absurd but I'll do whatever you want as long as you take the medicine. Hell, I'll stand on my head if that makes you happy," he said, still chuckling over my request.

Since he did not know what he was really doing, Kevin nonchalantly went through the motions of using the card. I didn't mind that he was just placating me. Results were all I was interested in. "Fire all weapons," I said silently, when he had finished.

"What movie did you pick?" I asked him.

"I didn't pick anything. The operator said something about 'Assimilation of Celebration.' I have no idea what the hell that means." I understood completely.

The battle was over and we had won! It had been a particularly bloody battle, but the power of love could not be defeated. Thank you all for fighting with me. The war is not over yet, but it won't be long now. Tonight we have irreversibly turned the tide.

I took the Haldol happily, knowing that it couldn't hurt me anymore. As I swallowed the pill a wave of exquisite pleasure passed through my body. Beyond that feeling, I also had another unusual reaction to the drug. Like a diabetic eating a box of chocolate, my brain went into an immediate sensory overload, knowledge was spewing into me from all directions.

"Don Mattingly is Don Corleone. Michael Jordan is number twenty-three, that was my number, I taught him how to play basketball," I said. I continued making ridiculous statements that I thought were very profound and brilliant. I couldn't understand why everyone was laughing at me. They were laughing out of relief that I had taken the drug as much as anything else.

As a final affront to my independence, my mother took my car keys away from me.

"What about my job interview tomorrow?" I asked. "I have to be at The Hilton at eleven o'clock. Is somebody going to drive me?"

"No. You can't go. You're in no condition. There will be plenty of other jobs, Dennis," my mother said. "First you have to get well." Although I was annoyed, I didn't bother to argue with her. There was no point in wasting my breath.

I went into my bedroom, gave everybody a half hour to fall asleep, and then began whispering to anyone who could hear me.

"You are going to have to start celebrating without me. Go to The Hilton at Short Hills tomorrow morning. To thank you for your help, you'll be entertained by the music of Mr. Carmine Coppola and Mr. Frank Stallone.

"Watch the highlight films. All sports, especially baseball, will tell a story. By understanding the games we play, you'll be able to understand more about me. Since baseball is my game, pay particular attention to the World Series films. Enjoy yourselves. I'll see you soon."

14

FOLLOW THE LIGHT

When I woke up Saturday afternoon, my grandparents were no longer super-gods, I was not God the Father, my son didn't exist anymore, and The Hilton had reverted back to a normal hotel. Despite being quite conscious of how wrong I had been on these counts and others, I was unphased by all the blatant mistakes I had made. I was still Jesus Christ. My erroneous beliefs were just minor setbacks on the road to enlightenment.

I attributed my miscalculations to my overactive imagination and then quickly forgot about them. In addition to all the previous signs I had received, the glowing headlights of my car were convincing proof that I was indeed "the light of the world." My power was immense!

Throughout the day I remained extraordinarily upbeat and optimistic about the future. I smiled a lot, and spoke in a soft, benign voice. Since I was love in its purest form, all selfish or hateful thoughts were now completely foreign to me. Instead, I was consumed by an exhilarating feeling of warmth that I wanted to share with the entire world.

The Haldol had little effect on my body. I was still bursting with the energy and vitality of a dozen men. I wanted to go outside and run five or six miles but my mother would not allow me to leave the house. I had to settle for doing a two hour workout consisting primarily of pushups and sit-ups on the floor of Thomas's bedroom.

No one mentioned The Pines to me, but I suppose that it was, at the very least, in the back of my family's minds. My car keys had not been taken away to prevent me from driving to Acme. They need not have worried about me making another trip to South Fallsburg. I was too concerned with saving the world to fret about an insignificant resort such as The Pines.

I no longer ascribed to the devil a human body, or even a physical presence. I now believed that the devil was a formless, shapeless entity as in Deirdre's dream with the singular ability to produce unprovoked, random acts of evil. He existed only on a spiritual level but was as real as any person. I took solace in the knowledge that his days were numbered.

At dinnertime, my brothers and I discussed tomorrow's Super Bowl game. We were all rooting for the Giants, but Kevin and Thomas thought the Bills were going to win. I couldn't sit idly by and listen to their ignorance. It was time for another lesson.

"Tomorrow is going to be the greatest Super Bowl ever. Both the Giants and Bills are going to play heroically, and the game won't be decided until the final minute. The Giants will win on a miracle play as the clock runs out. L.T. and O.J. Anderson will have key roles in the victory, and Jeff Hostetler will be named the game's M.V.P.," I said in one big breath.

"How do you know all this?" Thomas asked me. "Do you think you are Elijah or Jesus?"

I paused for a moment to consider an appropriate response to his question.

"I am who I am," I said quietly. Kevin, Thomas and even my mother howled with laughter. They all found my answer extremely amusing. They didn't know how long I had believed I was God and I guess they assumed that the thought would disappear in another day or two.

Super Sunday finally arrived. My brothers and sister each dispersed to different Super Bowl parties, so I was left to watch the game with my mother. She lasted about five minutes and then went upstairs to finish her class preparation for the upcoming week. I didn't mind being by myself, though. As a matter of fact, I enjoyed the solitude. I could watch the action without any distractions.

The game followed my script as closely as I could have hoped. When the Bills' kicker, Scott Norwood, barely missed his last second field goal attempt to give the Giants a 20-19 win, I pumped my fists in the air. "That's a miracle play if I ever saw one!"

I would have batted a thousand if O.J. Anderson had not been awarded the M.V.P. trophy. O.J. had been terrific, but my man Hostetler clearly deserved the honor. Did someone alter the voting? I wondered. My fears were vanquished when ABC, covering the Giants' locker room celebration, showed Hostetler hoisting his two young boys onto his shoulders. His sons were the real trophies. They were the only awards that mattered.

In Monday's *Post*, there was an article about Bill Parcells. The headline read: "God Was On Our Side!" I couldn't believe what I was reading. The Giants' coach was publicly admitting that God was the 12th man that had led his team to victory. He credited God's power as the key to the outcome of the game.

Parcells was completely out of character. Football coaches just aren't supposed to talk about such things. I thought back to the day his hair had turned white. This man had truly been blessed from above. In light of the war we were in, it was difficult to imagine why the outcome of the Super Bowl was so damn important, but I didn't question my Father's plan. Bill Parcells had merely verbalized something that the entire world had seen with their own eyes.

The article fueled my belief that I was the Messiah for quite some time. I knew that the world was not ready for this secret, however, so I never mentioned it to anyone.

During the next week, I stopped making predictions and kept my thoughts to myself. My family thought I was making rapid progress. Each day without a psychotic episode was construed as a small victory by them. They were confident that Haldol was the wonder drug that was going to return me to normalcy.

In reality, although Haldol effectively controlled my behavior, it merely camouflaged the symptoms of my illness. The drug was the equivalent of putting a band-aid over a bullet wound. Until I could admit to myself that I had suffered a bout with mental illness, I was never really going to get well. I fought against that notion with every ounce of my fiber. It was so much more pleasant to go on thinking that I was Jesus.

I don't know if it had anything to do with the Haldol I was taking, but over the next few weeks I experienced a rash of remarkably clear and vivid dreams. Virtually every one of them was about sports. I dreamed about all the guys I had played with and against during my career. In every other dream or so, I competed against a team of girls. The girls' teams usually won or were winning when I woke up.

By the end of February, everyone thought I was well enough to visit Kevin in New York. I wasn't thrilled about going into the City, but I wanted to see my brother. His frantic work schedule had prevented him from visiting Manalapan in quite a while.

After granting me a tour of the matchbox he called an apartment, Kevin treated me to a Chinese dinner and a movie. As we walked out of the theater and through the streets of Manhattan, we reached into the past and reminisced about some of the glory days we had shared. It was always a pleasure to recall the rites of passage we had gone through together.

While we continued walking, he changed the subject and said he was encouraged by the way I looked. From the very beginning, Kevin had expected nothing less than a full recovery from me. He believed that all I needed was a little time to get my thoughts in order.

When we returned to his apartment, my brother turned on CNN news. The U.S. had just initiated a ground attack against Iraq and he wanted to see what was happening. We both watched intently as General Norman Schwarzkopf gave a detailed report on the strategy that had led to Iraq's withdrawal from Kuwait. The war was mercifully over.

I felt no joy in my heart, just relief that the bloodshed had finally ended. Although the American casualty list was low, I grieved for the few U.S. soldiers and the thousands of Iraqis who had senselessly lost their lives in the hot desert.

At that moment I realized that I had no special powers to bring about world peace. I was just a man like everyone else, subject to the same human frailties and weaknesses as the next guy. I had never been so painfully aware of my own mortality.

That night Kevin and I talked well into the early morning. I fell asleep on his couch. As different as we were in some respects, many of Kevin's dreams were very similar to mine. We were both idealistic enough to want to change the world and leave it a better place than when we found it.

Like me, my brother had visions of greatness and wanted to do something on a grand scale. As an attorney with the money, power, and prestige his job afforded him, Kevin was in a position to actually do something about those dreams. I envied him for that. What could I do? Where was I going to make my mark? Those questions continued to plague me. Was I ever going to find the answer?

15

BACK TO REALITY

Sean came home from his training two days later and moved into an apartment with Starlight in Weehawken, New Jersey. He and Kevin called as often as possible, but they were both busy with their own hectic lives. I feared becoming a burden to them. My pride was one of the few things I had left, and I was determined to hold on to it.

After I no longer believed I was Jesus, the effects of the Haldol became more pronounced. The drug may have helped piece my mind together but it was wreaking havoc on my body. The constant fatigue that plagued me was becoming intolerable. I barely had the energy to brush my teeth and shower in the mornings. Doing anything remotely active was now completely out of the question.

The month of March was a blur. I usually didn't get up until one or two o'clock in the afternoon and then was back in bed by eight. Life no longer offered any challenges, so what was the point in kidding myself? In addition to seeing Dr. Miller for my medication, I began weekly counseling sessions with a psychologist named Dr. Dhillon. Dr. Dhillon was a kind Indian woman with whom I enjoyed talking, but there was not much she could do for me.

The few days that I rose before noon were when I managed to secure a handful of hotel interviews in Manhattan. I tried not to get overly excited about their potential but I aspired to resume a normal, independent lifestyle, and viewed my possible employment with a New York hotel as a tremendous opportunity. I was anxious to make a favorable impression with my prospective bosses.

During each of the interviews, I tap-danced around my illness but the Haldol made me appear lethargic and listless. As a result, I never even made it to the second interview stage. It killed me to know that had I been healthy, I would have had a damn good shot at getting one of those jobs.

I looked into the mirror on April 1 and saw a fat, severely depressed ex-mental patient. Tell me this is your idea of an April Fools joke, God. What the hell happened to my life? I want it back! The joke was on me. I was on my own. I was in a maddening "Catch-22." The drug that was keeping me sane was making my life a nightmare. There seemed to be no solution.

Dr. Miller and my mother both tried to get me to take an anti-depressant but I held my ground and refused their urgent pleas. The meant well, but were putting the horse before the cart. I was depressed because of what the Haldol was doing to my once proud body. More drugs were not the answer to my problem.

A couple of weeks later, my father invited me over to play a round of golf with him. We teed off at the municipal Blue Hill course in Rockland County. After carding a 55 on the front nine, I stopped keeping score. Despite my poor play, my father called out "good shot" whenever I managed to make semi-solid contact with my ball. I appreciated his support but I really didn't hit a good shot the entire day.

By the 15th hole I just wanted to get off the course. My futility took all the fun out of the game. It was yet another reminder of how far I had fallen. In addition to the woes of my golf game, I was also having a rough time physically. Walking the course with my heavy bag draped over my shoulder was testing my diminished stamina.

I didn't want to interrupt my Dad's fine round (he shot a 77), however, so I dragged myself through the finishing holes. As embarrassing as my pathetic performance was, I was still glad I had made the trip. The four hour round gave me a unique opportunity to have some relaxed conversations with my father. I cleared the air about a few things that were on my mind before I drove back to Jersey.

On Wednesday, April 24 I had a 9:00 a.m. appointment with Dr. Miller. It was a real struggle to crawl out of bed that early, but I was eager to get to the hospital. Each previous time I had seen him, I had asked Dr. Miller to change my medication and each time he had refused.

He felt that the Haldol had made me stable and didn't want to take any chances with a new drug. As I walked through the front doors of Centra-State I vowed to myself that today was going to be different. I was going to convey to the doctor exactly how insufferable my situation had become. Surely he would listen to reason.

"Hello, Dennis. How are you feeling?"

"Not too good, Doc. The Haldol is making me exhausted. I want to try a new drug," I said. He studied me carefully and then gave his standard reply.

"You know I don't want to do that. You've responded very well to Haldol. You just have to live with being a little tired. Hell, I'm tired too. I drink a dozen cups of coffee a day."

I wasn't interested in his caffeine addiction and was annoyed by his cavalier attitude. Tired, or even exhausted, was not nearly a strong enough adjective to describe the way I was feeling. If there was a word for it, it wasn't anywhere in the English language.

"You don't seem to understand the gravity of my situation, Dr. Miller. Either you change my medication or I'll go off the Haldol altogether. I can't live like this anymore." The doctor evidently saw how serious I was and finally acquiesced to my ultimatum. He prescribed a common anti-psychotic drug called Navane.

"Navane isn't as potent as Haldol, so I'm prescribing twenty milligrams a day instead of ten. Take it as soon as you get home."

When I arrived home, I happily showed my mother the Navane I had just picked up from the drug store. She had played hooky from school and was doing some work around the house. "That's great, Dennis. Maybe this medicine will help you feel better. You got a call from someone from The Helmsley Hotel this morning. They want you to call back. Here's the number," she said, handing me an ink-stained napkin.

I immediately called the hotel and learned that they had an opening for a front desk manager. I set up an interview for the next day at two o'clock. Things were definitely looking up. The Helmsley was one of the best hotels in New York City.

My good mood lasted until the effects of the Navane hit me about two hours later. I was completely unprepared for what the new drug was going to do to my body. It turned me into a dehumanized, slow-motion version of myself. The Navane made me talk, walk, and move at approximately twenty percent of my normal speed.

My frustration was exacerbated by the foolish hope that this new medication was going to help me lead a more productive life. Despite fighting as hard as I could, I was powerless to do anything about my condition. Now even my dignity had been rudely stripped away from me. There was nothing else left.

My mother immediately called Dr. Miller and told him what was happening. He said I had probably been overmedicated and instructed her to reduce my dosage to ten milligrams.

"The doctor said you'll be fine in a day or two. Sometimes it takes a while to get adjusted to a new medication," she reassured me.

"What ... about ... tomorrow, and ... the Helmsley?" I asked. She shook her head sadly.

"I'm sorry about that, Dennis. But I don't think you're ready to work yet, anyway. You just have to be a little more patient. You'll get there one of these days." For the first time in quite a while, I began to cry.

"Patient ... I've ... been ... patient ... for six ... fuckin ... months. When ... does ... it ... end? I ... just ... want ... to ... be myself ... again," I sobbed.

I was angry at the world and especially at God for putting me through this anguish. I didn't deserve this cruel fate. Seeing my pain, my mother took me in her arms and tried to console me. "I know how hard this is for you but you'll get through it. If anyone can beat this, you can. You're the toughest guy I know," she said, with as much confidence as she could muster.

Her pep talk helped a little, but I didn't feel too tough while I wept on my mother's shoulder. I felt tremendously weak and as fragile as a piece of fine china. My increasing dependency on her and the rest of my family was deeply humiliating and there was nothing I could to do to change it. I despised being a prisoner of my own body.

Dr. Miller was correct. My body returned to normal functioning in forty-eight hours. Although relieved, the trauma of my slow-motion experience lingered like a bad aftertaste. Regardless of how much they may or may not have helped me, I was never going to have the slightest affection for any anti-psychotic drug. The price I paid for my sanity was high. I often wondered if it was too high.

Navane was not as sedating as Haldol, but it still made me very tired. There were no other noticeable side effects, so I suppose the results were all I could have realistically hoped for. Nevertheless, I was far from satisfied.

On Saturday, my brothers dragged me into Brooklyn for the first annual Poly Prep Alumni baseball game. Because of my current status, I was hesitant about returning to my alma-mater. But Kevin and Sean refused to go without me. After a few hours of non-stop badgering, they finally convinced me that the game might help raise my spirits. Maybe knocking a hardball around the park was just what I needed to make me forget my hellish week.

Starlight and Thomas came along with us to see if we played as good a game as we talked. I wasn't nervous until we crossed the Verrazano Bridge and entered the borough of Brooklyn. As I drove closer to the school, the sight of my old hangouts (White Castle and Nathan's) made me break into a nostalgic smile.

"Wow. What a beautiful campus!" Starlight marveled as she caught her first glimpse of Poly Prep.

Aside from a few minor touchups, Poly hadn't changed much in the four years since I had last visited. In addition to an expansive outdoor athletic complex behind two main buildings, two ponds, four tennis courts, and many acres of well manicured grass gave the place a country club atmosphere. Nestled in the heart of Bay Ridge, Poly Prep was one of the last vestiges of 19th Century Brooklyn.

We arrived early enough to watch the end of the varsity game against The Trinity School. As I sat in the concrete bleachers and scanned the familiar ball field, I recalled some of my high school memories. Had it really been nine years since I had last stepped onto this field?

Kevin nudged me out of my trance. "Are you all right, Den? You look like you're a million miles away."

"I'm fine. I was just thinking about a few things."

I stared at the Trinity pitcher as he rocked back into his windup, but I wasn't paying any attention to the game. My mind drifted to a scene from the school chapel, during late November of my junior year.

It was the athletic awards ceremony, and I was proudly looking forward to receiving my first varsity letter in football. This accomplishment was going to remove the stigma of being a social outcast. No amount of money or fancy clothing could diminish what I had done on the playing field. After two and a half years of struggling for acceptance, I finally felt that I belonged at this school.

The Senior Varsity Club president, Peter D'Agostino, stood in front of a podium and announced the names of the letter winners in my class: "Cosidente, Guerrero, Hill, Lynch, Merone, ... Mu-hun," he said, crinkling his nose and making a funny face. Riotous laughter reverberated through the chapel. In a matter of seconds my moment of glory had become a public humiliation.

I wanted to crawl into a hole but I had to go up on the stage to accept my letter. I walked quickly with my head down, laughter still ringing in my ears. I had a fairly thick skin, but not this thick. The self-esteem that I had gradually built up was back to ground zero. Coach Foglietta handed me my letter and gave me a compassionate look, as if to tell me, "I'm sorry, Dennis. You didn't deserve that."

When the ceremony was over, I went into the bathroom and put my fist through the plasterboard wall. That's what you should have done to D'Agostino's face, I thought bitterly. Punching out the best athlete in the school would have gotten me suspended, but it would have also restored my self-respect. Ignoring his insult was one of the biggest mistakes I have ever made. I should have come onto that stage with my fists flying, regardless of the consequences.

As it was, I never again tried to fit in at Poly. I was content to be a loner, and prove myself in athletic competition. I suppose I missed out on the high school experience, but the success of my senior year was enormously rewarding. When I received outstanding player awards in football and baseball, my name was correctly pronounced both times. I was as relieved about that as I was happy to have received the recognition.

My brothers and I were disappointed when only a dozen ballplayers showed up for the alumni game. But one of these men was Peter D'Agostino. Although I hadn't seen him in ten years, I braced myself for another personal attack. This time I was going to take appropriate action to defend my honor.

Fortunately for him, Peter was friendly and cordial. He had probably long since forgotten the chapel incident. To him, it had just been a harmless goof to get a few laughs from his adoring student body. I happened to be the unlucky butt of the joke. If he had known how deeply it was going to hurt me, I'm sure he would not have done it.

Since we didn't have enough players for a game, we decided to take batting practice. I grabbed my glove and raced out to centerfield. Kevin and Sean were among the first men to hit and they both performed admirably. They still had a little pop left in their bats. As for me, I stumbled around the outfield like Joe Hardy in *Damn Yankees*. Every fly ball was a new adventure. When I jogged in to take my turn at bat I just hoped not to embarrass myself too badly.

I took a wild flail at the first pitch and missed it by a foot. Disheartened, I grabbed a handful of dirt and rubbed it into my sweaty palms. C'mon, Zeke. Swing like you mean it, I told myself.

"Lets go, Dennis. Show me that sweet stroke of yours," urged a raspy voice from behind home plate.

I didn't have to look back to realize that the voice belonged to my old coach, Harlow Parker. "Park" was a true gentleman, and as passionate about the game of baseball as I was. After my father, he was easily the best coach I ever had the pleasure of playing for.

I dug in and coldly eyed the batting practice pitcher. "Ping." The ball screamed down the right field line and skipped past an unsuspecting outfielder. To my astonishment, I proceeded to lash line drives all over the field. I was elated by my unexpected success at the plate, and Kevin and Sean were equally thrilled. "Way to go, Den." Knock the cover of the ball!" they yelled joyously. From the stands, Thomas and Starlight echoed their cheers.

I ended the show with a long drive that sailed fifty feet over the right fielder's head. I dropped my bat and watched the flight of the ball, ala Reggie Jackson. Before returning to the field, I sought out Park for a handshake. For a man of his age, he looked remarkably fit and healthy. His grip was firm and strong.

"You were one of the best hitters I ever coached. I loved to watch you swing the bat," he said, placing a gentle hand on my shoulder.

"Thanks, Park. Coming from you that means a lot to me," I replied, battling to retain control of my emotions.

"Nice sticking, Mul," Peter said to me as I trotted past him at his shortstop position. I nodded and continued on toward the outfield. For the first time in months, a little of my old swagger had returned.

Unfortunately, the glow of my performance wore off in a few days. So I could still hit a baseball. How was that going to help me earn a living? I sank back into a dark depression. By Thursday, May 1, I had reached rock bottom. It was impossible to envision my life getting any better. I was drowning in a pool of my own self-pity.

That night I went to bed right after dinner. I'm in trouble, God. I'm losing my will to fight. Please help me. It was the first prayer I had said since my days as the Messiah. Everyone in my family had agreed that it was prudent of me to shy away from anything of a spiritual nature but now I was desperate. There was no other place to turn. I shut my eyes and fell asleep.

Soon I was in the midst of a very vivid dream. The dream began with me standing on a Russian street. There were no distinguishing features to let me know where I was, yet I instinctively knew I was in the Soviet Union. At the end of the street was a baseball batting cage. I watched the comrades take some hacks and laughed at their ineptitude at our game.

While I was still laughing, two well-dressed young men grabbed my arms, escorted me into a dark chamber, and strapped me into a machine that looked similar to an electric chair. I was powerless to resist them. The machine was painless but, when activated, drained my mind of knowledge. The damn thing was killing off my brain cells at an alarming rate. This process was repeated a number of times, and each time I entered the machine I vowed to remember my past. I didn't know what the Russians were trying to find but imagined that my mind held a valuable secret.

The cycle was finally broken when instead of being brought to the chamber, I was taken to a doctor's office. The doctor was a small, gray-haired man with a kindly, cherubic face.

"I'm glad to finally meet you, Dennis. You've done extremely well," he said, smiling. Before I could blurt out a question, he gave me my answer.

"I'm sorry you've had to suffer so much, you've had it pretty tough. But there is a logical explanation for everything you've been through. We needed your mind to be completely open to what you are about to see. I think you'll enjoy it." He walked toward a closet door and motioned me to follow.

The doctor unlocked the door and held it open.

"Are you coming too?" I asked him.

"No, Dennis. This is something you must do by yourself. Have a good time." I walked through the door and into a beautiful nightclub. Before I became acclimated to my new surroundings, a cold hand slapped against my cheek. The slap wasn't meant to hurt me, it was merely intended to get my attention.

"C'mon, partner. Wake up. We got a lot to do, and not much time to do it in," said the man whom I presumed was my guide. Even without his cowboy hat and boots, this guy would have still looked like a character from a spaghetti western. I was not frightened by him, however. Behind his unshaven face was a pair of caring eyes. I could tell that he wanted to help me.

The cowboy led me to a round cocktail table. "Look and learn," he said, roughly pushing my head against its surface. I didn't understand what he was talking about until a wave of numbers flashed before my eyes.

The numbers were not random, nor were they insignificant. They were the dates of the most important historical events since the beginning of time. "You can't live in the past, Dennis, but you need to remember it so you don't repeat the same mistakes. Take the knowledge with you and don't look back," said the cowboy.

He hurriedly rushed me over to another table. This one was the language table. When I placed my head on it I was able to comprehend every known language on the face of the earth. I didn't know whether to speak Mandarin, German, or Swahili.

Finally, the cowboy brought me to the food and beverage table. This table showed me what I could and could not eat and drink. The guidelines were emphatically clear: alcohol, caffeine, and fatty foods were off limits, but I could consume as much milk, water, fruits and vegetables as I desired.

"Okay, partner. Put your feet up and enjoy the show," the cowboy said, pointing toward the stage. This is what it's all about." Prior to this time, the nightclub had been empty. But now, the cast of *Mame* appeared on the stage. I sensed a magical moment ready to take place.

The cast performed a beautiful song about love. I can't remember the exact words, but the music moved me to the verge of tears. In the midst of my self-pity, I had forgotten about all the love I had in my life. How could I have been so blind?

Suddenly, the cowboy, singers, and nightclub itself were gone. My dream wasn't over, though. I became a bright ball of light transcended above time and space. The feeling was indescribable. It was a delicious combination of peacefulness, intense pleasure, euphoria, and wholeness. I didn't want it to ever stop.

Just when I thought this feeling couldn't possible get better, it did! I was assimilated into a huge light, a light whose scope was beyond my comprehension. Despite its vastness, the light didn't attempt to overpower me. It merely wanted me to become a part of it. I was able to become fully absorbed into the light without losing my individuality. My pleasure increased a hundredfold. I had achieved Nirvana, Heaven or whatever else one might choose to call it.

When I began waking up, I fought hard to remain in my dream. No. Not yet. Just a few more seconds, I begged. I lasted another minute or two before gently regaining consciousness. I looked at my digital clock and saw that it was only 8:15. I hadn't been asleep for all that long.

My room was exactly as I had left it but I was never going to be quite the same again. I had always believed that God existed, but now I knew that he did. My subconscious mind was incapable of producing the depth of emotions I had felt. God had shown me a small glimpse of his true nature.

My dream gave me what I needed most: renewed hope. It also furnished me with the strength to start fighting again. I could still be someone to be reckoned with if I applied myself.

I tried to go back to sleep but was too wound up. I knocked on my mother's door and shared the dream with her. "That's very interesting, Dennis. What do you think it means?" she said, without much enthusiasm. I suppose she was wary of me having a relapse.

"Love is the key. We are all imperfect pieces of a big puzzle. When the time is right, we become one with God and join him in perfection. This interpretation is obvious, isn't it?" My mother bit her lip.

"I don't know. Dreams are funny things. Sometimes they are not as they appear to be."

I didn't let her skepticism dampen my spirits. It didn't matter what she thought. I understood exactly what the dream had meant. God had answered my prayer. Thank you, God. I appreciate your help. I'll take it from here.

The next morning I called Kevin at his office and animatedly described my dream. He let me finish without interrupting once. "That's a hell of a story, Den," he said, sounding impressed. "The last part sounds similar to near death experiences I've read about."

"Kev, I can't adequately explain the way I felt. It was unbelievable."

"How did it compare to sex?"

It didn't. It made sex seem like going to the dentist. He chuckled at my analogy.

"It's funny you dreamt you were in Russia. I had a dream concerning Russia last night, too.

"I was standing outside the Kremlin with one of my law school professors. It was a cold and rainy day, yet everyone was outside. We watched three Russian leaders being placed in coffins, and then buried in the ground. When the coffins were covered with dirt, everyone started to sing and dance. There must have been thousands of people dancing in the streets. That's all I remember. Hey, Den, I've got to go. One of the partners is asking for me. Talk to you soon. Bye."

In hindsight, I think it is quite possible that my brother's dream was a foretelling of the breakup of the Soviet empire. Even if it wasn't, it is still mighty strange that we both dreamed we were in Russia on that same night. I had never dreamed about Russia before that evening. Nor have I dreamed about it since.

16

RENAISSANCE MAN

That afternoon I ventured out to the library to do some research on my illness. I wanted to know exactly what I was facing, so I'd be better prepared to beat it. Do you have any books or schizophrenia, I asked a librarian. She gave me a queer look before directing me to the medical section. I found three pertinent books and sat down to read them.

I had two major symptoms of schizophrenia: grandiose delusions and loose associations. Believing that you are God is about as grandiose as you can get. I didn't settle for merely being a king or a president. Those roles would have been too limiting when compared to the power of the Supreme Ruler.

Loose associations were a term applied for taking unrelated information and trying to make it fit together. My thought that Coach Foglietta was a Catholic priest simply because his picture had been in my father's yearbook was a prime example of this. Hell, I was a master of loose associations. I brought it to an art form. My mind was capable of making a sophisticated connection between any two pieces of information.

Despite manifestations of these two symptoms, I did not hear voices or experience visual hallucinations, which were the most prevalent symptoms of schizophrenia. Therefore, I concluded that I was not a true schizophrenic. They did not yet have a name for whatever it was that I had.

I continued reading and skipped to the chapters on the causes of the disease. There were a number of different theories but the current consensus was that it was a bio-chemical imbalance. One joker, however, believed schizophrenia was the direct result of a domineering mother. Leave it to the shrinks to blame the mother. What an outrageous hypothesis! My mom was as gentle as a lamb. Reading something like that, in a fairly current textbook no less, showed me exactly how little was actually known about the malady.

I didn't completely buy into the bio-chemical imbalance theory, either. It seemed like just another convenient answer that was far too broad to be of any real value. The sad truth was that the doctors didn't know for sure what caused it. More research was desperately needed but the medical community had only recently accepted mental illness as a bona fide disease.

The great progress psychiatry had made in the past twenty years poignantly illustrated how much more there was to learn about the fragile human mind. I found it tragic that at a time when heart transplants were routinely performed every day, the research and treatment of brain diseases was comparatively still in its infancy. Maybe I should have been grateful that I wasn't locked in an asylum somewhere, but instead I was bitter that more effort wasn't being expended to help mentally ill people like me.

Finally, I read the chapters regarding treatment of the disease, which dealt mainly with anti-psychotic drugs. I learned that these drugs were considered heavy-duty tranquilizers. No wonder I was so damn tired all the time. Everything else I read reaffirmed what I already knew, except for one exceptionally unpleasant surprise: "One side effect of the drugs is a decreased libido in both sexes, and impotence in some men." I slammed the book shut in disgust. I felt as though someone had punched me in the stomach. When I thought about it, I couldn't remember the last time I had been sexually excited. I had never before had any problems in this respect, but like most males, it was an acutely sensitive subject for me. I was well aware of the fine line between being a stud or being a dud.

With all the other anxieties in my life, I didn't want to have to worry about my sexual performance. I tried my best to forget about it. What did I have to be concerned with, anyway? ... I didn't even have a girlfriend. Nevertheless, I started thinking about it more and more. The fear of being a twenty-six year-old eunuch was the best temptation yet for going off the medicine. What good was being sane if I couldn't even be a man?

When I came back to the house, my mother had early dinner waiting for me. After picking up my food, I went outside and got some exercise by walking around the block. During past summers, I had raced my brothers around the mile and a half loop, but now I was happy just to be walking. My perspective had changed dramatically in the last six months. I wondered if I would ever again be an athlete.

In a week and a half I was walking five or six miles a day. I explored parts of Manalapan I had never seen before. The pounds and inches slowly started to come of. I was quite pleased. The shape of my body contributed significantly to my self-esteem.

On Monday night, May 13, my mother drove me to Riverview Hospital in Red Bank. She had scheduled an interview for me with an out-patient mental health program called "Renaissance." The five day a week program was designed to help mentally ill people cope with their illness and become readjusted to the real world.

I was less than enthusiastic about being grouped with a bunch of crazy people, but after months of my mother's nagging I finally decided to give it a chance. I had to agree with her that I needed an impetus to get up in the morning, and it couldn't hurt to at least hear what this program was all about.

We arrived at Riverview at seven o'clock and followed the signs to Renaissance. That the program was located in the basement of the hospital did not make a particularly good first impression with me. "Here it is. First door on the right," said my mother.

We were greeted by the director of Renaissance, a blond, middle-aged social worker named Susan, whose close-cropped hair and round glasses gave her a distinctly intellectual look. After awkward introductions, Susan smiled and said, "C'mon, Dennis. Let me show you around." I was getting good vibes from this woman. She was relaxed and informal and did not seem to mind that I was keeping her late.

The program's modest facilities were spread among three rooms, a meeting room, a lounge area, and a game room with an old pool table in it. "Do you play any pool?" Susan asked me.

"Of course. I'm from Brooklyn." I had learned the game in a smoke filled pool hall on Coney Island Avenue. I wasn't a shark but I knew what to do with a stick in my hands. Only one guy at Albright could consistently beat me.

The pool table brought back memories of my freshman year in college. Every night after football practice, I spent three or four hours playing eight-ball with my new teammates and friends. With the indifference only a clique of eighteen-year-old kids could display, we jokingly referred to our college experience as the eight thousand dollar pool game. Our first semester grades suffered accordingly, but we all had a blast. For the first time in my life, I was one of the boys.

"As you can see, we also have a ping-pong table and a Universal weight machine in this room," Susan said, jolting me back to the present. Upon completion of the tour, the three of us returned to her office to discuss the program.

"Let me give you an overview of what we do here at Renaissance," said Susan, as my mother and I settled comfortably into our chairs. "The entire day is very structured and organized. In the morning, we have a group therapy session where everyone shares their thoughts and feelings with each other. If someone has a particular problem, we'll try to help him or her work it out."

My mother didn't seem impressed with this information. "What about individual counseling? Are there any one-on-one sessions?" she asked.

"Yes. We have an excellent staff psychiatrist, Dr. Beir, who is available two days a week. To be honest with you, though, his primary role is to monitor and prescribe medication. We can usually make much more progress in "group." Group therapy sometimes gets a bad rap but we've found it a highly effective form of treatment. The patients have quite a bit to offer."

By the time Susan had finished explaining the details, I had decided that I wanted to join the program. In addition to counseling, Renaissance also provided a wealth of social interaction. Following lunch in the hospital cafeteria, afternoons were usually spent in a public place such as a mall or a state park. Other special outings were also planned from time to time. It would be good for me to get out of my house and spend some time with other people.

"Well, that's Renaissance in a nutshell. Tell me what brought you here tonight, and whether you think you can help you," Susan said. My mother and I gave her a brief summary of what had happened to me at The Pines and in the ensuing months. I was uncomfortable discussing my illness, but Susan listened without judging me. She was very supportive and understanding, as well as a little intrigued by my unusual case.

"You look terrific now, Dennis. You're functioning extremely well. Just don't go off the medicine again," she said.

"Thank you," I responded, masking my irritation at her choice of words. I hated the word "functioning." It made me sound like a machine. Normal people were never described as "functioning" well, that distinction was reserved for the mentally ill who were lucky enough to blend into society without drawing too much attention to themselves.

Undaunted by the inadvertent slight, I told Susan I would like to give the Renaissance program a try. "It might help me to be around others who can relate to what I've been through. Maybe I won't feel so isolated," I said.

"I agree. I'd like to get you started right away. You need Dr. Beir's approval before I can process any of your papers. He's here tomorrow afternoon. Can you find a ride to the hospital?" Susan asked.

"Sure. I'll take my car in. I'll see you tomorrow."

On the ride home my mother was bubbling with excitement.

"This is exactly what you need. I have a real good feeling about this program," she said spiritedly.

"I hope you're right. At least it will give me something to do." I would have probably benefited more from the program in February, but I suppose it was better late than never. I was anxious to get back into mainstream life and Renaissance appeared to be a good first step toward achieving that goal.

Before I went to bed that night, I flushed my Navane pill down the toilet bowl. I knew I was taking a big risk with my mental health but felt it was something I had to do. I wasn't satisfied with just functioning anymore. I wanted to live life with the same energy and vitality that I had enjoyed before October 20th. Nothing less was acceptable. I had been patient long enough.

My decreased libido was the final straw that compelled me to stop taking the Navane. I could accept the side effects of being tired, dull, and even uninteresting, but I could not tolerate the threat the drugs posed to my masculinity. If and when I met a nice girl, I wanted to be operating at one-hundred percent efficiency.

Since I had finally come to terms with my illness, I thought I was well in control of my mind. I didn't anticipate any problems but, even if the delusions did happen to return, I could always go back on Navane and everything would be fine again. What could possibly go wrong?

I woke up early on Tuesday morning feeling young, free, and ridiculously happy. It was as if I had been reborn. I took a slow, leisurely walk to Acme and rejoiced in my good fortune to be alive. The air, the trees, the birds, and the faces of the people I came in contact with were all so beautiful.

To top it all off, there was not a cloud in the sky. The warm spring sun heightened my euphoric mood, but I wouldn't have cared if I were in the middle of a hurricane. I had my body back. It should have been illegal to feel this good.

I was still flying when I drove to Riverview to meet with Dr. Beir. My unrestrained joy eliminated any nervousness I might have normally felt.

"Hello, Doc. I'm Dennis Mulhearn," I said as I entered the psychiatrist's office.

"Hi, Dennis. Have a seat. I just finished talking with Susan about you. Why don't you tell me about yourself." Dr. Beir's dark beard, large stature, and general demeanor reminded me very much of Burt Lewis. The two men could have been brothers.

I talked for a while about my life and my previous mental history. Dr. Beir listened attentively. He was obviously trying to evaluate my current state of mind. When he asked me why he should let me into the program, I related some of my minor delusions and the corresponding loose associations I had inferred from them. I stopped short of telling him about my Messianic delusion, however. I didn't want the man to think that I was a complete basket case.

The doctor found my answer satisfactory, anyway. "That's fine, Dennis. I think this program might be able to help you." He shook my hand and welcomed me to Renaissance. Since they didn't like to start people in the middle of the week, I was going to have to wait until next Monday to begin. That was fine with me. I had all the time in the world.

The next day, while I was mowing the front lawn, I developed a severe headache. Ignore it. Your body is just suffering a withdrawal from the drugs, I told myself. Nevertheless, the throbbing persisted for quite some time. It became so bad I seriously considered going back on Navane, but decided to try to tough it out. I was greatly relieved when the pain finally went away on Thursday morning. I felt as if my brain had passed a litmus test. There was going to be nothing else that could stop me from here on in.

Everyone in my family commented on how well I looked. They all thought the Navane was the cause of my rejuvenation and I was satisfied to let them continue thinking that. There was no need to rock the boat. My cover was blown on Friday night, however, when my mother discovered one of my pills floating in the toilet.

She was furious until I told her I hadn't taken the drug in five days. "I don't need any drugs anymore. I'm fine. I have a right to determine what I put in my own body," I said.

"Yes. But you can't make a rational decision when you're sick," she replied. "What happens if you have a relapse? We'll never get you to take the medicine."

We discussed our options for a while. My mom could see that I was doing well and had to reluctantly admit that I had gotten much better since Monday. She was not, however, as eager to gamble with my mental health as I was. She wanted me to go back on a lower dose of Navane and gradually ween myself off it. Her idea made good sense but, after my four day reprieve, I was unwilling to put even the tiniest trace of an anti-psychotic drug back into my body.

I finally made a proposal she could live with. I told her that if for any reason she thought I needed to go back on Navane, I would take it without an argument. I gave her "power of attorney" over my body. That was the best I could do. "Okay, Dennis. I hope you're right and you don't need the medicine. Let's just see what happens," she said wearily.

When I walked into the basement of Riverview Hospital on Monday morning, I felt like I did not belong there and that I was making a big mistake. I almost turned right around and went home but, fortunately, Susan was the first person to see me as I hesitantly stepped out of the elevator. "Hi, Dennis. I'm glad you could make it. Let me introduce you to the other Renaissance members. We have some wonderful people here," she said, leading me into the lounge.

There were a dozen other men and women in the group, ranging in age from eighteen to forty. They were all pretty friendly and seemed surprisingly normal for the most part. With one or two exceptions, I would not have been able to detect anything wrong with them if I had met them in any other environment. These people had widely varied ethnicity, religious beliefs, and socio-economic backgrounds, yet they shared one all-inclusive common denominator: they were clinically diagnosed as either schizophrenic or manic-depressive.

Despite their encouraging positive behavior, I felt a little superior to them. All the out-patients were taking anti-psychotic drugs similar to the ones I had just freed myself from, and I arrogantly thought that this made me the most normal person in the program.

As much as I empathized with the other patients for their difficult plight, I admired them for their courage. Society was embarrassed by these people but I thought they were true heroes. I respected them for fighting against daily adversity that would paralyze most people. Their illnesses did not prevent them from having the same dreams and hopes as everybody else, it just made realizing those dreams much more difficult.

My first day at Renaissance went smoothly. I met the rest of the staff at the morning group therapy session. In addition to Susan, the small staff consisted of a counselor, Geri, an R.N., Mar, and a recreation therapist, Frank. May and Geri were well-dressed, articulate professionals, and as pleasant as Susan. I seemed to be in capable hands. I also took an immediate liking to Frank.

Frank was a short man with wide shoulders and big feet. Although he had very little hair left and wore a pair of thick glasses, he was a rugged outdoorsman with a passion for fishing. The proud father of three young children, he was a devoted family man as well. What I liked most about him was the way he spoke to the people in the program. He spoke to us as equals, as though we were friends he had met at a bar. Of all the healthcare professionals I had encountered, he was the first person who did not display even a hint of condescension every now and then. I really admired him for that.

I didn't say anything of value in group therapy. I just listened to my peers talk about their problems. Whenever I was thrust into an unfamiliar environment, it always took me a few days to get over my shyness. I hoped people didn't interpret this as snobbishness or arrogance. I just needed some time to warm up to new faces.

After a free lunch, Frank packed us into a blue Dodge van and took us for a nature walk in one of the local parks. I kept to myself but I enjoyed the exercise and fresh air. Walking had become one of my great pleasures in life.

Before I left for the day I met with the van driver, Gloria, and gave her directions to my house. Starting tomorrow, I was going to be picked up at nine and dropped off at four. Since the nearest parking spot was three blocks away from the hospital, I appreciated the service. I didn't worry about what the neighbors might think.

A full week had passed since I went off Navane, and I thought I was completely out of the woods. My thoughts were as ordered and rational as they had ever been. My mother watched me like a hawk and couldn't find the slightest fault with my ability to reason. Even she started to breathe easier. Her son had made it all the way back. Or had he?

17

BATTLING THE DEVIL

Unfortunately, things began to turn sour again on Thursday. It started in the morning, when Gloria picked me up in front of my house. Seven persons usually rode in the van but today there were only three persons on board. I sat in the back next to a girl name Krista.

"Morning, Dennis. You look good today," she said brightly.

"Thanks. So do you," I replied. Krista was a diminutive twenty-three year-old brunette, who lived in Manalapan on the other side of Route 9. Originally from Queens, New York, she had been in Renaissance for four years, and had made remarkable progress by all the accounts I had heard.

I was her last pickup, so Gloria headed directly to the hospital. After brief experimentation earlier in the week, she had decided that Route 520 was the fastest and most direct main drag to Red Bank. I might have been able to enjoy the scenery of the winding country road had we not passed right by the Marlboro State Psychiatric Hospital every day. This venerable institution was the home of some of New Jersey's most chronically and severely mentally ill people.

Marlboro's large, castle-like fortress of a building sat high atop a hill and was surrounded by a barbed wire fence. At least one or two police cars continually guarded the front entrance. A few of the out-patients at Renaissance had the misfortune of spending time there and their horror stories frightened me. Marlboro was the one place I wanted to avoid at all costs.

Farther along 520, we passed Brookdale Community College in Lincroft. "That's not a bad school. I once took a summer course there," I said to Krista. She said, "Yea. I know. I went there for four years." That's impossible! I thought. Brookdale's only a two year college. I never considered that her illness had prevented her from matriculating full-time.

My mind took off at warp speed. Krista had been studying about me! Under an assumed name, my Uncle Harry had been one of her professors at Brookdale. Was it merely a coincidence that this girl was from Queens, while I was from Brooklyn (Kings County)? I was again starting to see the big picture.

One of the unpleasant side effects of Krista's medication was that it caused her to perspire profusely. I didn't know this at the time. I reached over and wiped her sweat away from her cheeks with my fingers, thinking that the droplets of moisture were tears of joy.

This girl was Cory Malone! Her body was an illusion. A kiss from me would restore her to her true form. I gently put my arm around her. She didn't resist but she started to tremble ever so slightly. She knew that I knew who she was. Now I just needed to be alone with her, so that I could plant my magical kiss on her lips.

I didn't get the chance in the morning. She clung to her friend Mary like a sock to a sweater. Perhaps she knew the exact moment in time we were supposed to come together. In group therapy, I stared at Krista from across the room. She stole quick glances at me and then hurriedly looked away, her right foot furiously tapping against the linoleum floor.

Be patient, Cory. We're almost there. I'm not going anywhere, I told her with my mind. I knew exactly how she felt. I was ready to crawl out of my skin as well. Every time I looked up at the clock, the damn thing seemed to be moving backward. Finally, we broke for lunch. I excitedly bounded out of my seat.

Krista approached me in the hallway. Even in jeans and a T-shirt, she looked exquisitely feminine. "Uh, Dennis ... I don't know how to say this, but your affection is making me very uncomfortable. I hope I'm not being nasty but I'd appreciate it if you kept your hands to yourself."

She apparently noticed the shocked expression on my face. "It's got nothing to do with you. You're a real nice guy but I happen to be gay. I'm only attracted to women," she said. "Let's see if we can still be friends. No hard feelings?"

"No. No hard feelings, Krista." I shook her hand stiffly. "I understand. I'm sorry I bothered you."

Before I had time to consider the meaning of what had just occurred, a tall, slender young man named Jay asked me if I wanted to shoot a game of pool. "Sure. We have a few minutes before lunch. Rack 'em up." Jay had been to Renaissance previously, but this was the first day I had seen him here.

There was something unusual about him. He looked at me with longing desire in his eyes. Was he gay, too? When I sank my eight-ball shot, I figured out who my opponent was: Jay was really Cory! His searing eyes were a dead giveaway. We looked at each other and didn't say a word.

I was confused. Why had Cory taken a male body?

The thought of kissing another man repulsed me but I reminded myself that it wasn't really a man I'd be kissing, it was Cory. His body was yet another illusion. While I hesitated, two other male patients walked into the game room. "C'mon, fellas. The cafeteria's closing soon. We better get going," one of them said.

I ate by myself at a corner table. When I returned from lunch, the urge to kiss Jay was gone. Cory had left his body. I was very angry with myself. My homophobia had ruined a terrific opportunity and now there was no telling how long I was going to have to wait for another chance.

I spent the rest of the day looking for Cory in the face of every person I encountered but I did not have any luck. My belief that I'd be able to recognize a delusion was incorrect. I didn't think there was anything wrong with what I was doing. It made sense to me. Cory was moving from body to body to hide from the evil forces that were trying to keep us apart. She was out there somewhere, waiting for me to discover her.

Friday was an uneventful day at Renaissance. I didn't have the desire to kiss anyone, nor did I get any other delusional thoughts. I interacted beautifully with my peers and the staff. By all outward appearances, I had it all together. Later on, a couple of the outpatients told me that they were wondering what the hell was wrong with me. They said I seemed almost too well-adjusted.

When Gloria dropped me off in my driveway, Thomas was outside practicing his golf swing on the front lawn. "Hey, Den. I feel like playing some golf. You want to go to Pinebrook?"

"Sure. If we leave now we can get eighteen in."

Pinebrook was an Executive Course next to the Covered Bridge development in Manalapan. Despite its shortness of length, its slick greens and devilish pin placements made the course a difficult challenge.

We bought our green fees and walked up to the first tee. The usually crowded course was virtually empty. "I can't believe no one's here on a beautiful day like this," Thomas said. I did not share his surprise. The course was being specially reserved for me and my brother.

Although I hadn't picked up a club in over a month, I expected to play a perfect round. "Let's see—sixteen birdies and two eagles should come out to about a 52. If I can hole a couple of shots from the fairway, I'll be able to get into the forties," I said. Thomas thought I was joking but I was completely serious.

Whenever I played golf, I usually relied on one basic swing thought such as "hit through the ball" or "turn your shoulders." On this day, however, I wasn't going to have to concern myself with the mundane mechanics of the golf swing. "Power" was the one thought in my mind as I boldly stepped up to my ball.

Unfortunately, I wasn't at the gym. I took a mighty swing and shanked my tee shot onto the adjacent street. It took me another eight strokes just to reach the green. What's going on? I'm not supposed to be doing this, I moaned. Instead of overpowering the golf course, it was swallowing me alive. "Concentrate harder. Think about what you're doing," advised Thomas. My brother knew he was in for a long day on the links.

My play had not improved by the fourth hole and my temper was boiling. After each skull, shank, or top, I fired the offending golf club into the ground. If anyone had seen what I was doing, I would have been thrown off the course. My disgraceful behavior took away all the enjoyment of the game for Thomas. He just wanted to finish the round and go home.

On the 12th tee, I figured out what I was doing wrong. I was using the wrong clubs. All the clubs I had been using were made of metal. How could I possibly hit the ball correctly with those artificial materials? I needed to get back to nature.

There was only one wooden-headed club in my bag. My trusty old 4-wood. When I had received a new set of metal woods at Christmas, I didn't have the heart to relegate it to the garage or the trunk of my car. I kept it in my bag as a nostalgic reminder of my days on the Kissimmee Golf Course. The club was chipped, warped, and held together by masking tape, but these facts were irrelevant now. I needed to strike my ball with a natural substance and my 4-wood was the only tool I had that was made of wood. I pulled it out and began using it on every shot from tee to green.

My scores improved but Thomas was vexed by my unorthodox strategy. "You can't do that! You need to play this game with a different club on every shot," he yelled irately. He had long since lost his patience with me.

"Oh, yeah, Lee Trevino once played a round with a Coke bottle glued to a stick," I retorted. The 4-wood felt good in my hands; it was the only club I needed.

"Let's skip the next two holes. We can cut across and play the 18th, Thomas said, after we had finished 15. That I parred the previous two holes with my 4-wood did not alleviate his annoyance with me. I was quite agreeable to the suggestion, however, as soon as I sunk my final putt, the 18th green was going to start spinning and my party was finally going to begin. Everybody I had ever loved was going to join me on the green.

While we waited for a group ahead of us to finish playing the hole, a young boy who introduced himself as Chris approached us on the tee. "Mind if I finish up with you guys?" he asked.

"Sure. No problem," Thomas said, happy to be talking with someone else. I scrutinized the boy carefully. "Are you Cory?" I asked with my eyes. He responded by working on his backswing. I took that as a definite no.

I let Tom and Chris hit first and then stepped up to the tee. The 18th hole was an uphill two-hundred and twenty yard par 3 that actually called for a 4-wood shot. My ball floated up to the green, landed softly, and came to a stop in the back fringe.

I watched Chris walk down the fairway with a decidedly masculine gait. He was not Cory but he was a significant person in my life nevertheless. We had not met him on the final tee by accident.

Thomas and Chris both chipped up close to the hole, but their shots were incidental. My score was the only one that mattered. When I walked over to my ball, I saw an older man standing on the green, instructing young Chris as to the line of his putt. He was probably his dad or grandfather, but I imagined that the man was an angel sent from Heaven to record my heroics.

I studied my twenty-five foot birdie putt from every conceivable angle before I was ready to play the shot. My aggressive putt brushed the side of the cup and rolled six feet past the hole. Thomas and Chris putted out, and watched me look over what I hoped would be my final stroke of the day.

Since he had no idea about the importance of me making par, Thomas was disgusted with my snail-like pace of play. "Hurry up. I'll meet you in the car," he said, storming off toward the parking lot. Chris and the angel also left, leaving me all alone on the green.

This was the way it was supposed to be. It was all between me, my golf ball, and the elusive hole in the ground. My stroke was solid, but I misread the break and missed the putt to the right. Surprisingly, I wasn't the least bit angry. "Everything happens for a reason." It wouldn't be long before I'd get another chance to redeem myself. I triumphantly raised my 4-wood over my head with both my arms fully extended toward the darkening sky. "The kingdom, the power, and the glory are yours. Now and forever."

Kevin, Sean, and Star were already home when we got back to the house. After Tom and I showered, we all went to Freehold to see the movie *Only The Lonely*, starring John Candy and Ally Sheedy. Candy played a robust Irish cop from Chicago, a bachelor name Danny Muldoon. I had seen quite a few movies without any connections, but this one was speaking directly to me.

The name of the main character was the first clue. In college, a few of my friends used to playfully call me Muldoon. I found this coincidence very interesting. When Candy takes his date (Sheedy) to an empty Comiskey Park, I became sure that he represented me. Who else would bring a girl to a deserted baseball field?

Muldoon still lived with his overbearing mother and continually imagined her dying a macabre death. I didn't realize that the man was simply having paranoid fantasies. Instead, I believed that the film was confirming what I had previously suspected: death was not real. Although I didn't understand the nuances of the illusion, I felt certain that this mystery was going to be revealed to me soon. The role of Muldoon's mother was performed with flair by Maureen O'Hara. She portrayed a bigoted, nasty woman who selfishly interfered with her son's life. For the first time I realized that my own mother was an evil, ruthless person. I was going to have to watch her carefully, her motherly concern was merely a clever façade.

I had no inclination to sleep when I came home from the theater, so I read a book Thomas had recently given me: *Star Trek: The Lost Years*. I read with great interest because I believed that the three central characters were a metaphor for the Trinity.

Spock was God the Father; McCoy was the Holy Spirit; and Kirk was Jesus Christ! Their personalities matched my image of what the three-in-one God represented. Spock's knowledge and wisdom, McCoy's compassion, and Kirk's fearless bravery combined to make the perfect being. Individually they each had serious flaws, but when they were together no life-form could match them.

There were two coincidences in the book that kept my mind busy for a while. First, Kirk's commanding officer was nicknamed "God" and was rumored to have mystical powers. Second, the evil Vulcan villain's name was Zakal. In earth language, Zakal was translated into "desert storm."

After I finished reading the final chapter, I turned back to the inside jacket of the paperback and saw that the book had been published well before all the problems in the Middle East had even begun. What did this mean? What was the author trying to tell me?

I reread the book again but was still unable to solve the riddle. Only after reading it for a third time did I finally see how the plot pertained to the war and to me. I congratulated myself for my perseverance; the answers were always there if I looked hard enough for them.

Saturday was a beautiful sunny day with the temperature in the mid-eighties. The low humidity made it an ideal beach day. Deirdre had to work but Starlight and my three brothers and I squeezed into Sean's car and headed for the shore. We decided to go to Point Pleasant Beach, my favorite. There were a number of beaches closer but none nearly as festive.

The highway turned into a parking lot as we approached the shore, but I didn't care. Nothing could diminish my enthusiasm.

"Do you guys know what day it is today?" I asked.

"It was Saturday the last time I checked," replied Kevin.

"Yes, but not just any Saturday. Today is May 25, 1991, the five-year anniversary of my Albright graduation and of Hands Across America. This is going to be a great day!?

"Yea, Den. Whatever you say," Thomas mumbled. Nobody suspected I was beginning to lose my marbles again. Aside from my typical over-statement, I had done nothing out of the ordinary.

By the time we arrived at the beach, my old delusion had returned with a vengeance and a new twist. I was God the Son again, but that wasn't the best part: Cory Malone was now God the Daughter. Along with God the Father, there was also a God the Mother. The female half of the equation had been deleted from the Bible. Why I don't know. Maybe the men who had written the Bible had intentionally edited out the sections on the feminine deities, or perhaps there are missing chapters buried beneath the deserts of Israel.

In any event, it only seemed logical that the Supreme Being should have a feminine partner to share his glory. Likewise, as the Son of God, I deserved someone with a heart as pure as mine. Although Cory and I were spiritually brother and sister, there was nothing incestuous about our relationship. We were both primordial components of the original nuclear family and our genes were thus totally separate.

The colorful carnival-like atmosphere of Point Pleasant's boardwalk provided plenty of stimuli to feed my delusion. The roulette wheel in particular caught my attention. In addition to the numbers on the wheel, there were four large spaces that read: MOM, POP, SON and SIS. This was all I needed to see. I plunked down five dollars on myself (the Son space) and watched the wheel spin round and round. The arrow finally came to a stop in the middle of the POP space. I didn't mind losing, though. My Father was simply showing me that he was the boss. In the pecking order of the world, I was number two. I could live with that.

My brothers and Starlight stopped at a concession stand to get something to drink, but I went right down to the beach. I carefully spread my beach towel over the white sand, laid down on my back, and began soaking in the rays. The sun was the source of my power. It held all the answers to my questions. Countless new thoughts and ideas came flooding into my brain as the pulsating sun beat down on me with unyielding intensity.

After my body had absorbed an incredible amount of knowledge, Starlight tapped on the arm and said, "You better get out of the sun, Dennis. You're burning up."

"That's okay, Star. Don't worry about me, I'll be fine." My pale skin had turned bright red and my face felt like it was on fire, but I was not concerned. My sunburn was the price I had to pay to regain my power. I could easily handle the pain.

I sat up and gazed out toward the sea. The salty aroma of the ocean seemed to be calling me to it. Taking a running start, I dove in head first and luxuriated in the cool, sensationally refreshing water. My three brothers followed my lead and tentatively tiptoed their way into the water.

Thomas had brought a tennis ball with him and the four of us tossed it around for a while. Even at twenty-six, I still loved to play catch. When I retrieved an errant throw, I drifted off by myself until the water was up to my neck. As I looked out at the blue ocean stretching for as far as my eyes could see, I expected Cory to come swimming toward me at any moment. One kiss from her and the world was going to be perfect again, just as in *The Little Mermaid*. Our kiss was the key that would unlock mankind's unlimited potential.

"C'mon, Dennis. How long have you been standing there? We're gonna take off now. Everybody's getting hungry," Kevin said. I reluctantly returned to land and followed my brothers into the car. We stopped at the first McDonald's we saw along the highway. My diet had recently taken on gargantuan importance, so I judiciously ordered a fish sandwich and a container of milk.

Kevin offered me a bite of his McLean Deluxe cheeseburger, and I took one before I realized what I was doing. I immediately regretted this foolish decision. The burger tasted fine but I was disgusted with myself for consuming animal flesh. My body needed to be kept pure and meat was loaded with contaminants that could potentially weaken my spirit.

Kevin was starting to show some anxiety about my behavior. He was the first to notice that I was slipping back into my fantasy world. I misinterpreted his concern and love for me as a sign of unspeakable betrayal.

By nightfall I had decided that he was my evil twin. This belief stemmed mainly from an old Star Trek episode, "Mirror, Mirror," in which the crew of the Enterprise encounters a parallel universe. Since I was the embodiment of goodness and love, he had to be evil and hate. His kindness and integrity was a brilliant charade. The balance of power was shifting, however, and I was going to replace my brother as the ruler of this universe.

I spent the night replaying children's fairytales in my mind. There were important lessons to be learned from *Cinderella, Little Red Riding Hood*, and all the other stories children grow up with. The information I gathered from them was going to help me orchestrate a real life happy ending on a world wide scale.

I watched the sun come up from my bedroom window and saw that it was going to be another glorious day. The last fairytale to pop into my head was *The Tortoise and The Hare*. Inspired by the theme of this fable, I took a very long, very slow walk around my block. I believed that the slower I walked, the more enlightened I would become.

When I was halfway around the block, I picked up a stick, carved a heart into a telephone pole, and wrote Cory's and my name in it. I was the perfect guy and she was the perfect girl. Together we were going to change reality. My excitement over this was immeasurable. Wherever she was, I was sure that she shared my feelings.

Twenty minutes later, I had only advanced another thirty or so yards. I turned my head to watch a bird fly by and saw Kevin sitting in my car, approximately fifty feet behind me. I wondered how long he had been spying on me. I smiled and waved to my traitorous brother.

He pulled up beside me and rolled down the passenger window.

"Let me drive you home, Den. You've been walking around the block for two hours. I'm worried about you."

"No. Since when is walking against the law? I want to finish my walk. I'll be home in a little while." I moved away from the car. Kevin continued to follow me around the block. He looked unusually worried and justifiably so. I was taking all his power from him. After a few minutes, he chugged past me.

The stress of seeing me flip out again made Kevin physically sick. When I returned from my marathon walk, he was lying in Thomas's bed with a heavy blanket draped over his body. In spite of myself, I felt sympathy for my brother.

There was still a very small part of me that was sane and knew he was the last person on earth who would ever hurt me. Unfortunately, this part of me was overpowered by my delusion that my twin was my opposite and therefore my arch enemy.

I'm eternally grateful that I didn't try to physically harm him in any way. I believed that our battle was being fought on an intellectual level, so violence was not needed. I had never been violent to begin with but who knows what I might have done had I thought my own life was in jeopardy. With my sanity hanging by a precarious thread, my delusions made me dangerous to myself and to everyone around me.

"I have to get back to New York. Please take the medicine before I go. I think you need it," Kevin said, trying to hand me my pill container. I shoved his hands away from me.

"No. I haven't done anything abnormal. Why are you doing this to me?"

"Taking three hours to walk around the block is not exactly normal. Trust me, Dennis. You look like you're in a trance, the medicine will help you."

Kevin had what appeared to be a valid argument but I was not swayed by his reason. As persistent as he was, I was twice as stubborn. I was not going to let him force me to take the drugs. In a battle of wills, he could not win.

My mother called from her girlfriend's house and Kevin apprised her of my actions. He put me on the line and she also urged me to take the medication. She didn't have the courage to speak with me face-to-face, but I already knew she was on Kevin's side, so I wasn't surprised.

"Remember your promise to me," she said. "You have to live up to your end of the agreement."

"All right, I'll take the damn drugs." I disgustedly handed the phone back to Kevin.

My logic was simple. I had to let my brother and mother continue to think that they were getting the best of me. The only way I could accomplish this was by swallowing the Navane. Kevin looked extremely happy when I finally relented and took the pill in front of him. The son-of-a-bitch couldn't wait to get back to the City and plot a new strategy to keep me in check.

That was fine, though. I'd have my day in the sun. The race wasn't over yet. Not by a long shot.

After Kevin left, I carefully dialed Cory's number.

"Hello." The sound of her voice nearly made me drop the phone. I didn't know what to say to her.

"Uh … hi … this is Dennis. I … uh … just wanted to see how you were doing. How was Virginia?"

"Oh, it was great. I had a real good time there."

"When did you get home?"

"Yesterday. My father picked me and my boyfriend up from school. Listen, I'm cooking dinner for my parents so I've got to run. I'll talk to you soon. Bye."

The phone call left me numb. Why was she so abrupt and who the hell was this boyfriend? I theorized that perhaps her phone was being tapped and she had tried to send me a coded message; maybe the "parents" she had referred to were God the Father and God the Mother.

Regardless, I decided then and there not to call her again. I had to assume that it was very possible she did not yet have the self-awareness that I had.

She needed more time to understand her crucial role in the world. She'd contact me when the time was right. Once again, I needed to be patient. I seemed to have a surplus amount of patience these days. After waiting nearly two millennia, I knew I was only inches away from the finish line.

Sunday night was the last time I swallowed the Navane all week. I developed a great talent for trapping the pill between my tongue and the roof of my mouth. Again, no one suspected a thing. I was also becoming increasingly adept at hiding my delusions. I could carry on a lucid, intelligent conversation while attempting to solve the mysteries of the universe in my mind. It was almost as if I had achieved a dual consciousness.

During my second week at Renaissance, I broke out of my shell in a big way. I monopolized eighty percent of the group time with pompous, long-winded speeches about peace, love, happiness, and the senselessness of pain and suffering.

Geri and the staff encouraged me to get my feelings off my chest and I happily obliged them. They knew I was a troubled young man but had no idea as to the extent of my rapidly expanding delusions. They tried to find out what was making me feel this way but I refused to talk about my past. It was time to move forward and start planning for the future.

The other people in the group were no longer mental patients; they were now my twelve apostles. Their honor and courage had given them the privilege of being the first people in the world to hear my powerful message. By the end of the week my authority was unquestioned. I was the unspoken leader of the Renaissance group. With their help, I was going to lead my lost sheep out of the wilderness and into Paradise.

Kevin called a couple of times during the week and once again became an ally. There was no specific reason for such a dramatic turnaround in my thoughts I simply disregarded my "Parallel Universe" theory. I did have enemies, though. Powerful enemies. On Saturday, I learned that my sister was one of them.

I was watching a ballgame in the family room, when my favorite picture inexplicably fell from the wall. The portrait was of the five Mulhearn children, circa 1975. I held baby Thomas in my arms while Kevin, Sean, and Deirdre gathered around us.

I picked up the picture frame from the floor and discovered that the glass had cracked right across Deirdre's face. My brothers and I were all smiling brightly, but she was wearing an evil frown. I immediately knew why the crack had separated her from us: Deirdre was the Anti-Christ! No wonder she was spending more and more time at the Wilsons. The girl was deathly afraid of me.

There were other dangers lurking everywhere, the phone, for instance. My phone number was 446-6644. Anyone who had ever read Revelations or saw *The Omen* knew that 666 was the sign of the devil. The double 4's represented the power that surrounded the beast. Baseball's homerun king, Hank Aaron, wore number 44, as did Reggie Jackson. At the beginning of this season two of the game's best current sluggers, Howard Johnson and Darryl Strawberry, had both changed their numbers to   as well. That these two men had recently become orn- gain   hristians was hardly a coincidence.

By Memorial Day my delusions had intensified. As sick as I had been in December and January, there had always been a fragment of doubt in my mind about my true identity. But now even that fragment was gone. As sure as I knew that the sky was blue, I knew I was the Messiah. The perfect world I had dreamt about was coming to fruition. It didn't matter that the rest of my thoughts were discombobulated and fuzzy; I was beside myself with happiness.

Kevin and Sean both came home for the three day weekend to keep an eye on me and I hadn't given them anything to worry about on Saturday or Sunday. They were hoping to enjoy a relaxing, quiet Memorial Day. My mother woke up bright and early and said she was going to the beach with her friend Risa.

Before she left the house she asked me for directions to Point Pleasant. It was a smart move on her part but I wasn't fooled by her bluff. She was really going to New York City to try to determine how to prevent me from taking power. I was one step ahead of her, however, and she didn't know that I knew what she was doing. This was the only edge I was going to need.

Deirdre and Starlight both had to work but my three brothers and I were invited to a party in Freehold. The host of the gathering was a close friend of Sean's named Pat Mullaney. Pat was a tall, blond-haired guy who could have passed for a California surfer. Despite his outwardly quiet personality, he had a wild streak in him as well. The man knew how to throw a party.

When we arrived at Pat's house there were already roughly twenty people milling around the backyard. Some were lounging by the built-in pool, while others were engaged in a friendly co-ed game of volleyball. Loud music was blaring from two stereo speakers that had been brought out onto the deck.

The smell of barbecued hamburgers and hotdogs filled the air, and there were plenty of liquid refreshments as well. A key of beer and two large coolers filled with wine coolers, soda, and juices were strategically placed in a shady spot under a huge tree.

Pat put his beer down and came over as soon as he saw us walk into his backyard. "Hey, it's good to see you guys. I'm really glad you could come. C'mon. Let me show you the house." He proudly walked us through his new home and introduced us to some of his friends along the way.

It didn't bother me that Pat was the only person I knew there, because I assumed that everybody at the party had been specifically chosen to share this day with me. Some of my most worthy followers had assembled to pay homage to me. Five or six of these followers were wearing gold crosses around their necks as symbols of their loyalty and devotion. Seeing the crosses made me burst with pride, but even without the symbols I still would have been flying as high as a kite.

After grabbing a bit to eat, Kevin, Pat, and I joined in a game of volleyball, while Thomas and Sean chose to remain on the deck and observe the action. I guess it was kind of hard for them to play volleyball with a cheeseburger stuffed down their throats.

I had played some volleyball in my time and was fairly good at the sport. Although we weren't even keeping score, Kevin and I both played to win. We were the only two fools willing to dive onto the hard ground to make a save. That was the only way we knew how to compete.

I was having fun batting the ball around, but the game took on a whole other meaning for me. It provided an excellent opportunity to pass along some of my power to my faithful flock. My method for doing this was simply a touch from my hand.

As a result of this belief, I high-fived everyone in sight after each play. My teammates must have thought I was just one hell of an exuberant athlete, but I could feel a tremendous amount of energy pass through my body to theirs every time I touched one of their palms. I was happy to share my gift with them.

After a while, people lost interest and the volleyball game broke up. I went into the house to get to a drink of water from the kitchen sink, and heard a low roar coming from the living room. Four die hard baseball fans were sitting on the sofa, watching the Yankees–Red Sox game.

"How we doin'?" I asked.

"Not too good. Boston's up two runs in the ninth inning."

The Yankees weren't dead, however, two men had reached base ahead of Mel Hall.

"It looks like I got here just in time," I said. "Hall's going to hit one out."

"Yeah, that would be nice."

"It will happen. Just wait and see."

The muscular slugger deposited the next pitch deep into the right field seats. He circled the bases with both fists in the air as the Stadium crow erupted, and the entire Yankee bench mobbed him at home plate. I shared the Yankee players' elation. This game was only the beginning.

The New York Yankees were a team of destiny. Their weak pitching staff and lack of a quality third baseman were irrelevant. Nothing was going to prevent them from being crowned World Series Champions. It was part of my Father's plan.

I walked back outside onto the deck but my feet weren't touching the ground. The U2 song, "In God's Country," played on the radio. I thought that the song was an anthem dedicated to me and stood there soaking in the glory.

My euphoria had reached its zenith.

My mom didn't get home with her friend Risa until eight o'clock. Her suntan did not change my belief that she had gone to New York. I couldn't trust anything she did anymore. She was no longer the kind woman I had loved.

After making two cups of coffee, she joined Risa outside on the deck. "C'mon out here and talk to us, Dennis."

"No thanks. I like it inside." I was not about to let myself be lured into one of her traps.

The microwave clock was the final piece of evidence that proved to me my mother was evil. Although it was pitch black outside, the clock read 3:27. My mother was playing with my mind. She had turned the clock back and was trying to make me go crazy! I believed that she was either the daughter of the devil or his bride, and therefore was terrified to see my power increasing every day. She would do anything she could to try to stop me.

My mother and her friend were chased inside by a pack of hungry mosquitoes. They were sitting on the family room couch when I went into the kitchen and poured myself a glass of Pepsi. I swallowed the soda in one big gulp and let out an obnoxious belch.

"That wasn't very polite, Dennis. Apologize to Risa," said my mother.

"Fuck you."

"What. What did you say to me?"

"You heard me. Fuck you, you bitch!" My mother was shocked and embarrassed by my uncharacteristic outburst.

She brought me into her bedroom and tried to talk to me. Kevin had gone home but Sean and Thomas were still there. They followed me into the bedroom, not really knowing what to expect.

"What's wrong, Dennis? What did I do? Don't you know that I love you?" my mother asked me. I answered her by violently pulling her head towards me and kissing her hard on the mouth.

"Fuck you," I whispered. Thomas immediately recognized what I had done and said, "He just gave you the kiss of death, Mom. That was the same kiss Michael Corleone gave his brother Fredo in *The Godfather II*." I smiled to indicate that my brother was correct.

"I'm going to my room now, Mom. I don't want to have to look at you anymore. The sight of you makes me sick." Sean and Thomas did a good job in calming my shaken mother down. I'm glad they were present.

"He's sick, Mom. He doesn't know what he's doing," I heard Sean say as I shut the door behind me.

My mother was able to reach Dr. Miller at his home.

Sean knocked on my door and opened it cautiously. "Dr. Miller's on the phone. He wants to talk to you," he said.

"Good, I'm interested to see what he has to say." The doctor spoke in a low, hushed voice generally reserved for funerals. I explained that there was no need to worry about me. I had everything under control. He instructed me to take two Navane pills and a sleeping pill he had previously prescribed. Since I now thought that he was one of the generals in my army, I did exactly as I was told.

Along with her worries about my sanity, my mother was now physically afraid of me for the first time. I had frightened the poor woman to the point where she now feared for her life. She slept with three large kitchen knives placed underneath her bed that night.

While my mother tried in vain to get some sleep, I sat up in my bed and thought about what I had done to her. I realized that she, Deirdre, Kevin, and everyone else in my family were all good people who loved me very much. There was no logical reason for any of them to want to hurt me. My despicable actions must have devastated my mother. I owed her a big apology in the morning.

Despite recognizing that it was dangerous to fear the people closest to me, my continuing denial of my mental illness didn't allow me to admit to myself that I had been having paranoid delusions. Also, the belief that I was Jesus remained firmly entrenched in my mind. As delusions go, this one was as strong as they get.

Dr. Beir received a full report of my antics and immediately upped my dosage of Navane to twenty milligrams. I believed that the drugs couldn't hurt me anymore, so I took them without an argument. Nevertheless, I stayed euphoric all week. My friends at Renaissance were great, my family was great, I was great, and life itself was great. The near future was going to get even better. I woke up every morning hoping this was the day I would see Heaven on earth.

Kevin came in again over the weekend. He, Thomas and I drove to the Manalapan Recreation Center on Saturday afternoon to shoot some hoops. The multi-faceted sports complex was one of the finest in New Jersey. The well-kept basketball courts were a far cry from the bent rims and glass-laden cement courts we had grown up with in Brooklyn.

After shooting around for a few minutes, the three of us played a game of Horse. I won with a baseline shot from beyond the out of bounds line. "So you can shoot. Let's see what you can do against some defense," Kevin said, handing me the basketball. The medication took away most of my quickness but I was still able to beat my twin by hitting long-range shots from the perimeter.

Kevin and I were equally competitive. His defeat did not sit well with him. "Damn. I can't believe all the lucky shots you're throwing in. Let's go again."

"Sure. You must be a glutton for punishment."

Again, I gave him a sound whipping. He and Thomas shook their heads in wonder. They didn't know my secret. As God, I was the greatest athlete in the world. It was not possible for me to lose.

We were all set to leave the park when a middle-aged man named Ron walked over and asked us if we were up for a game of two-on-two. "Okay. One quick game of eleven. Winner's ball," I said, "you can play with me."

Thomas wasn't much of a basketball player but he was Larry Bird in comparison to Ron. I couldn't find any fault with Ron's effort but he had poor coordination and terrible hands. My two brothers exploited my teammate's weaknesses and took a 9-5 lead.

Like all great players, I personally took over the game at this point. I stole the ball from Kevin and then buried five consecutive jump shots. Kevin and Thomas were determined not to let me make the winning shot. They double-teamed me, leaving Ron wide open underneath the basket. I flipped the ball to him and watched him clank it off the rim.

Kevin took advantage of this miscue and swished two fall away jumpers over my outstretched hands. When the last bucket floated through the hoop, Ron began walking off the court. "No, Ron. The game's not over yet. You have to win by two," I informed him. Inspired by his second chance, Ron rebounded a missed shot and passed the ball to me at the top of the key.

I faked Kevin off of his feet and went right around him for an easy lay-up. Unlike Ron, I did not miss. "That's it. Game's over," I announced.

"What are you talking about? Let's finish up," said Thomas.

"Yeah. We should play until someone wins," Ron agreed.

"No. A tie is good." I picked up the ball and began to walk toward my car. My brothers shrugged their shoulders and thanked Ron for the game.

I stopped the game because I was afraid of losing it. If I lost, I was not the infallible Jesus Christ as I thought. I rationalized my action by telling myself that the tie game had balanced the scales of the world. I had taken an important step toward achieving the beautiful symmetry necessary to create perfection. A tie is good, a tie is great, a tie is Perfect!

I continued going to the Renaissance program every weekday and enjoyed the time I spent there. The program's format provided me a wonderful opportunity to preach my word. When I wasn't preaching, I was taking on all challengers in pool. A few people came close, but no one was able to break through and beat me. That none of my competitors were any good was an insignificant detail. I believe that I would have found a way to defeat Willie Mosconi himself if he should have happened to walk into the basement of Riverview.

18

CENTERFIELD

During the second week of June I saw Dr. Beir twice. He wasn't happy with my progress, so he switched my medication to Stelazine. I was pleased with this change because the new pills were light blue, my favorite color. This new anti-psychotic drug was very potent but I was hardly affected by it. I began referring to Stelazine as "my candy" and convinced myself that the drug was no more harmful than an M & M.

On the afternoon of Friday, June 14, Frank took us out for a walk in Holmdel Park. By that time I had become a connoisseur of all the parks and malls in Central Jersey. I liked Holmdel because it had a series of fitness stations along the walking trail. None of the other outpatients were into exercise, so Frank and I competed in a friendly personal battle of our own.

He was exceptionally strong and a worthy opponent. Nevertheless, I always managed to pump out one more pushup or chin-up than he did. My mind would not allow me to lose any competition of strength or skill. At the last fitness stations, I found a tattered Polaroid photograph that was lying upside down on the ground.

The dark photo was of a balding, pot-bellied man standing in the middle of the park. Upon closer inspection, I saw that he was wearing a Yankees shirt. The shirt wasn't just a regular T-shirt, either, it looked as if it were an authentic Yankees uniform top.

I had followed the Yankees closely since Memorial Day and was undisturbed by their losing. They were still the team of destiny. I studied the picture carefully and tried to discern what it meant. Had God the Father given me another sign?

I continued to stare at the Polaroid during the van ride back to the hospital. When we reached Riverview, I had comprehended my Father's brilliant plan for me. The Yankees were floundering because they were missing one key ingredient for success. Me! I was the missing piece of the puzzle that was going to lead the team to glory.

In the tradition of Joe D. and The Mick, I was going to patrol centerfield and play the game as it had never been played before. As an unknown rookie from out of nowhere, I was going to rock the baseball world to its foundation. I'd bring new meaning to the term "The Natural."

What a perfect script. After months of suffering, my Father was rewarding me by making my lifelong dream a reality. Any boy who had ever wrapped his fingers around a bat or slipped his little hand inside a mitt had at one time or another harbored fantasies of baseball stardom. This dream usually died a quick death and by the teenage years was replaced by thoughts of girls and cars.

Due to my early success and my love for the game, however, I thought I was going to be a major-league ballplayer right through my twenty-first birthday and beyond. Even after three mediocre college seasons, I expected to have a breakthrough senior year that would have the scouts knocking on my door.

Unfortunately, I finished my last year at Albright with yet another disappointing showing. My teammates regarded me as a solid ballplayer but I knew I hadn't even scratched the surface of my ability. I felt I should have been the premier player in the league, yet I struggled just to reach the .300 batting mark. The pitching wasn't that much better than it had been in high school and my body was far stronger than it had been then. I couldn't understand why I wasn't excelling.

Ironically, I concluded my career kneeling in the on-deck circle at the University of Scranton, desperately hoping for one last at-bat, one last swing. Scranton's leftfielder made a spectacular diving catch to end the game and the season. The play was a fitting final footnote to my undistinguished collegiate career.

But now my career was reborn. I was going to play against the best players and in the best ballparks in the world. While the personal satisfaction and enjoyment I'd get from playing for the Yankees would be substantial, there was a higher purpose to my Father's plan. As an unparalleled superstar, I'd have a tremendous forum to expound my ideas. New York's sports crazed media could help me spread my message all over the globe.

The details of my baseball fantasy were remarkably clear. The Mets were going to win the National League and face us in a subway series. On the twentieth of October I was going to step in against Brooklyn-born pitcher, Johnny Franco, and win the series by launching a homerun completely out of Yankee Stadium. As I rounded the bases, millions of people were going to see

God the Father perform a miracle that would reveal me as his Son. Everything was going to turn out exactly as I had planned. Now all I had to do was wait for my birthday to come again.

Two days later, my brothers, Deirdre, and I drove to Pearl River, New York to visit our father on Father's Day. Because he had been unable to find suitable work, he and Willie had been forced to move into a small apartment in Pearl River at the beginning of April. I spoke to him by phone every week but hadn't seen him in person in quite some time.

The day was relaxing and pleasant for everyone. Willie prepared a delectable lunch for us, and then we moved to the living room for some lively conversation. While we talked, we watched the final round of the U.S. Open Golf coverage on the tube. When Thomas mentioned the most recent Yankees game, I broke in and informed everybody of my intention to wear the pinstripes. This declaration was met with bemused laughter. Nothing I did or said shocked my family anymore.

"Let me know how your tryout goes, Den. I might want to take over for Mattingly at first base," Kevin said. His sarcasm didn't bother me. He and everyone else had been conditioned to be skeptical of the things they did not understand. How in the world could I explain to him that he was the twin brother of God? I'd have the last laugh when I stepped out onto the Yankee Stadium field and showed the world my power.

The golf action on T.V. was exciting as the two leaders, Payne Stewart and Scott Simpson, battled down to the wire. They both sank clutch putts on the final green and finished in a tie for first after completion of regulation play. Since I had predicted a Stewart victory on Thursday, he was a shoe-in to win tomorrow's 18-hole playoff.

"Bet the ranch on Payne," I told my father. "He can't lose."

"I already bet the ranch. I lost it in the Giants-Redskins game."

As soon as I returned home I sat down in my room and wrote a long letter to the Yankees' General Manager, Gene Michael. I told him that I had mastered the game of baseball and was the one player the Yankees needed to win the pennant. I concluded the letter by asking for a special tryout at Yankee Stadium. I hoped to get a response from him soon, so I could begin to get the team back into the race.

I shared my baseball fantasy with the Renaissance group on Monday morning. Geri attempted to head me off at the pass.

"That sounds great, Dennis, but it's not going to happen. Scouts are paid a lot of money to watch players and sign them out of high school or college," she said. "You're not going to get a tryout based on a letter. You have to learn to accept reality."

"I don't accept reality; I want to change it. October 20 will mark the beginning of a new reality. After that day nothing will ever be the same." "What's going to happen, Dennis?" asked Frank.

"I'm going to hit a homerun to win the World Series for the Yankees. Following that, I'm not quite sure. I'm looking forward to seeing what happens myself."

Geri was exasperated with me. She didn't know what else to say, so she moved on to somebody else in the group. It was probably a wise decision. Continued questioning would have only reinforced my delusion. As it was, I spent the rest of the session daydreaming about tearing up the American League. I was still daydreaming when Gloria dropped me off in the afternoon.

After I watched Payne Stewart win the U.S. Open playoff on T.V., I drove to the Rec Center by myself. My red, white, and blue A.B.A. basketball was the only companion I needed. A couple of mothers were playing with their toddlers in the sandbox but the six basketball courts were all empty.

I walked directly to the half court circle of the first court and focused my eyes on the distant basket. I knew exactly what I had to do. My Father wanted me to sink a shot from this spot. He wanted to test me to see how strong I had become.

I took careful aim and fired a basketball style throw the length of the court. The ball banged off the top of the backboard and bounced right back to me. After ten subsequent attempts I had only managed to hit the rim twice, and my right arm was starting to get distressingly sore. "Let's go. This has to be your last try. You arm needs to be strong for the Yankees tryout," I told myself.

It was time to pull out all the stops. I chanted my now familiar "Power, power, power" mantra and let her fly. I knew the shot was good as soon as it left my fingertips. The ball whistled through the hoop without touching the rim. Swishhh! I raised my two fists to the heavens and exalted in my achievement. There were no limits to what I was capable of accomplishing.

Fresh off my stirring triumph on the basketball court, I had no interest in seeing Dr. Beir on Tuesday. I had nothing personal against the man, but as a psychiatrist he was trained to see the world on a rigid, one-dimensional level. He would never be able to understand the concept of destiny. Nevertheless, Geri insisted that I meet with him. She wanted to give him a crack at breaking through my baseball delusion.

"So, Dennis, I hear that you think you're going to be the next centerfielder for the Yankees. Is that true?" he asked.

"Yes, that's right." I reiterated the details for him. Dr. Beir alternated between looking at me and his notes. I could almost feel him working out a strategy in his mind.

"Take a guy like Cal Ripken, Dennis. Do you realize how many ground balls he's fielded, and how many swings he's taken in the batting cages to be able to perform the way he does.?"

"Sure. Thousands. Maybe tens of thousands."

"Exactly. You haven't played baseball in six years. What makes you think you can play the game at its highest level? When have you practiced?"

I carefully considered the doctor's questions before answering him. "I've practiced every day of my life. Right here," I said, tapping my forehead with my index finger. Dr. Beir evidently wasn't impressed with my mental powers. He scowled at me and then studied his notes again.

"I'll be very blunt with you, Dennis. I'm not happy with what I'm hearing. You're getting dangerously close to being readmitted into the hospital."

"Go ahead. I don't care. What can they do in the hospital that hasn't already been done to me?" Dr. Beir decided not to put me into the hospital. Instead, he upped my medication to 30 milligrams of Stelazine and told me to see him next week.

The increased dosage still had little effect on me. Over the next couple of weeks I spent nearly every night playing basketball at the Rec Center. Let's see. Who is going to have the honor of playing against Christ tonight? I'd say to myself as I made a slow entrance from the parking lot. In each pickup game I participated in, I competed as though I were playing in The Final Four. My teammates and foes alike deserved to see me at my absolute best.

I played with and against a multi-ethnic field of ballplayers: African-Americans, Puerto Ricans, Asians, Jews, Italians, and just about every other nationality were represented at the Center. A few years ago all the black guys had played on one court while the white guys played on another. Now I was delighted to see that everyone was playing together. The integrated games gave me a chance to test my skills against the best athletes in the area, black or white.

Remarkably, my delusion elevated my game to a new level. I sincerely believed that I was the greatest hoopster to ever lace up a pair of sneakers. Since I didn't know I was out of my mind, I parlayed this unfounded (yet very real) confidence into some impressive performances. While I thought I was Jesus, it was not uncommon for me to hit sixty or seventy percent of my three-point shots.

During the last days of June my delusions became more and more focused on sports. I believed that God the Father had invented sports as part of his elaborate plan to achieve world peace. The cities with major sports teams were going to play a key role in the revitalization of the world. The various colors of their respective teams represented all the different races of men. White, black, yellow, or red, we were all human beings made in my Father's image. Athletic competition was going to be the common thread that linked us together as one.

Therefore, Yankees shirts, Mets caps, and alley-way basketball hoops replaced rosary beads, stained glass windows, and statues of the Virgin Mary as the new icons of the day. As the greatest game ever, baseball was especially sacred. Every diamond in America was a church, and Yankee Stadium was my grand cathedral.

I had written Gene Michael a second letter a week after the first one but still had yet to hear from him. His negligence was costing the Yankees dearly. The team was skidding further down the standings each week. They desperately needed my bat in the lineup. Although annoyed by the delay, I wasn't worried. There was still plenty of time for me to lead the Yankees to their first title since 1978.

At times I didn't think I could wait another minute to play for the Yankees. As excited as I was about my immediate future, I was equally bored by the very dull present. During those times I reminded myself that I needed to be patient. I'd made it this far; the rest of the way was going to be easy. My infinite glory was only months away.

In the meantime I had to derive pleasure from other sources. I learned how to procure great contentment from some of the simple things in life. The smile of a young child, carefree laughter of friends and family, or even a certain song on the radio, was often enough to keep me happy for an entire day.

As June turned into July, the Stelazine slowly began to wear me down. I stopped driving to the Rec Center and started going to bed by eight o'clock. Also, the drug was extremely successful in making all of my loose associations disappear.

I still tried to make connections but the matching pieces of the puzzle were missing. Nothing fit into place anymore. Even my baseball delusion was slowly fading. "Maybe only my spirit is going to lead the Yankees," I rationalized in a weak cop-out.

Unfortunately, my Messianic delusion was still as strong as ever. I held firm to the belief that I was Jesus Christ. Regardless of what was going on around me, I unequivocally refused to accept the slightest possibility that I was not God. Although I never came right out and told anyone I was Jesus, I continued to preach about peace, love, and morality. As Christ, I was first and foremost a teacher.

I accompanied Kevin to a Fourth of July party in North Jersey. I knew most of the people there from Muhlenberg, so I felt comfortable. I mingled and socialized expertly with my brother's friends. No one suspected that there was the slightest thing wrong with me.

I didn't have a bad time at the gathering, but the euphoria I had felt on Memorial Day was conspicuously absent. Since I had anticipated a truly spectacular day, the party was a big letdown. I didn't even bother to stay for the fireworks display at night. Three days later, I regained my euphoria in a rather unusual way.

"Dennis, I'm going to mass now. Why don't you come with me, it might do you some good," my mother said as she knocked on my door. Aside from two weddings I had attended, I hadn't been inside a church in eight years. The idea filled me with excitement, anyway, I still didn't believe in organized religion, but perhaps my holiness could liven up a traditional Sunday service.

The church my mom attended was named after Saint Thomas More. It was conveniently located at Gordons Corner Road, just a half mile from the Acme shopping center. Saint Thomas was an ultra-modern facility that would have offended many older Catholics. The automatic sliding-doors, low ceiling, bright lights, and paucity of icons, combined to give it the bland flavor of a school auditorium, rather than the impressive splendor of a more traditional Catholic Church.

I sat in one of the back pews with my mother and absorbed the unsolicited praise of hundreds of Manalapan residents. Their rhythmic chants, prayers, and songs were all aimed directly at me. It was quite an emotional experience. I felt enormously uplifted by the endless stream of accolades being heaped upon me.

Communion was the grand finale. When I ate the holy water and swallowed the holy wine, all my worries and concerns instantly disappeared. I had reclaimed a part of me that had been missing for a while. The entire church seemed to be filling up with love. All the babies stopped crying, and the faces of the churchgoers glowed with joy. I was filled with a tremendous amount of pride for who I was, for what I had done in my first life, and for what I was about to do in this life.

I arrived at Renaissance on Monday morning with renewed enthusiasm. The catchy church tunes from the day before were still dancing around in my head. Before group therapy, I joined Frank and two of my friends, Mary and John, for a brisk walk through Red Bank.

A few minutes into the walk we heard loud organ music coming from one of the homes. "That's weird," said Frank. "You don't usually hear church music this early in the morning." I did not share his opinion. Although I didn't know the name of the street we were on, the number of the musical house was 41.

After I ate my dinner that night, I drove to Chi-Chi's. My patience with Cory was wearing thin. I couldn't wait another day to see her. I quietly walked into the restaurant and sat down at a corner stool in the Cantina.

"Hey, Dennis. It's about time you showed your face in here. What can I get you?" said the bartender.

"How are you, John? I'll have a club soda please."

Before I had finished the first sip of my soda, Cory sauntered over and ordered a drink from the service bar. I had hoped she would be working, but this precise timing was beyond my expectations. She had gained five or six pounds in the hips but to me she still looked as beautiful as ever. She appeared stunned to see me sitting there, though.

"Hi, Dennis," she said, reluctantly making brief eye contact.

"Hi, Cory."

I tried to strike up a friendly conversation with her but she cut me off. "I'm sorry, I don't have time to talk. I'm very busy. I have to get back to work." She might as well have hit me over the head with a sledgehammer. I angrily stormed out of the bar without saying goodbye to anyone.

Why is she being so cold to me, God? Doesn't she know who I am? Her reaction to my presence was incomprehensible. The girl looked as though she were afraid of me. I rolled up the windows of my car, turned the volume of the radio up full blast, and screamed like a wounded animal. Cory's rejection left me nearly in a state of shock. Somehow I managed to drive home without getting into an accident.

In reality, it was probably the best thing that could have happened. For the first time since May, I began to seriously question who or what I was. Cory had punched a giant hole in my last remaining delusions: that I was Christ and that she was destined to be my mate. Her brush-off left these beliefs hanging in mid-air. No amount of rationalization could alter what she had done.

During the next couple of weeks it became harder and harder to continue to believe I was Jesus Christ. All my senses told me that the very thought was silly, yet I clung to my delusion like a drowning man holding on to a life-preserver. In my heart I knew I wasn't the Messiah but I didn't want to admit to myself that I had been crazy for all this time. Despite my denial, my ability to reason was slowly returning. Rational thoughts were gradually replacing my fantasies.

I made a breakthrough in the group therapy session of Wednesday, July 24. Geri was on vacation, so Susan was sitting in for her. "Okay. Who would like to start this morning?" she asked. I cleared my throat and began to speak. "I'll start. I've got something important to say today.

"For a long time I thought I was going to make the world a perfect place. Believe it or not, I actually thought I was Jesus Christ. Today I finally realize that I don't have the singular power to save the world. I'm just like everybody else. I've been very sick but I'm going to get better. I want to thank all of you for helping me reach this conclusion. I couldn't have done it without you."

"That's great, Dennis. I feel like standing up and cheering," said Susan. I felt surprisingly good myself. I didn't go through the post-psychotic depression I had experienced on New Year's Eve. Instead, I felt a great burden being lifted from my shoulders. I didn't have the awesome responsibility of being the Messiah anymore. I could just be a normal person and try to enjoy my life again. Even as a common man, life held great promise.

Through the end of July and into August I continued to make steady progress and my delusions became a thing of the past. As each day passed I became more centered in reality. This reality, however, was not always pleasant. I battled some minor depression and fought the fatigue caused by the Stelazine, but all in all I was doing remarkably well. My frame of mind was as positive as could be expected considering the circumstances.

On the third Saturday of August, Starlight fixed me up with one of her friends from Lord and Taylor, the department store in which she worked. Renee was a twenty year-old brunette with long legs, high cheekbones, and big brown eyes. She was not, however, nearly as naïve and innocent as her age might suggest. Indeed, Renee prided herself in being a bit on the wild side. She had a boisterous personality and was not shy about expressing her opinions.

On our first date I took her to the movies and then to the Manalapan Diner for a cup of coffee. I was under the impression that Starlight had told her about my illness, so I was surprised when she asked me what I did for a living. I took a deep breath and tried to summarize my situation for her.

It was quite embarrassing to have to talk about my mental illness but I thought I needed to get everything out in the open. When I had finished speaking, I sat back in my booth and waited for Renee to react.

"I'm glad you were honest with me, Dennis. I had no idea."

"I'll understand if you don't want to go out with me again. I thought you already knew."

"Don't be silly. It doesn't bother me at all. If anything, I admire you for being able to bounce back. You're nice to talk to. I'd love to see you again." I was extremely impressed with her attitude. Not too many women would be willing to overlook such a serious flaw in a man. Renee was obviously a person of great substance.

I began dating her on a regular basis. In a very short time our relationship became intimate. The Stelazine didn't make me impotent as I had feared, but it did have a noticeable effect on my libido. I was unable to have sex with the frequency or intensity to which I had been accustomed. Although Renee was patient and understanding, I was mortified by my sub-par performance in the bedroom. I now had the sex drive of an old man.

My inadequacy in this area became the dominant thought in my mind. I spent hours on end worrying and sulking about my lack of virility. That I could function at all was of little consolation. I was bitter about being cheated out of the prime years of my sex life.

I spoke with Dr. Beir and discussed my problem with him. His solution was to lower my daily dosage of Stelazine to ten milligrams. The decreased dosage helped, but not enough to satisfy me. Despite everything that had happened, I once again contemplated going off the medication. On Friday, September 6, that's exactly what I did.

19

BIRTHDAY WISHES

"Blow out the candles and make a wish," my mother said, placing my birthday cake in front of me. "C'mon, Kev, give me a hand. It's your birthday too," I said to my twin brother. I wished for good health and prosperity for all my friends and family, and extinguished the candles in one breath. Kevin was there with me but everyone knew that the party was really for me alone.

About eight of my friends from Renaissance, my brothers and sister, Renee, and a couple of my closest friends from Chi-Chi's, had come to help me celebrate a new year, and what I hoped would be a new beginning. My biggest wish had already come true I had been drug-free for six weeks and was still completely sane. I didn't think I was Jesus, and I could watch a movie without drawing any bizarre conclusions from it.

My mental illness had disappeared as suddenly as it had arrived. All the delusions and loose associations had stayed away. The first few days off the drugs had been more frightening than any conceivable nightmare. I was terrified of losing control over my mind again. Only after the third week or so was I finally able to relax. My dangerous gamble had paid big dividends. The circuits of my brain had reconnected and I was back operating at full capacity in every aspect of my life.

I would like to say more about my recovery but there really isn't much more to say. The mystery of mental illness is that there is no definitive reason for why certain individuals become afflicted and even less explanation for why some of these people regain full control over their thought processes while others flounder in various states of psychosis for the rest of their lives.

After going off the anti-psychotic medication twice and regressing further each time, no certified psychiatrist in the world would have allowed me to discontinue the medication again for at least a year. Indeed, some conservative doctors would have *never* permitted me to do so. Yet for me, the third attempt proved to be a charm. I didn't stop to ask why I had been so fortunate. I just counted my blessings. For once, my stubbornness had worked to my advantage.

I sliced the first wedge of cake and handed it to Renee. I was pleased that she had come to my party, but her appearance was a largely a formality. We both knew there was no magic between the two of us anymore. Although we never officially broke up, we hadn't seen each other since the end of September. As highly as we thought of each other, we had some basic personality conflicts that made a serious relationship all but impossible. I don't think I was extroverted enough for her and her interest in the bar scene was a big turn-off for me. These and other intrinsic differences, largely the result of our age variance, made us slowly drift apart.

Nevertheless, I deeply appreciate the few weeks that I spent with her. She accepted me at the weakest and most vulnerable point in my life and asked for nothing in return. A less compassionate woman could have easily crushed me. Instead, Renee gave me back my confidence and provided the incentive to go off the Stelazine. I hope she finds a great guy some day. She deserves one.

The party was a rousing success. My friends seemed to all be having a fun time. After we quickly disposed of the cake, a bunch of us played a touch football game on the front lawn. The crisp October winds blew against the back of my neck as I reached out and snared a long touchdown pass.

My friends' and brothers' spirited yells were music to my ears. I was very happy, but unlike my delusional euphoria, this happiness was firmly rooted in reality. As lucky as I had been to get where I was, I knew that I still had a long way to go.

When the last guest had left, my mother, Kevin and I sat down on the living room couch and discussed my future.

"Well, Den, what are you going to do with your life? Do you have any ideas?" Kevin asked.

"Not really. I'm kind of in the same boat I was in before I went to The Pines. I'm still looking to find my niche out there. I'm going to leave Renaissance soon, though, I'll miss my friends but it's time to move on."

My mother and Kevin nodded simultaneously. Knowing me as well as they did, they had both anticipated this decision for a while.

"What about a job?" my mother asked.

"I'm not real worried about finding work right now, Mom. My disability check will be enough to tie me over for a few months. I want to devote a lot of my time to writing about what happened to me this past year. Starting tomorrow, that's going to be my number one priority.

I stood up, excused myself, and started walking into Thomas's bedroom. "Where are you going?" my mother called out.

"The World Series is on. I don't want to miss a pitch this year," I replied.

"I'll be there in a minute, Dennis," said Kevin. "Who would have bet on two last place teams playing for all the marbles. Anything can happen in baseball."

Yes, Kevin. In baseball, as in life, anything can happen. The immortal poet Yogi Berra put it best when he said: "It ain't over 'til it's over." Words cannot express the relief I felt that this chapter of my life was over. With my joyous birthday party, I had come full circle. The turbulent, year-long rollercoaster ride had finally screeched to a grinding halt.

My memories of that year are still vivid and often painful. But having come through unscathed, I think that in the long run the experience may prove to be enriching. As I struggled to differentiate between my idealism and the realities of what can sometimes be a brutal world, I learned a valuable lesson: I'll never play centerfield for the New York Yankees or single-handedly lead the world to paradise, but I can still make a difference with what's left of my life. Every person can! We all have the power to touch so many others. In the end, regardless of our religious or spiritual beliefs, what we do with this power is all that really matters.

EPILOGUE

April 1, 1993

Time marches on. It is hard to believe that two and a half years have passed since my unforgettable week at The Pines. As I edited this book, I sometimes wondered exactly what really happened up there in the Catskill mountains. I'll probably never learn the entire truth unless I am lucky enough to run into Evan Harris one day.

The last eighteen months have been good ones for me. I have enjoyed excellent health, frequent laughter, and as always the unconditional love of my extraordinary family.

Moreover, in May of 1992 I met at Jack LaLanne's of all places Elaine, a beautiful young woman who accepted me and loved me despite my flaws. She has patiently stood by me this past year while I devoted most of my time and energy into writing this book. In addition to her encouragement, she has played an active role in helping me finish this work. Her typing skills and editorial advice have been invaluable. Elaine is everything I imagined Cory Malone to be and much, much more.

I have not yet looked for a full-time job because my writing has simply taken too much of my time. I felt that anything less than my full attention would detract from the quality of the book. Perhaps now, with this story purged from my system, I can again sift through the *New York Times* classified ads and choose a new career direction.

As I look back at the tale I have told, some of the events I have recounted seem surreal. Was that really me … could I have done that? I ask myself. Nevertheless, writing this book and reliving those memories was not a chore or a burden. I consider myself blessed to have recovered my mental faculties enough to be able to record my thoughts and feelings on paper.

I know that this book will probably not make much of a dent in removing the social stigma of mental illness (and there is still most definitely a stigma attached to the disease). If, however, I have cleared up some of the common misconceptions and incorrect presumptions most people have about it, then I have achieved my primary objective.

Was I truly a schizophrenic? I'm not sure and I don't care. I prefer referring to my malady as mental illness because, frankly, I do not like being labeled. There is strong evidence to suggest that there may be as many as a dozen separate diseases currently lumped together as schizophrenia. Additionally, many of the symptoms of manic-depression overlap those of schizophrenia.

As if that weren't bad enough, the majority of people still think schizophrenia means multiple personality, ala Sybil. Indeed, I frequently come across newspaper and magazine articles in which the writer carelessly uses the term in this manner. In actuality, schizophrenia means "out of touch with reality," and afflicts one percent of the population.

I hope this book has shed some light on the subject but, sadly, my personal contribution to the cause represents only a few grains of sand scattered along the vast Jersey shoreline. Not until the general public has been thoroughly educated about mental illness will the disease stop being unfairly perceived as what Dr. E. Fuller Torrey refers to as "the leprosy of the twentieth century."

There have recently been some excellent books and television shows about schizophrenia and that's a good start, but much more needs to be done. A comprehensive program providing up-to-date and forthright information about mental illness should be made a mandatory part of the high school curriculum. Funding for out-patient programs similar to Renaissance needs to be made more readily available. Most importantly, research efforts need to be increased substantially.

Persons with mental illnesses usually have relapses because they stop taking their medication. Health professionals seem shocked by this revelation but they shouldn't be. The anti-psychotic drugs control the symptoms of the disease but their debilitating side effects destroy a person's already tenuous self-esteem. We have to find new drugs that treat the disease itself and not merely the abnormal behavior associated with it, while at the same time keeping the side effects tolerable.

But therein lies the paradox. How can any doctor treat a disease that is unidentifiable? The brain is the most complex organism in the human body— the very essence of who we are— yet it is also the least understood. Until more is learned about the causes of mental illness, the medical community will continue to grope in the dark in search of elusive answers.

In the meantime, society as a whole can start treating the victims of this dreadful disease with the compassion and understanding they deserve. Imagine the terror of not knowing whether your next thought is going to be a sane one!

I wish I could give more definitive advice to others suffering from mental illness, but I don't have any easy answers or solutions. I have only this observation to offer: the most important thing to realize is that you are not alone out there. Millions of people have shared remarkably similar experiences and many of them have gone on to lead happy, rewarding lives. Personally, I owe a huge debt of gratitude to Renaissance for removing me from my isolation and making me see this simple fact. I might still be delusional had I stayed in my mental cocoon.

There are a number of books on mental illness that are well worth reading. The best of these is *Surviving Schizophrenia: A Family Manual* by Dr. E. Fuller Torrey (Harper & Row, 1988). It is a practical guide that sagely graphs the complex issues a schizophrenic patient and his or her family will be forced to confront.

Dr. Torrey understands that schizophrenia is a disease which affects entire families, and not just individuals. My family was woefully unprepared to deal with me, but they instinctively responded to my break from reality with heroic stoism. Their love, patience, and unwavering support played a large role in my recovery, and I will never be able to find sufficient words to adequately express my thanks.

I have followed the standoff in Waco, Texas between David Koresh and federal agents with keen interest. There is no doubt in my mind that Koresh truly believes he is the Messiah. What fascinates me is that he amassed so many loyal followers who are willing to risk their lives for him. This tragic episode is a poignant example of the dangers of religious fanaticism and Messianic delusions, yet I hope this book has made it clear that not all would-be-messiahs espouse violence, which is the unfortunate stereotype perpetuated by people like Koresh.

As for me, when my delusion that I was the Savior vanished, so did most of my religious fervor. I have not been to church in quite a while and, although I still have a strong faith in God, have no desire to go back any time soon. It's not that I fear any possible ramifications of going to mass; I simply prefer to keep my spirituality a personal matter.

My general feelings on religion are now similar to what they were before my psychosis propelled me into my Messianic delusion. The subject still intrigues me but I no longer worry about finding answers to esoteric questions that were never meant to be comprehended. I could probably write another book based solely on my religious and philosophical beliefs and maybe someday I will. For now, however, I will concentrate on living one day at a time and being the best friend, brother, and son, I can possibly be.

AFTERWORD

Ah, but a man's reach should exceed his grasp,
Or what's a heaven for?

—Robert Browning

May 14, 2015

My twin brother, Dennis John Mulhearn, died on August 24, 1993, less than five months after he finished the *Epilogue* of this book. He was twenty-eight years old.

The night before, Dennis had hosted most of my family for dinner at his restaurant, Tony Roma's, a rib joint on Broadway in New York City. He had worked there as Assistant Manager for only a few weeks. Dennis had a wild, glassy, far-away look in his eyes that night, which was punctuated by his manic, hyperbolic, over-the-top ranting. We all knew that Dennis had relapsed. He was in the unpredictable and terrifying grip, once again, of mental illness. This realization, especially considering the valor of Dennis's effort to heal, was heartbreaking for all of us.

On the morning of August 24, Dennis ditched work, headed to the Port Authority Bus Terminal, and purchased a Greyhound ticket to Washington, D.C. He no doubt had some grand political motive in mind when he boarded the bus to our nation's capital.

The bus stopped in Baltimore, Maryland for a quick break. Dennis departed. According to the Baltimore Police Report, he walked to the Korean War Memorial outside Baltimore Harbor, just a stone's throw away from Camden Yards. Dennis, with Bible in hand, stepped on top of the memorial, a concrete map of the Korean war zone depicted on custom made tiles, and engaged in some bizarre ritual prayer.

Two twelve-year-old boys were playing catch with a pink spaldeen at water's edge. An errant throw sailed into the harbor. Dennis, without even removing his sneakers, jumped into the water and began paddling towards the spaldeen. But he could not swim so he quickly went under. Numerous people, mostly tourists, observed this unfolding tragedy, but—unlike at Police Camp, when Dennis was a child—no Good Samaritan emerged to jump into the water and save my brother. The Baltimore Police pulled his lifeless body out of the harbor an hour or so later.

It is no small irony that the elusive spaldeen, that pink rubber ball, meant a great deal to Dennis. He featured a spaldeen as the prized gift from his beloved paternal grandfather to his imaginary daughter in the short story he wrote about a magical game of stickball that he played with our grandfather and his brothers (*see* pages 68-69, *supra*). In real life, shadowed by delusion, Dennis's quest to retrieve a spaldeen led directly to his sudden departure from this world.

I believe that to Dennis the spaldeen was a symbol of love. Love from grandfather to grandchild, from father to child, and from child to parent. In the clutch of his last delusion, Dennis probably attached extraordinary, perhaps even supernatural, powers to a simple pink rubber ball. To him, it was not just a cheap piece of rubber, but a vital talisman which would protect, bind, and unite his family.

Dennis never reached the spaldeen that was thrown into the Baltimore Harbor. For him, in this world, it would always remain elusive. But he succeeded in a higher, more important mission: Dennis taught me, my siblings, my parents, and all who were fortunate enough to know him, how to live with a full and open heart. The heart, always, must take the lead from the head, the gut, or a combination of the two. This is not always painless, for the heart bleeds far more easily and profusely than the head or the gut, but it is the only way to live. The only right way, at least. Dennis taught us this lesson by how he lived his life.

Dennis's story, this story, at the end of the day, is about courage, hope, and, most importantly, the power of love. Dennis believed with every fiber of his body that love conquers all. Crippling illness, inexplicable tragedy, rotten luck … all can be overcome with the force of love. No one could ever tell Dennis anything to shake his belief in this bedrock conviction.

As Dennis often said, "love is the medicine." And he was a master physician who liberally dispensed prescriptions of compassion, empathy, and genuine concern for the less fortunate amongst us. Despite his own ordeal, Dennis refused to wallow in self-pity. He always believed that he could will himself to get better, to live not just an ordinary life, but an extraordinary one.

This steadfast belief, unfortunately, came at an extraordinarily steep price. Dennis was unwilling to take the anti-psychotic drugs that he needed. He gambled with his mental health because he refused to live at anything less than his physical best. He was not content to merely "function." Dennis believed that his gamble had paid off but in the end, of course, it did not. His zest for life's finest pleasures, and his stubborn refusal to sacrifice physical prowess for mental wellbeing, ultimately betrayed him. But, still, one can't help but admire Dennis's bravado and courage.

The manuscript of this book—which Dennis painstakingly typed with two fingers on a now anachronistic word processor—has been tucked away in one closet or another for more than two decades. The pain of losing Dennis—which felt like a slow but unending incineration of the best part of me, with my eyes taped open to make sure I viewed every ghastly image (like the protagonist in *A Clockwork Orange*)—made it difficult for me to pick up, let alone read, the manuscript.

But time soothes, if not heals, all wounds. While reading and editing this book these last few months, a part of Dennis came alive. I heard his gentle voice, saw his crooked smile, felt his rage and frustration, courage and fear, and, first and foremost, felt—once again—the extraordinary power of his love.

One of the most tragic aspects of Dennis's untimely death was that he did not live long enough to meet his nephews and nieces: Sean's sons, Michael Cid and Blake Lee, Deirdre's children, Christian Thomas Michael and Alexandra "Lexi" Lee, Thomas's daughter, Sophia Ann, and my son, Dennis Luke. These beautiful and spirited children were each denied the gift of knowing their Uncle Dennis.

Yet it is my fervent hope that all of these children will read *Grand Delusions* when they become adults. Perhaps then they will recognize that Dennis's account of his harrowing battle with mental illness reveals a fundamental truth: that a part of him, the part that loved those closest to him, was actually touched by the divine. This is neither blasphemy nor my own delusion, but, rather, my firm conviction.

I see it most in the bright, inquisitive and trusting face of Dennis's namesake, my son. While Dennis Luke is his own person, I believe with all my heart that my brother's spirit is connected in some way to this child: guiding him, protecting him, and helping to teach him to be a good and noble man. I have no proof of any of this, of course. Only faith. But sometimes faith is enough. Sometimes it has to be.

My brother Dennis lives in a world without boundaries or conflict, where dreams—no matter how wild or far-fetched—are nourished, and nothing, absolutely nothing, is beyond the imagination. Or his grasp. Take that on faith. That is Dennis John Mulhearn's legacy. This book is his enduring gift.

—Kevin Thomas Mulhearn

ABOUT THE AUTHOR

Dennis John Mulhearn was born in Brooklyn, New York on October 20, 1964. He and his twin brother were the oldest of five children of Thomas Lee Mulhearn, a New York City police officer, and Mary Ann Mulhearn, an early education teacher.

From 1978-1982 Dennis attended Poly Prep High School in Brooklyn, where he was a star athlete. He played varsity football, baseball, and basketball, and earned outstanding player awards for his performances on the gridiron and diamond. Dennis then attended Albright College in Reading, Pennsylvania, where he played both football and baseball.

Upon his graduation from college in 1986, Dennis embarked on a quest to find real meaning in his life. He rejected the corporate world of New York City in search of a higher and deeper purpose. This quixotic quest, however, was not without pitfalls.

On October 20, 1990—his twenty-sixth birthday—Dennis had a mental breakdown after being fired from a new management job at a hotel in the Catskills. From that day forward, Dennis battled mental illness, most notably prolonged periods of Messianic delusions. During these phases, Dennis had a firm and unshakeable conviction that he was God, and that his mission was to bring peace, love, and joy to the world.

Dennis finished Grand Delusions, which he worked on for more than a year, just a few months before his death on August 24, 1993.

Dennis was blessed with a loving nature, a bright mind, extraordinary strength (both physical and spiritual), inspiring grit and determination, and an unyielding resolve—never weakened by his own horrific ordeal—to make the world a better place.

Those who knew and loved Dennis John Mulhearn will never forget this one-of-a-kind man.

www.ingramcontent.com/pod-product-compliance
Lightning Source LLC
Chambersburg PA
CBHW081413270326
41931CB00015B/3265